*For Trudi, Gabby and Bryn.*
*Your support is always amazing.*

*BIG MUCH.*

# CONTENTS

# WARREN GATLAND

# IN THE LINE OF FIRE

## THE INSIDE STORY FROM
## THE LIONS HEAD COACH

With Gerry Thornley

HEADLINE

800 705 311

First published in 2017
by HEADLINE PUBLISHING GROUP

First published in paperback in 2018
by HEADLINE PUBLISHING GROUP

1

**Picture Credits**

All photographs © INPHO except for page 16 (bottom right) which is © Getty Images.

Cataloguing in Publication Data is available from the British Library

Paperback ISBN 978 1 4722 5249 4

Typeset in Bliss Light by CC Book Production
Printed and bound in Great Britain by Clays Ltd, St Ives, plc

Headline's policy is to use papers that are natural, renewable and
recyclable products and made from wood grown in sustainable forests.
The logging and manufacturing processes are expected to conform to
the environmental regulations of the country of origin.

FSC
MIX
Paper from
responsible sources
www.fsc.org    FSC® C104740

HEADLINE PUBLISHING GROUP
An Hachette UK Company
Carmelite House
50 Victoria Embankment
London EC4Y 0DZ

www.headline.co.uk
www.hachette.co.uk

---

*Wednesday, 6 July 2016*
*Lions Head Coach interview, Sofitel London Heathrow*

It's a pretty hard job to say no to. John Feehan, the Chief Executive Officer of the British and Irish Lions, had contacted me a few weeks before, asking me if I'd be prepared to put my name forward for the role of Lions Head Coach again. Taking a Lions squad to Australia was one thing; taking one to New Zealand less than a week before the first tour game was quite another. It had already been described as 'Mission Impossible'. Graham Henry, Head Coach on the 2001 Lions tour, would subsequently call the itinerary 'suicidal'.

But that's why we're involved in professional sport: to take on challenges and test ourselves, and to achieve the unexpected. So I was quite relaxed about the whole process as I put together my presentation on my laptop over the previous two weeks, before driving from Cardiff to London that morning.

They had interviewed Scotland's Vern Cotter before me, and I had to wait a while before I was called in. It was between Vern and myself, as Ireland's

Joe Schmidt had decided not to put his name forward. In a small meeting room, I was interviewed by John, Tom Grace, the Lions Chairman, Gareth Davies, a Lions Board Member, Charlie McEwen, the Chief Operating Officer, and Gerard Carmody, their Director of Operations. John Spencer, the Tour Manager, was not in attendance as he was recovering from illness, while Andy Irvine, another Board member, took part via a conference call as he was on holiday with his family. The screams of his grandchildren enjoying their break made for an unusual backdrop to the interview.

I was asked to make a presentation for about half an hour, before taking questions for another thirty minutes or so. I gave a timeline for the tour, going through the schedule, and outlined the history of the Lions in New Zealand, where they'd won one series out of eleven in 1971. I spoke about the ethos and culture of the Lions, bringing four nations together, that you have to do it a little differently, given its history and values.

I talked about the challenges of New Zealand, which is the hardest country to tour, and the demands of the schedule, which had been agreed long before the interview process. I spoke about the quality of opposition we would be facing, with the five Super Rugby teams, the Maori All Blacks and three Tests, and also the potential for bad weather.

I referenced my involvement in 2009 and 2013 as Assistant and Head Coach, and drawing on those experiences, emphasised that harmony off the field was paramount. Initially, my thoughts were that the Lions would need a squad of thirty-seven players, as in 2013, and stressed the need to keep them all engaged and fully part of the tour until the end. For most of the players involved, they were frontline internationals who were used to being first-choice or at least being in their country's Test twenty-three, so an all-embracing team ethic involving the entire squad was critical.

I spoke a little about the hangover from the last tour to New Zealand in 2005: the injury to Brian O'Driscoll there and its bitter fallout, how the appointment of Alastair Campbell had antagonised the New Zealand media and public, and the series whitewash. A lot of negativity surrounded that tour, which emphasised the need this time round to engage with the community, with fans, clubs, local hospitals and charity organisations, and also the need for players to room together, which they hadn't in 2005.

Another key aspect for me was my understanding of the New Zealand culture. Drawing on my experience of taking Wales to the World Cup there in 2011, the Lions needed to be prepared. New Zealand is different. It's such a long way away. You have to accept the *powhiris*, the traditional Maori welcome ceremonies. The Lions had to do everything they could to be ready for that, so that nothing would come as a shock to the players.

This was also when I first raised the issue of protecting the match-day squad of twenty-three as much as we possibly could for the first Test, as we had done in 2013, by bringing in additional players a week before the first All Blacks game.

I also talked about the announcement of the coaches and support staff, and the medical team. When I made the presentation, I suggested leaving this until after the 2017 Six Nations, but that would prove to be too late. Logistically we would need to finalise and confirm the coaches and support staff before then.

Four years previously, I had remained as Head Coach with Wales during the autumn campaign of 2012, but this time I thought it was important to take a step back sooner, to be more neutral and give players from the other three countries more opportunity to be selected by watching more games. Outlining the All Blacks' Test programme in 2016, I also felt this would give me more opportunity to have a closer look at the opposition.

Furthermore, the commercial commitments involved in being Head Coach of the Lions are incredible, and in 2012 and 2013 I hadn't been prepared for the demands of the Lions' major sponsors. The Lions are not like individual nations, who receive a percentage of the TV rights. Commercial sponsorship drives the Lions' revenue, but those demands had taken me by surprise four years earlier.

I also spoke about the importance of the relationship between the Head Coach and the Tour Manager, the Logistics Manager and the commercial team, and I highlighted the need for some continuity of staff from the Australian tour. With the Lions, you can't reinvent the wheel, and a level of trust can help to fast-track preparation time.

I then went through the list of potential assistant coaches and support staff: Joe Schmidt and Rob Howley as possible Attack Coaches; Steve Borthwick as Forwards Coach; Andy Farrell and Paul Gustard in Defence; and Neil Jenkins as Kicking Coach. I wanted Paul 'Bobby' Stridgeon for Head of Strength and Conditioning; Brian Cunniffe, who had been involved in 2013, to oversee the sports science once more; to retain most of the medical team from 2013; and again have Rhodri Bown and Mike Hughes plus one more overseeing our analysis.

I also wanted 'Rala', Patrick O'Reilly, as bagman again. When you're touring with the Lions you need people with personalities, who have a sense of humour. Rala has been there and done it. I know what the Irish players think of him and I'd been involved with him myself with Ireland. He's a unique character. Never mind a father figure, he's almost like a grandfather figure to the players, and they just love him. He's always in a good mood, so positive, and the players congregate in his room the night before games to clean their boots and have a chat. You can't buy that. Bobby is like that too, and the two of them are just gold dust. Good humoured and good people.

Near the end of my presentation, I suggested I was the best qualified person for the Lions job, having been an Assistant Coach in 2009 and Head Coach in 2013. I felt that my experiences coaching Ireland, in England with

Wasps, and Wales, gave me an important understanding of the cultural differences between the players.

I also believed I had a pretty good understanding of what a Lions tour meant to New Zealand, being a Kiwi, having played against the Lions, and knowing how excited their public already were that the Lions were coming.

In concluding my presentation, I said I'd be able to handle the pressure that comes with the job, internally and externally, and, if necessary, I had the ability to make the tough decisions.

When questions followed, Tom Grace asked: 'How would you feel if you were offered the job, or if you weren't offered the position?'

I thought about that for a few seconds and said: 'Tom, I feel that I can't lose.'

There were a few puzzled looks so I added: 'Look, if you offer me the position, it would be a huge honour and I'd be privileged to take the post, and I'd give you everything I've got. I'd give you one hundred per cent in New Zealand and do the best job I can. And if you don't offer me the job, then I'll think: "Well, thank God for that. I've probably dodged a bullet."'

They saw the irony in that, knowing how tough a task this would be.

It was genuinely how I felt too. Having experienced 2013, I knew how hard it is on the management and the coaches, and especially the Head Coach. You're in the spotlight every day. Everything you do, every decision you make, is scrutinised.

By comparison, the players can step in and out of the spotlight. The matches are, of course, tough, but if a Lions tour is not successful – and that can happen for any player – they can return to their clubs and their national teams without it necessarily impacting on their career.

For the coaches on the other hand, even Ian McGeechan, and certainly Clive Woodward and Graham Henry, they shoulder more of the burden of responsibility if the Lions fail. The Head Coach won't emerge with any credit, because there are so many people with opinions and judgements about any and every decision you make.

Being Head Coach of the Lions in 2013 was definitely the toughest thing I'd ever done. This was definitely true of the last week in Australia, after leaving out Brian O'Driscoll for the decisive third Test. The vitriolic criticism shocked me.

Selection is a matter of opinion. That's all selection is, and we all have our own opinions. I thought it was the right decision at the time but it was one of the hardest things I've ever had to do as a coach, not only making that decision but delivering the news, particularly as I had huge respect for Brian.

I had given him his first cap in 1999, and then was his Coach again after a gap of eight years in 2009, and once more in 2013. I was incredibly impressed with the knowledge he had accumulated in the intervening time, his maturity and understanding of the game, and his ability to bring the best out of those around him through his leadership.

We made a decision that we thought was right, which doesn't mean that you don't reflect on it and question whether it was the correct call. There are still some people who disagree with the decision, which I understand and respect. But that's why you're given the job of Head Coach. You make what you think is the right call at the time.

I came out of that 6 July meeting still feeling fairly relaxed about it all. By the end of the interview, coaching the Lions again was something I really wanted to do. But whatever happened, I was in a good place. If it was meant to be, they'd appoint me. If not, then I was comfortable with that as well.

● ● ●

About three weeks later, towards the end of July, John Feehan rang me and asked me if I'd like to accept the position. I immediately said yes. My contract wouldn't start until 1 September and they wouldn't be announcing it until a week later. In the meantime, Ger Carmody had been doing all the recce stuff, and other bits and pieces.

I was in Fiji on holiday with Trudi, Gabby and my parents-in-law, Margaret and Terry. Bryn had his own rugby so couldn't be with us. We were sitting outside our apartment finishing dinner when John Feehan's number appeared on my phone. I took the call inside while the family waited for the news. We thought we might hear the outcome of the interview while we were on holiday. I came back outside and said: 'The Lions job is mine if I want it!'

Gabby said: 'Well what did you tell him?'

'I said yes.'

There was great excitement and more wine poured. For Trudi and my extended family, coaching the Lions in New Zealand would be pretty special, although it had to be kept secret. They couldn't tell anyone until the official announcement.

'I'm telling you, but don't tell anyone else,' I said. 'Just keep it quiet for a few weeks.' This was going to be especially hard for Terry to keep secret, but he did a great job.

The Lions still had to have another board meeting and this was during peak holiday season. They also had to send me my contract, and we had to agree a deal, which takes a little bit of time, and inform the Welsh Rugby Union. They were happy enough for me to accept the position if offered, but we still had to complete the process of seconding me to the Lions for almost ten months.

So I sat on the patio on a balmy Fiji night, chatting with the family, and thinking about what I'd just taken on. It was meant to be, after all. I was going home with the Lions.

## WAIKATO KID TAMES LIONS

I first became aware of the Lions in 1971 when I was seven.

My dad, Dave, played a bit of club rugby at number 8. He and my mum, Kay, were both from Waikato. Like almost all Kiwi boys, I started playing rugby at five when my dad took me down to the local rugby club, and I got indoctrinated from a very early age into thinking that rugby was invented in New Zealand. That's actually what I believed! Back then the All Blacks were the best team in the world, always had been and always would be. So to discover that other countries played rugby, and were any good at it, came as something of a shock.

Growing up in New Zealand, your view of life is so narrow. You don't realise how small a country you live in, or how isolated you are from the rest of the world. So for the Lions to come to New Zealand in 1971, play some great rugby and win that Test series had quite an impact.

In those days, rugby was very much the fabric of the community, and the Lions undertook long tours reaching into every part of the country. People followed them and kept the press clippings. They got to know all the Lions players by name and what sort of people they were.

The 1971 Lions stopped off in Australia for two matches, losing their first game to Queensland, and then played another twenty-four matches in New Zealand. Waikato in Hamilton was the third of those, on 29 May, which was a Saturday, and the Lions won 35–14.

I didn't see that game. My grandmother, Doris Gatland, lived around the corner from Rugby Park in Ulster Street. Relatives and friends would park there and walk to the stadium. I could easily have been at her house as a young kid while they all went and watched the game.

With the Lions playing two games a week, there tended to be a significant difference between their Saturday team and their Wednesday team. The Lions won the first Test in Carisbrook 9–3, before the All Blacks won the second in Christchurch, at Lancaster Park, 22–12. It was the Lions' only other defeat of their tour. They won the third Test in Wellington 13–3 and the fourth was a 14–14 draw, so the Lions secured the series 2–1.

My memories of listening to games on the radio or watching them on TV are blurred. We didn't have a television then. At the time, colour TV was relatively new, and there were just two channels, TV1 and TV2. That was it.

On Saturdays, I would have been playing rugby at eight in the morning and the Tests would have been televised in the afternoon, so I would have watched them in my junior club in Hamilton, Eastern Suburbs.

You were brought up believing that the All Blacks were invincible. It must have been quite a shock for the country to lose that series, and it definitely had an impact on me. But I was a young kid. I didn't really understand the game, as I'd only just started playing myself.

The Lions came back again in 1977, and this time I watched their game in Hamilton. They left the UK in early May and returned home in mid-August, having played twenty-six matches. The Lions lost the first Test in Wellington and won the second in Christchurch. A week after that game they played in Hamilton and beat Waikato 18–13.

I just remember a massive crowd. Waikato had a reasonable side, with a few All Blacks. The New Zealand scrum-half Kevin Greene played that day and I recall the game being reasonably close.

The All Blacks won the third Test at Carisbrook in Dunedin, 19–7. The fourth and final Test took place in front of 58,000 at Eden Park, with the All Blacks scraping through 10–9 to secure a 3–1 series win. It must have been incredible to be there. Dougie Morgan scored all the Lions' points that day with a try, conversion and penalty, and the Lions led 9–6 going into injury time only to concede a match-winning try by Laurie Knight. Most people felt the Lions were a little unlucky not to draw the series.

I was thirteen and playing at my school, Te Awamutu College, just outside Hamilton, to where my parents had moved. I went to school there in 1977 and 1978 before I went to Hamilton Boys.

Lions tours were more regular back then, whereas now they only come to New Zealand every twelve years. When the Lions returned in 1983, I was nineteen and had just left school. I was playing in the Under-21s at Hamilton Old Boys, and was at Waikato University Teachers' College.

The Waikato game in Hamilton was the second-last match of the tour and the Lions had already lost the series 3–0 at that stage, with a fourth Test to come, but they beat Waikato 40–13. The first three Tests had been quite close, but for the last one at Eden Park they must have had one foot on the flight home. They lost that one 38–6.

Growing up as young players in New Zealand, we were absorbed in our own little world. While we might watch some of the Lions games, we didn't have a massive amount of interest until they come to our region. Then, there was almost a fever about the Lions being there.

● ● ●

When the Lions returned to New Zealand a decade later, it was completely different. I was twenty-nine and played against them for Waikato. There were two standout things I remember about that game. We'd won the New Zealand Championship the year before in 1992 and we were a little bit disappointed at being given the last midweek fixture before the final Test of what was now a three-match series. We wanted to have a crack at the Saturday side, a match-day squad as close to the Test side as possible. Being New Zealand champions, we felt we deserved the opportunity to go out there and make a statement.

It was interesting, because we learned afterwards that the Lions players had never heard of some of our players, not even the likes of our openside Duane Monkley. They knew all about him that day. He scored two tries and was awarded the man of the match.

They'd just won the second Test in Wellington to level the series, before playing us the following Tuesday afternoon. We were pumped up. That was a big game for the Lions too; their last game before the series decider. If they performed, and won, that would set the tone for the following Saturday.

But even before we went on to the pitch, I knew we were going to win that game. It was just one of those rare days, maybe just three or four, in your career, when you get a feeling in the changing room. Our Coach was Kevin Greene, who had played for Waikato against the Lions in 1977 and was then an All Black, and we had John Mitchell as captain and number 8.

Mitch would look at you with his steely blue eyes. Second-rower Brent Anderson would walk diagonally across the changing room, pacing back and forth. Some of the backs would hide in the showers to keep away from the forwards because we were a little bit wild at the time.

Waikato had a tough bunch of forwards. I was hooker and part of a good scrummaging and mauling pack. Those were also the days of rucking, when, if you got on the wrong side of the ruck, you got a good shoeing.

We had trained the previous Tuesday and Thursday evenings and came into camp on the Monday and stayed together that night. We had heaps of experience in that side. Six of the pack had played over 100 games for Waikato.

Despite it being a Tuesday the old Rugby Park was absolutely packed. There was an incredible atmosphere as everyone had taken the afternoon off. It was a good farming area, and farmers would come from out of town. Some beer would have been drunk in those days, and all the kids would sit on the ground around the pitch, so there was a definite buzz about the place.

We kicked off long and when the Lions kicked the ball out, I said to Richard Jerram, our number 6: 'I'm going to push this lineout a bit further.' He tapped it down and Brent Anderson peeled around the back of the lineout and ran straight at Stuart Barnes, the Lions fly-half. We made some yardage, came back on the short side, and scored through winger Doug Wilson, in the first minute of the game. I don't think the Lions touched the ball for the first twenty minutes. We absolutely smashed them.

If Barnesy had commentated on that game, I'm pretty sure he wouldn't have given himself man of the match. It wasn't a bad Lions backline, but they got hammered up front.

The best player on the field for the Lions was Will Carling, who scored a try in the last minute. My respect for him went up that day. He was the England captain at the time, and could have been demoralised about being in the dirt-trackers again on the final week of the tour and not involved in the Test match, but he played exceptionally well.

'The Day Gatland Scored a Try to Help Smash the Team He Now Coaches', read one headline years later when I became Lions Coach. The truth is, I scored a few as a player. In 140 games as a hooker for Waikato, I think I managed seventeen tries. I scored our last one that day on the left wing, when Monkley popped it to me. I ran around towards the posts to narrow the angle. It wasn't the most elegant dive in the world. It was more like a belly flop after falling onto my knees first.

I remember talking to some of the Lions players afterwards and a couple of them saying: 'Jesus, you come to New Zealand, and you play against the All Blacks, and the best player we've come up against on tour is Duane Monkley. Never heard of him.'

In my opinion, Duane was the best player I know never to have played for the All Blacks. He was phenomenal defensively and a great athlete but just didn't fit the mould at the time. They didn't think he was quite tall enough in those days. At Waikato, we were always up against the big three provinces, Auckland, Wellington and Canterbury. They had the best press machines behind them, writing stories about their teams and pushing players. We didn't get much media coverage, so it was a fight for our players to get recognition.

In that year we had Craig Stevenson at loose-head and Graham Purvis, an All Black, at tight-head. I took Craig and Graham to the barbers for matching flat-top haircuts. It was to help our scrummaging trick, called 'hang heads'. At the scrum, we'd spear into the opposition and drop our heads down. Then, when the ball came in, we'd snap back up into their chests and snatch half a metre.

We had two more All Blacks in the second-row, Steve Gordon and Anderson, as well as Mitch at number 8, while Richard Jerram was the blindside flanker. Simon Crabb was our scrum-half, and 'Fozzy', Ian Foster, was our number 10. He was a good outside-half, he controlled things with a good kicking game and was pretty quick as well.

In midfield we had Rhys Ellison, who would go on to play for Munster and marry a girl from Limerick, Karen. I went to school with Rhys. He was a couple of years behind me, went to Otago for a few years and had just come back to Waikato.

Our outside-centre, Aaron Collins, went to Scotland to play rugby and is still there. Wayne Warlow and Doug Wilson were the wings, and our full-back, Matthew Cooper, kicked three penalties and a couple of conversions that day. He had scored twenty-three points on his All Blacks Test debut against Ireland the year before and was on the bench in all three Tests against the Lions.

For the rest of us, it was the only time we ever played the Lions. Waikato had played against Wales in 1988, and Australia a couple of times. We had beaten Wales and had drawn with and beaten Australia. We had also had victories over Samoa and Argentina, but we had a loss to South Africa. So we had a decent record against international touring teams, but as a player you looked on a match with the Lions as a once-in-a-lifetime opportunity. It wasn't just a national team. You were playing the Lions, the best players from four nations. That was huge motivation. The Lions' record in the past, against provincial teams, had been pretty good, although on that tour they had beaten six provincial sides while losing to Otago, Auckland and Hawke's Bay. It was a chance to make a little bit of history.

Waikato had never beaten the Lions before. Their most famous victory had been in 1956 against South Africa. In those days, South Africa used to bring a Springbok head with them, and would present it to the first provincial team that beat them on tour. Many times they had toured New Zealand and taken the head back with them because no provincial team had managed to win against them.

When the full-time whistle blew at Rugby Park, the score was 38–10 to us, and everyone just ran onto the field. You don't get that nowadays, but one of the great things about playing for Waikato was the fans' loyalty and how vocal they were in supporting you. They were smacking their cans together or ringing their cow bells all through the match.

We had a good night and partied pretty hard. That was the reward. In those amateur days Waikato gave you a gold pin, a little *mooloo* badge (*mooloo* is a cow and was the Waikato mascot), if you beat a touring team. They didn't come around very often. If you won, you also got to keep your jersey. Over the years I gave most of my stuff away, but I still have that jersey in a drawer at home in Hamilton.

That day was one of the three most memorable wins of my playing career. The others were also with Waikato: in 1992, when we won the New Zealand Championship by beating Otago, and at the end of 1993 when we beat Auckland for the second year in a row, at Eden Park, for the Ranfurly Shield. They'd held it for seven or eight years and were unbeaten at home for a long, long time.

But that Lions victory was up there with those two.

I was incredibly proud of being an All Black and playing for them seventeen times, despite the fact that I didn't play any Tests. I had played against plenty of provinces or clubs on tour, and it was always a massive honour, but nothing like those victories playing for Waikato.

There was no official dinner after that Lions game, but we went to a local bar and a few of the Welsh boys were out on the beers. We'd had official dinners in the past, but this time there was just a function at the ground afterwards, with stand-up food and some drinks, and a few speeches by their touring manager and captain, and our chairman at the time. Mitch said a few words as well.

Most of the people of Hamilton and a good few beyond were out and about that night. There must have been a fair amount of absenteeism on the Wednesday morning. I don't know if I went into work the next day. I presume I did.

They were good days, and that day playing against the Lions was certainly one of the best.

# 2

## MUTINY ON THE BUSES

### Lions to South Africa, 2009

When you're an international coach in the UK and Ireland, the Lions are never too far away. I was appointed Irish Head Coach in February 1998, after Brian Ashton had resigned one round into what was then the Five Nations. I was thirty-four.

Almost twenty years on, I copped plenty of flak for not picking enough Scots for the Lions, and I know how they feel. Back in 2001, when Graham Henry was the Lions Head Coach for their tour to Australia, from an Irish perspective I didn't feel we were represented fairly either.

In the original squad of thirty-seven players, there were eighteen English, ten Welsh, and three Scots, along with six Irish players, Brian O'Driscoll, Rob Henderson, Ronan O'Gara, Keith Wood, Jeremy Davidson and Malcolm O'Kelly. The seven players later added to the squad did, however, include David Wallace and Tyrone Howe.

I certainly felt Denis Hickie should have been in the squad, and maybe one or two others. But the Irish players suffered more than anybody because of the outbreak of foot and mouth disease across the UK and Ireland that year. After beating Italy in Rome and France in Dublin, Ireland's remaining three games in the Six Nations, against Scotland, Wales and England, were postponed until the autumn, and so were held after the Lions tour.

There was a plus-side though. After Ireland lost to Scotland in Murrayfield in early September, we were a pretty motivated team when we played Wales in the Millennium Stadium, a game Ireland won 36–6, and when England came to Dublin aiming for the Grand Slam a week later, Ireland were again winners, 20–14.

A significant motivating factor for us was that so many Welsh and English players had been selected for the Lions and so few Irish.

● ● ●

In 2009, Ian McGeechan asked me to come on board as one of his assistant coaches on the Lions tour to South Africa.

By then, having coached in Ireland, I'd also coached in London with Wasps and won a Grand Slam with Wales in 2008, and in addition to the Irish and Welsh players I'd coached, there were four Wasps players in that squad. I'd also gone back to New Zealand to coach Waikato in 2005 and had gone to the third Test in Eden Park that same year.

Graham Rowntree, Rob Howley, Shaun Edwards and Neil Jenkins were also part of the coaching ticket and we had quite a few meetings. Geech had done most of the planning himself before the tour.

After the disappointment of 2005 in New Zealand, plenty of people were questioning whether the Lions could survive in the professional era. Was the concept still viable? Was it a relic of the amateur era? Was there room for it in the busy rugby calendar? Yes, it generated interest and money, but the results had been bad, losing five Tests in a row after leading 1–0 in the series in Australia in 2001. The 3–0 whitewash in New Zealand had been a hammering.

I think the 2009 tour was a real crossroads for the Lions. Our whole motivation was to regain some respect for the jersey, and by the end of the series we felt we had achieved that.

We didn't lose any games leading into the first Test, but got caught a little bit with our pants down in that game, thinking we were probably in better shape than we were, because we'd won the warm-up games pretty comfortably. We'd had a couple of tough matches, but South Africa hadn't released any of their Test players to their provinces.

We had problems in the scrum in that first Test. Sometimes it happens with a prop, but for whatever reason Phil Vickery had a bad day against the Beast, Tendai Mtawarira. Looking back on it now, I think we probably should have made a change sooner. We debated it in the coaches' box, but we waited until after half-time before we brought on Adam Jones as a replacement. By then we were already 19–7 down, and soon fell 26–7 behind, before scoring two tries to make it 26–21. But in the end, we ran out of time.

We should have drawn the second Test. In fact, we should have won it. We were reasonably well ahead in the first half. I think it was disgraceful that the touch judge, Bryce Lawrence, bottled out of not recommending a red card for Schalk Burger when he raked his fingers across Luke Fitzgerald's eyes in a ruck. We could see it clearly from where we were, and it was only about ten yards away from Lawrence. The incident occurred in the first minute of the game, but it should have been a straight red card and that would have been game over. Burger ended up receiving an eight-week suspension for it, which shows he should have been red carded. A yellow card was just a cop out.

Even then we were leading 16–5 until the last kick of the first period, when François Steyn kicked a huge penalty from his own half. We were still leading by eleven points going into the last quarter.

Brian O'Driscoll put in a huge hit on Danie Rossouw but it left both of them poleaxed. Rossouw went off but Brian stayed on, whereas today he would have come off for a head injury assessment. Players didn't have to go through the HIA protocols back then and Brian was caught out in the next play when Bryan Habana cut through our midfield to score.

We then replaced him with Shane Williams, but soon after that we also had to take off Jamie Roberts. Ronan O'Gara came on, and we shifted Stephen Jones to midfield for the last dozen minutes, when we were 22–18 ahead. Another option we didn't consider at the time was putting Mike Phillips to 12. After Morne Steyn converted Jaque Fourie's try in the corner, Stephen's penalty made it 25–25.

A draw would have kept the series level, but we all know what happened next. With seconds to go, Ronan probably should have kicked the ball out from his own 22, but instead he put the ball up in the air, chased and clattered into Fourie du Preez to concede a penalty. With the last kick of the match, Steyn sealed the series for South Africa.

I felt for Ronan. Regardless of whether he should have got the ball off the park, he was trying to keep the idea of winning the series alive. Players have to evaluate all of this in the space of a few seconds. He opted for an up-and-under, but unfortunately he caught du Preez when he was in the air. If he'd just held off him a bit, that would have been fine. But the penalty was awarded, and with that we lost the series, when it should have been either 1–1, or 1–0 to them with one drawn, and a decider to come in Johannesburg.

One of the most memorable events on that tour was the mutiny on the buses, on the Sunday after the second Test. As it had been such a long season for most of the players, we decided to give them two or three days off before the third Test. A safari trip was booked, and so two buses took the squad to north of Pretoria. All of a sudden one of the buses pulled over for some of the players to take a toilet break. At this point, some of the guys on the other bus said: 'We don't want to go.' By this they meant the safari, not to the toilet.

This led to a big debate on the side of the road. In the end, it was agreed that those who wanted to go on the safari took one bus, and the other one turned back to the hotel in Pretoria, for those players to hang out in the city for a few days.

When we went to Noosa for a couple of days in 2013, the Sunday after the second Test, a group of us flew over to Fraser Island. Others went surfing, some went on jetboats, and a few guys played some golf. Everyone got the tour out of their system in their own way.

In 2009 it was the same. Those who went back to Pretoria had a few beers on the Sunday night, and chilled for a few days, before we started training again on the Wednesday. All the work had been done at that stage. We weren't going to re-invent the wheel, or change our game too much, in the last week of the tour.

I learned from that too. What everyone did on rest days while on tour should not have been prescribed. In South Africa, I think the idea was right – giving the players a break and having a cultural experience – but this should have come with an option to stay behind in the hotel for those who wanted to.

Give the players a choice. Treat them like adults and let them do what they want to do. Thanks to that unscheduled toilet break, we stumbled upon the best solution.

Ironically, apart from Paul O'Connell, I had coached all those players who wanted to pull out of the safari trip: the likes of Andy Powell, Mike Phillips, Tim Payne and Simon Shaw. So I said to our Manager, Gerald Davies: 'There are a few Welsh players who want to go back and a few Wasps players, and

Paul. I think I should go and look after them.' However, Paul then 'got the guilts'. He felt he'd abandoned the squad. But we went back, had a few drinks in the hotel bar and a sing-song which we all enjoyed.

The second Test had been one of the most brutally tough Test matches I've ever seen. Both teams had several injuries, and Burger had been suspended while O'Driscoll was out of the tour, so both sides made lots of changes for the final Test.

It may have been a dead rubber, but in order to regain respect for the Lions jersey, we simply had to win that match. A second consecutive series whitewash would have meant eight Test defeats in a row and provided plenty of ammunition for those who wanted to kill the Lions.

Shane Williams was on fire in Johannesburg and scored two tries. Riki Flutey had a good game, so too Phil Vickery after what happened to him in the first Test. We had picked Ugo Monye for the first Test but dropped him for the second, and I've always wondered about that decision. He botched a couple of try opportunities in the first Test, but I still felt we should have kept faith with him.

I remember that discussion between the coaches. I said: 'Yes, he didn't score the tries but he put himself in a position to score them, and maybe the next time, given the same opportunities, he will finish them.' Ultimately, Ugo sat out the second Test, but we brought him back in for the third, and he played really well and scored.

We won well, 28–9, but we still felt that at a minimum the series should have been drawn. It was also the least Paul O'Connell deserved. Paul was a strong character and a real motivator, and I think he did a great job as captain.

For the most part, I kept my head down and did my job as the Forwards Coach. I remember Geech, before one of the Tests, saying to me: 'Would you present the jerseys, as a former All Black and a player who has played against the Lions?'

'No, I won't do that,' I said. 'I think, to do that you need to have earned respect as a Lion.'

I'd only been part of the Lions as an Assistant Coach and I hadn't earnt that level of respect yet. Geech often tells that story, and says that by me saying no to him, it meant that I understood the Lions, and what it means to the players and people who have been involved.

Certainly Geech's experience has given him an understanding of the Lions like no one else. What shone through for me on that tour was his love and passion for the Lions, having been involved in the 1974 and 1977 tours as a player, and five tours since as a coach – four of them as Head Coach.

That was hugely beneficial for me. As well as all of his own experiences, he'd seen successful tours and some not so successful, where coaches had tried certain things that hadn't worked. By tapping into his knowledge, I was able to get a 360-degree view of what went into coaching a squad of disparate parts which would prepare me for future Lions tours.

A key aspect of 2009 was reverting to the core values of the Lions, not least in engaging with the community. This is something the Lions do more than any other team. Geech stripped it back and made the Lions not only play some good rugby and win over our fans but also the South Africans. We were very, very conscious of that, and made ourselves a popular touring party by visiting local schools, clubs, townships and hospitals, and holding open training sessions and engaging with the media. We gave a lot of kit away as well to one of the children's charities.

All this gave me a huge grounding in what the Lions are about. Until then, I had been this Kiwi who had played against them or watched on from the outside. I was aware of the mistakes that Graham Henry made, and which he admits he made, in 2001, as well as those by Clive Woodward four years later. But after working with Geech, and also talking with other coaches and players, I could try to create a winning formula of my own.

It was on that tour that I fully realised the impact of the Lions jersey. They're all pretty proud to play for their own national team, but you see it when a player puts that Lions jersey on for the first time, especially for a Test. As a coach you don't have to motivate him. If anything it's the opposite. He's absolutely on the edge. It's the same as the impact that an All Blacks jersey has on a New Zealand player. That's what struck me as much as anything else on that tour, what the jersey means to the players.

You see it before the players even leave these shores, on what we call 'Messy Monday', when the entire Lions squad assembles for the first time to register and get fitted for all their gear. They're like kids at their first day at high school: a bit nervous around each other, not too sure of their surroundings, shaking hands and making polite conversation. Yet within a couple of weeks, strong bonds have already been formed.

They might only see each other once a year if they're playing an international, or they might not see each other for a few years, but once you've had that experience on tour as a Lion, it's there for life. No one can ever take it away from you and these players don't just want to be Lions, they want to be winning Lions, because that's the ultimate.

Even though as a scratch team you're playing, traditionally, one of the best three teams in the world, away from home, with limited preparation time, the expectation is still to win.

To win a Test series is the pinnacle. I don't think people fully recognise and respect how big an achievement it is to be a winning Lion. It's a hard thing to do; about as hard as it gets.

# 3

## THE BIG CALL

## Lions to Australia, 2013

Who might have thought that my next appointment with the Lions would start off from a hospital bed in New Zealand?

Initially, the Lions management had talked about selecting the Head Coach to Australia after the 2011 World Cup, and the people in contention were Ireland's Coach Declan Kidney, Scotland's Andy Robinson and myself. Wales did pretty well in New Zealand and reached the semi-finals, but then the Lions decided to defer their decision until after the 2012 Six Nations.

Wales ended up winning the Grand Slam, Ireland came third with five points and Scotland finished with the wooden spoon. It wasn't too much of a surprise then that Andy pulled out of the process, so it was just myself and Declan who were interviewed for the Lions job.

The Welsh RFU had agreed to release me in March, but in April I fractured both my heels when falling ten feet onto concrete while cleaning the windows of our holiday home in Waihi Beach in the Bay of Plenty. This delayed the announcement until September, when I was finally confirmed as Head Coach. Although I assumed the job then, a deal was agreed with the WRU whereby I could continue as the Welsh Head Coach in the November Test window before stepping aside to concentrate solely on the Lions.

Having had a stint as the Lions Assistant Coach four years previously in South Africa was hugely important. The thing with the Lions is that despite what certain journalists or people on the outside might say, it is a unique concept and previous experience helps.

The 2005 and 2009 tours had shown that the limited preparation time placed more value on continuity in selection, for both the playing squad and coaching team. One of the biggest decisions a Lions Coach is ever going to make is choosing a tour captain, and I had no hesitation in making Sam Warburton the youngest ever at twenty-four. The logic was sound. I just felt that if he was fit and playing well, he had a good chance of being in the Test side and, in any event, I have no problem in picking someone else to be captain of a Test side even if they're not captain of the tour.

Sam had achieved significant success as Welsh captain at the 2011 World Cup, and in the team that won the Grand Slam in 2012 and went on to retain the Six Nations title in 2013, even though he didn't captain the team in the final game against England. No one else in the four countries had experienced that same level of achievement in those two years before the tour.

I was surprised when some of our selections attracted more attention than they deserved. We picked Dylan Hartley in the original squad before he was suspended and then called in Rory Best. There had been quite a lot of criticism for not selecting Rory in the first place. One significant impact in the modern game is the increasing influence of social media, where everyone has an opinion. In my view, it can be a vent for parochialism, from country to country, more than an outlet for reasoned debate.

Dylan is definitely an extremely competitive individual and his disciplinary record hadn't been the greatest with his club Northampton, although it had been pretty good with England. There were a few bigger concerns as we came to finalising our squad. Paul O'Connell had been injured and hadn't played a lot of rugby, and it was the same with Brian O'Driscoll. I think Brian was really concerned he wasn't going to make the tour. Not being able to take one or both former Lions captains would have been a significant blow given their experience and ability.

On the final Saturday of the Six Nations, in an Anglo-Welsh showdown at the Millennium Stadium, England were going for the Grand Slam and Wales were looking to retain their title. Wales won 30–3. It was almost like a final trial for places in the Lions squad. One example was Alex Cuthbert, who scored both tries that night. Others were Ian Evans and Dan Lydiate, who made it into the travelling party at the expense of Chris Robshaw.

Another big call was in the backroom team and deciding to pick Andy Farrell ahead of Shaun Edwards as Defence Coach. That wasn't an easy one for me. I'd worked a huge amount with Shaun, but I just felt that it was good to bring in a different voice from another environment. I respected him, and I know how disappointed he was at the time. They're both excellent coaches, and Andy is hugely rated, having been involved in professional sport from such a young age. He also understands cultures, and especially winning cultures.

● ● ●

It was decided that the Lions should stop off in Hong Kong to play the Barbarians on the way to Australia. Initially, it wasn't a fixture I would have wanted. I'd have preferred to go directly to Australia, with a full week there to prepare for the first game against Western Force.

We had another problem on the night of the game in Hong Kong for which I was completely to blame. Some of the management had done a recce during the day from the hotel to the ground and, not wanting to arrive there too early, I put back the team meeting. But I completely underestimated the traffic in Hong Kong, even on a Saturday evening, and we only arrived at the ground about thirty-five minutes before kick-off.

As the bus crawled along at a snail's pace, Andy Irvine, our Tour Manager, was becoming quite animated and I was sitting there thinking: 'This is entirely my fault. Great start, Gats.' But at the same time there was no point in getting too stressed. There wasn't anything we could do about it.

The officials put back the kick-off by ten minutes due to our late arrival, although they were not obliged to do so. The boys hopped off the bus and quickly got themselves organised. No one said a word. No one complained. A problem that was of my own making was turned into a positive experience. The players, the coaches, the medics and the rest of the staff all handled a crisis situation calmly.

As any coach will agree, at some stage on tour you're going to have to deal with an issue, whether it's a late bus, something breaking down, a change in the weather conditions or a crisis off the pitch. Not everything can run smoothly, but not letting those experiences affect the squad is key.

Such was the heat and humidity in Hong Kong, managing the players through that game was also difficult; making sure they rehydrated by engineering stoppages and bringing the whole bench onto the pitch early.

We'd had a training session on the Thursday during which players were clearly in distress. I remember, particularly, the heat really affected Richard Hibbard. It was about 40 to 41 degrees, and he really struggled that day.

We had the option of going on two flights to Perth but we decided to all fly together, the players flying business class while the staff flew economy. There was a slight problem in that there were only thirty-six business class seats on the plane and we'd selected thirty-seven players. One player was going to have to fly economy. I had to choose, and the unlucky one was Richard Hibbard. You could say that it wasn't his week. 'Hibbs' is a great tourist, but you have to keep him in his box every now and again. He knew it was my decision, and he was on the fines committee, so he had his revenge by fining me for making that call.

Overall though, and surprisingly, it had turned out to be quite a beneficial stopover. Yes, it was really hot and humid in Hong Kong, but we had some good conditioning for a few days, and to break up the trip, acclimatise, play a game and get a good victory was really pleasing.

You could say that the quality of the opposition that night didn't make for the best preparation, but even for our first game on Australian soil, against the Western Force, their Coach Michael Foley chose what was virtually a second string side and we won that game comfortably too.

Even at that early stage, the injury problems started to mount. We had lost Gethin Jenkins right at the outset and then Cian Healy suffered ankle ligament damage against the Force, so we called up Alex Corbisiero and Ryan Grant as replacements.

Another feature of that game in Perth was Leigh Halfpenny's kicking. He kicked eleven out of eleven, whereas Johnny Sexton had started the Barbarians game and missed three out of five. Furthermore, one of our other full-backs, Rob Kearney, was carrying an injury and wasn't involved in the first few games. With Leigh kicking like a machine, the decision about full-back and goal-kicking for the first Test was virtually decided in those initial two games.

Next up was the Queensland Reds and, in contrast to Foley, Ewen McKenzie picked a strong team, and even though he wasn't allowed to play his Wallabies they gave us a good game. They tried to run us off our feet, starting at 100 miles an hour, and we were stressed for a while. They were a seriously good side and played with an intensity and tempo that made it a furiously fast game. We won 22–12, which doesn't tell the story of the match, and in fairness to us we entered into the spirit of it as well. It was also great to play at Suncorp Stadium before the first Test, where Australia had an excellent record.

We only took two '10s' to Australia, so Stuart Hogg played at outside-half against a Combined New South Wales/Queensland Country team, who we put away 64–0. The way we started that game it looked like it might be eighty or 100, but our level dropped in the second half. It was a messy performance after the break, with a little white line fever.

With Michael Cheika coaching the Waratahs in our next match, they were never going to take the Western Force approach a week out from the first Test. The Waratahs were really aggressive, with plenty of off-the-ball incidents – holding, grabbing, late hits. They were definitely out to unsettle us and in particular Johnny Sexton who of course Cheika knew well from his time as Leinster Coach.

But the boys handled all of that stuff and we played really well against the Waratahs, winning 47–17 with five tries. Jonathan Davies was especially good that night. Brian O'Driscoll had a little bit of an injury, and he came up to me afterwards and said: 'How good was Jonathan Davies?'

After the Waratahs game I thought we needed to protect as many of the Test-playing team as we could against the Brumbies the following Tuesday in Canberra. That's why we called up Shane Williams (who'd been playing in Japan and was in Australia doing media work), Christian Wade and Brad Barritt. We emptied a strong bench before the hour mark and that made a bit of a difference. In fact, I probably brought the replacements on earlier than planned because the game was close and I wanted to win, but we came up just short, losing 14–12.

●　●　●

Going into the first Test at the Suncorp Stadium in Brisbane on 22 June 2013, I was acutely conscious that recent history wasn't on our side. The Lions had lost to Australia in 2001, lost to New Zealand in 2005, badly, and then lost to South Africa in 2009. You had to go back sixteen years to South Africa in 1997 for the last series win.

We probably would have picked Jamie Roberts in that first Test, but he picked up an injury against the Waratahs. We thought the midfield performance in that game, of Jamie and Jonathan Davies, had been the best of the tour. Brian O'Driscoll might have been on the bench but he probably wouldn't have started if Jamie had been fit.

Brisbane was a nail-biter from start to finish. We knew how important it was to win the first Test. At the very least, it ensures that everything is on the line until the last game. Israel Folau, on his debut, scored two tries that night in the first half, but George North scored a brilliant 60 metre try of his own. He was possibly the best finisher and gamebreaker in world rugby at that point. We led 13–12 at half-time and in the second period, after Alex Cuthbert finished really well under the posts, we needed another penalty by Leigh Halfpenny to keep our noses in front. We were a little lucky that James O'Connor was initially kicking for them that night, and between him and Kurtley Beale they missed five out of nine kicks, with Beale missing with the last kick of the game. Leigh, in contrast, kicked six out of seven for us and we sneaked home 23–21.

Paul O'Connell suffered a fractured arm in that first Test, but we kept him on the tour for his presence off the pitch. Geoff Parling was then pulled from our final midweek game against the Melbourne Rebels to replace Paul in the second Test, so we made Dan Lydiate captain for the Rebels game. Dan was quite rousing and vocal in the changing room. I hadn't seen that side to him. Several players performed very strongly in that 35–0 win over the Rebels, so much so that they forced their way into the picture for the third Test.

We could have clinched the series in Melbourne. The second Test was a tight game and we led 15–9 until the last five minutes, but Australia had a good second half and came on really strong in the final quarter, eventually getting a try by Adam Ashley-Cooper which they probably deserved. Leigh Halfpenny did have a kick on full-time to win it from halfway but it dropped short. Australia had come through by a narrow 16–15.

I remember in the tunnel afterwards seeing some of the Wallabies' players in tears. I could see how much it meant to them, and the relief they felt because they brought so much emotion to the occasion. I thought: 'They can't get to that emotional pitch again in the third Test, and I know there's another level in us.' So I said to the players: 'I think we can go up another level and bring more emotion to the third Test.'

I had experienced something similar in the past when Wasps played Leicester in Martin Johnson and Neil Back's last game at Welford Road. As a coach I completely underestimated the emotion of that night and what it meant to Leicester. Two weeks later, we played them in the Premiership final, and put forty points on them.

You never forget how emotional this game can be at the highest level, and sometimes a team just want it a little bit more than the opposition. The problem is, when a performance hinges so much on emotion one week, it can be very hard to reproduce it just a week later.

In the second Test, we hadn't brought Owen Farrell on for Johnny Sexton, when maybe we needed a bit of a change. Owen's a different type of player and I had a conversation with Andy Farrell afterwards, saying to him: 'Just because he's your son, don't be afraid to have an input, to say "have you thought about bringing Owen on?"' Andy hadn't suggested that in the coaches' box, and it wasn't until I went back over the video that I felt maybe we should have made that change. So we were in more of a mind to bring him on in the third Test.

But, of course, with Jamie Roberts fit for that game, the bigger call was recalling him, moving Jonathan Davies to outside-centre, and leaving out Brian O'Driscoll. It was a big decision, very much based on Jamie's performance against the Waratahs.

Brian had given us everything. He made a lot of tackles in that second Test and I think Australia were looking to go down his channel. That decision made it a very challenging week. I repeat, it was the hardest thing I've ever had to do as a coach, having given Brian his first cap, to then be the first person to drop him in his rugby career.

I knew there was going to be a fall-out, but it was nothing like as I expected.

We made other big calls. We recalled Mike Phillips for Ben Youngs, who like Brian didn't make the bench as we opted for Conor Murray as back-up. We recalled Alex Corbisiero for Mako Vunipola, Richard Hibbard for Tom Youngs, Toby Faletau for Jamie Heaslip, and with Sam Warburton out, we called up Sean O'Brien and made Alun Wyn Jones captain.

Yet all the focus was on Brian and myself. Everything else went under the radar. There wasn't any finger pointing at any players or media focus on them. They could just concentrate on their own performance, and not worry too much about outside noises.

What we also learnt from the experience was making sure we discussed who should be put up for media before a big match. Brian did media on the Monday so the journalists assumed he would be playing and probably be captain. If we were thinking of making a change, Brian shouldn't have done media and it wasn't fair on him.

What made it even harder for me was that I could have taken the soft option of putting him on the bench. The outcry wouldn't have been anything like the same. It may have softened the blow a little for Brian as well.

But as Manu Tuilagi was fit again, I just felt that, if it came to it, for ten or fifteen minutes, given his size and pace, the impact he could have coming off the bench might be more destructive. Sometimes you're looking for a difference off the bench and Brian, to me, seemed more of a starter.

Toby Faletau played well against the Rebels and we felt that he deserved an opportunity. Plenty was made of the decision to start ten Welsh players, but I felt they could do a job. Ultimately, just as significant was the impact of the bench. I don't think enough was made of how important the replacements were.

One of those was Tom Youngs, who had started the first Test. An example of why I like him so much is that he admitted to me: 'It's the right call. I'm absolutely f*****.'

'Are you OK to be on the bench?' I asked him.

'I'll give you everything I've got coming off the bench,' he said, and he did.

On the Sunday after the second Test, we went up to Noosa for a few days of R&R, just to get away from it all, before travelling to Sydney on the Wednesday. It was the end of a long tour at the end of a long season.

For the third and final Test, with the series in the balance, while we made some changes in personnel, we didn't change our game plan much.

We dominated them in the scrums. Corbisiero scored early. With their scrum under huge pressure, his opposing tight-head Ben Alexander was sin-binned and replaced in the first half. On any other day, Corbisiero would have won the man of the match, but Leigh Halfpenny kicked virtually everything that night, eight from nine, and counter-attacked well.

We brought on Tom Youngs, Mako Vunipola, Dan Cole, Richie Gray, Justin Tipuric and Conor Murray quite early. I thought the Welsh boys in the settled combinations could start well, but definitely the bench was significant. If we'd had another Test match, Conor Murray would have started it. He began the tour as the third choice, and ended it almost being number one.

The Wallabies came back at us just after half-time, making the game close for a while, but then we scored three tries. With fifteen minutes to go, we knew we'd won the match. The final score read Lions 41 Australia 16 and with that we had won the series too.

When it was all over, I was relieved more than anything else. There had been a huge amount of pressure on the coaches, as there always is on a Lions tour because so much of the focus is on the selection, the coaching and the tactics, and this was particularly true that week.

Some people had gone out on a limb thinking that Australia, having won the second Test and finished quite strongly, were the team with the momentum going into the third Test and would win the series 2–1 from being 1–0 down. That is exactly what had happened in 2001, so plenty of journalists had become quite critical of me, the other coaches and the Lions in general.

I understand journalists play a game themselves. You're banking on a result going the way you forecast, which justifies your views. When the result goes the other way and they realise they're wrong, some journalists are capable of putting their hand up afterwards and admitting that. But there are other journalists who, when the result flies in the face of their argument, can still never admit that they were wrong.

That tour, and even winning the series, was an emotional rollercoaster.

The first question in the press conference afterwards was: 'Warren, you must feel justified in your selection and dropping Brian O'Driscoll after that result?'

If I had said yes, that would have been the headline. Gatland Feels Vindicated.

I just said no, that it was the hardest thing I've ever had to do as a coach.

I wondered at the time, and have done since, whether or not it was the right decision. Was it the right call? Would we have still won the game if

Brian had been playing? All those sorts of things. But I didn't want to give anyone the opportunity to turn the result back onto me and in the process create something negative again.

Before the full-time whistle, I had gone to the side of the pitch to start congratulating all the players and the staff. I wanted to experience that moment and celebrate the victory with the team. But when I went onto the field, there was a row of cameras in front of me. *'Click. Click. Click.'* I stopped to let them take photos from about twenty metres away. How many photographs could they need?

'Come on guys, give me a chance to get to the players?' I said.

They just wouldn't move. They kept a line in front of me. I walked a little more toward them and said: 'OK guys, you've had enough.' They weren't budging.

The players wanted to do a lap of honour and say thank you to the fans. I wanted to join them and be a part of it, but unfortunately the photographers had formed an impenetrable defensive line.

'Ah, f*** you then.' I turned around and walked back into the changing room. I had some precious time there on my own. I sat down, opened a bottle of beer and almost shed a tear. It had been an emotional week. I was completely on my own for those ten minutes before people started to come back in. It was surreal.

That evening there was an official function for both squads in the Sydney Opera House. I spoke to the Wallabies' Coach Robbie Deans and he wasn't too hopeful about retaining his job. That was a difficult night for him.

The boys all went out and had a big night, but I went back to the hotel and had a relatively quiet evening. When we met up the next day, some of them hadn't slept at all and were still celebrating. The parties went on for a day or two. Winning a series with the Lions doesn't happen too often so they deserved it.

The players and the management were good people to tour with and the celebrations made all the hard work worthwhile.

My wife Trudi and daughter Gabby had been on holidays there for a few weeks, and as a surprise a friend of ours, Michael Holland, flew my son Bryn over for the last game. Unfortunately, the plane was delayed and he missed the match. Still, he had a good night out on the town and flew back to New Zealand the next day.

Trudi and I went to Fiji for seven days. I've never needed a week's break from rugby so much in my life.

## 4

## 'WE REALLY ARE
## IN THIS TOGETHER'

---

**Build up to Lions to New Zealand, 2017**

*Tuesday, 6 September 2016*
*Management meeting, Edinburgh*

Three years on from my last stint as Lions Head Coach in Australia, the wheels were back in motion as the toughest tour of them all was coming up in less than nine months' time.

I had of course been offered the job of Lions Head Coach to New Zealand back at the end of July and accepted the position, but it had taken five to six weeks to get the contract sorted before the official announcement of my appointment could be made.

We were staying in the Caledonian hotel and it was a pretty full-on two days. I had a meeting with all of those who had interviewed me for the job, along with Charlie McEwen, the Lions' Chief Operating Officer, Anna Voyce,

Head of Commercial and Dave Barton, Head of Communications. I'd caught up with Charlie on 30 August, and Dave on 1 September.

I had to do a photoshoot with Billy Stickland and Dan Sheridan of Inpho, the official photographic agency with the Lions. The idea was to do the photoshoot secretly for publication at my official unveiling as Lions Head Coach the next day. We drove to a hill overlooking some monuments, where I took off the top which had been covering my Lions jersey. Puzzled tourists were clearly wondering what was going on.

We also did some photos outside the offices of Standard Life Investment, one of the Lions' commercial sponsors. Someone took a sneaky shot and posted it on social media with the caption: 'No secret who's going to be appointed the Lions Head Coach tomorrow.' That didn't go down well.

## Wednesday, 7 September
## Head Coach announcement, Edinburgh

Another jam-packed day, of about seven or eight hours, including interviews with rights holders, various one-on-ones and press conferences with the online, radio, daily and Sunday media.

At the main press conference, after the formal announcement of my appointment, I was asked various questions about the detail of the tour to New Zealand. One of those was about calling up replacements towards the end of the tour, and I said: 'That's one consideration. One thing that I spoke about in the interview process is that the hardest game is the Chiefs game before the first Test. How do you protect that Test match twenty-three? I know Wales are in the [Pacific] Islands, Scotland are in Australia, England in Argentina and Ireland in Japan – so there is potentially an opportunity to maybe bring in four or five players to sit on the bench.

'That is my thought process at the moment. It [protecting the Test twenty-three] made a massive difference in 2013. We had players on the bench, but not exposing the fifteen to having to be involved, that is important. It's about getting the balance right. You don't want the squad to be too big and unwieldy, [but] how do you keep it small enough so everyone feels a part, feels like they have an opportunity, so you are not carrying two or three just for the sake of it?

'Maybe Clive got the model right in 2005 in terms of having two different squads, but then if you are having two teams, an A and a B, do you devalue the jersey? There are all those debates and discussions to have. To me, it's about making the jersey special; how do you keep the squad intimate and small enough that everyone feels special and part of it?'

I was asked if it would be difficult to bring in five new players for one game, and I said: 'We did that a bit in 2013 with Shane Williams and others. Bring your boots guys, there's a chance! Look, those are my thoughts at the moment . . . Those are things I've discussed with the board and they'll fall into place in the next six months.'

## Thursday, 8 September to Wednesday, 21 September
## Recce visit to New Zealand with Ger Carmody

Ger wanted to show me all the stadiums, rugby training pitches, gyms, pools, hotels and R&R venues that he'd looked at, and it was also a good opportunity to take in some All Blacks games in the Rugby Championship. We flew out on the Thursday, arrived on the Saturday and went to the All Blacks–Argentina game that night, which, conveniently, was in Hamilton.

Argentina played really well in the first half. They got in behind the All Blacks a few times, scored a try early on through Santiago Cordero and after fifty minutes it was 24–22 before the All Blacks ran away with it to win 57–22. Argentina made Aaron Smith tackle quite a bit and got a few offloads away and used their wingers up the middle off '9' to get in behind the All Blacks. I thought that could be a useful tactic for the Lions.

The following Saturday, 17 September, myself, Ger and Trudi went to the New Zealand–South Africa game in Christchurch. The night before they had an All Blacks reunion, which was the first I'd ever been able to attend. It was held in the newly built Cardboard Cathedral which had replaced the Christchurch Cathedral that had been damaged in the 2011 earthquake.

As the newly appointed Lions Coach, I was mentioned as a 'special guest'. But I wasn't the enemy within. There was no fuss made of it. They're good rugby people in Christchurch. Everyone knows how it works.

The All Blacks won reasonably comfortably, 41–13, the next day, and at this point you're questioning how good South Africa truly are.

Ger went home the following Wednesday. We'd identified our preferred hotels, grounds, gyms and so forth, but then it was up to him to negotiate prices. It had been a productive two weeks, and a good opportunity to get to know him. I'd brought him over to our beach house for a night and a day's fishing before going to Rotorua the next day. He'd never fished in his life but he caught a few, so he was happy.

We'd come across each other quite a bit through Wales–Ireland games, but we hadn't really got to know each other. I developed a huge amount of respect for Ger. He's very loyal to the people he works alongside. He'd worked with Eddie O'Sullivan, Declan Kidney and Joe Schmidt, and he'd never say a bad word about any of them or the other people he'd worked with. I admired that. It takes a special person to keep their own counsel.

I stayed on and travelled on the Friday to Argentina for their game against the All Blacks the next day. Typical of the All Blacks, they were leading 7–3 coming up to half-time when they scored three tries in five minutes, the third a length of the field try from a kick-off, and that was the game.

The All Blacks had a thirty-hour trip to Durban for their game against South Africa a week later, as there's no direct flight from Buenos Aires to Durban. So I skipped that, and came back to New Zealand, leaving on the Sunday and arriving on the Tuesday, and then left for South Africa on the Friday.

That was an interesting experience. I arrived in Johannesburg to catch a connecting flight to Durban, but the queue to get through customs was so long that I missed my flight. There wasn't another flight until the next day. I thought: 'Jeez, what am I going to do here? Bugger this.' I hired a car and drove from Jo'burg to Durban, which took me six hours.

I had to stop for petrol on the way at about 1am, which was a little hair-raising. It was raining as well. I arrived at my hotel in Durban at 3am to much relief. The glamour of being Lions Head Coach!

The game was mainly notable for just how poor South Africa were. The All Blacks won 57–15, scoring nine tries to nil. I caught up with John Mitchell, my old Waikato teammate, and watched the game from the president's box. A few people were asking me what I thought was wrong with South African rugby. I didn't know enough to give an opinion. Two of the All Blacks' tries were off driven lineouts, and that's something you never do against the Springboks. There were plenty of discontented people in the president's box after the game.

I flew home via Jo'burg the next day and this time made my connecting flight.

A fortnight later, on 22 October, I went to Auckland with Trudi to see New Zealand play Australia in the final Bledisloe Cup match. Australia took the game to the All Blacks for much of the night. They were unlucky to have a legitimate try ruled out five minutes into the second half which would have put them level at 15–15 with a conversion to come.

But then the All Blacks, typically, scored three tries and won 37–10. It was a record eighteenth win in a row, and they extended their unbeaten run at Eden Park, which dates back to 1994, and of course this is where two of the upcoming Lions Tests are to be played.

Their strength and depth were unrivalled and they were playing with a huge amount of confidence. Having seen them five times, what struck me most was that they never panicked. They could be under pressure and not score for twenty or thirty minutes in a close game, secure in the knowledge that an opportunity would come, and then *Bang!* They were so clinical.

On the Saturday morning before the game, the *New Zealand Herald* portrayed the Australian Coach Michael Cheika as a clown, in a green top with the Wallabies' crest. I thought that was disrespectful to him and the Wallabies.

It was also the game where some of the New Zealand crowd booed Quade Cooper when he came on as a replacement. My reaction was: 'Ah c'mon, we're better than this.' They'd been doing this for a few years and it was time to get over it.

## Sunday, 23 October
## Return to UK

I flew back to the UK, and then went to the Lions Captains' Dinner in the Shelbourne hotel in Dublin on the Tuesday. That morning, I met Ger and John Feehan before a Lions management catch-up meeting in the afternoon.

The only ex-captain not there was Sam Warburton. He could not attend because of his club's training schedule. I was having a beer with Brian O'Driscoll when Martyn Phillips, the Welsh Rugby Union CEO, asked Brian: 'Out of all the people you could have on the Lions coaching staff to New Zealand, who would you take?'

'It's got to be Bobby [Paul Stridgeon],' said Brian.

Bobby had been on the 2009 and 2013 tours as a strength and

conditioning assistant, and Brian appreciated how important he was for the squad's dynamic, and the personality, humour and entertainment value he brought.

A week later, on Tuesday 1 November, at the press conference for the launch of the Lions jerseys for the tour, I was asked about the New Zealand–Australia game 10 days previously. I'd seen the *Herald*'s portrayal of Cheika on the morning of the game under the headline 'Send in the clowns'. All I said was: 'I was at Eden Park watching the game a couple of weeks ago and, as a Kiwi, I was embarrassed. There was still a portion of the crowd booing Quade Cooper. Get over it. Then there was the clown stuff in the *NZ Herald*.

'One of the things I am proud of as a Kiwi is showing humility. The All Blacks try to do that, but there's a proportion of New Zealanders that have a little bit of arrogance and not humility . . . You can be proud, but you've still got to show humility and respect. In the past, New Zealanders have prided ourselves on that and been humble about the success of the rugby team. It was the first time that I've sat there and thought, "We're better than this."

'I don't think the All Blacks are doing that. Obviously there's history between [Steve] Hansen and [Michael] Cheika that's come out on a few occasions, but the squad and team have tried to play things down.'

The *NZ Herald* got me back the next day when they portrayed me as a clown. It's all very well having an opinion, it seems, but if you criticise people who can dish it out, they can't take it.

*Saturday, 5 November*
*Ireland v New Zealand, Soldier Field, Chicago*

Ger and I flew to Chicago on the Friday and watched the Maori All Blacks play the USA. That night and the next day, I learned one invaluable lesson about being in America. If you don't have the Uber app on your phone, you're in trouble. It's almost impossible to get a taxi.

Before Ireland ended the All Blacks' eighteen-match winning run, I had mixed emotions. If the All Blacks won and continued their sequence until the following summer, they'd have gone into the series against the Lions on a run of twenty-three consecutive victories, scoring freely and feeling invincible. Sometimes though, the best thing that can happen to a successful team is a poor performance or even a defeat. That can re-ignite everyone in the squad.

That was a selfish perspective.

However, as the game evolved in front of a sell-out crowd, you could only admire the way Ireland took the game to the All Blacks, turning down kicks at goal to go for tries and leading 25–8 at half-time. When Ireland went 30–8 ahead, it looked like they'd win but, typical All Blacks again, they came roaring back to within four points, and you thought it was going to be another one of those days for Ireland.

But they carried on playing, moved it wide, and when Simon Zebo kicked in behind, they caught Julian Savea behind the goal-line and then Robbie Henshaw scored from the resulting scrum. In the last few minutes, the All Blacks uncharacteristically looked fallible.

As a coach against the All Blacks, you try to convey the message to your players that if you let them on to the front foot and they play with confidence, they're almost unbeatable. But if you put them under pressure they can make mistakes like anyone else. And that's what happened here.

That's what I saw, but when I made a few comments along those lines, I was criticised again in the New Zealand media. I thought Conor Murray was outstanding and Robbie really came of age as well. He's a good kid and a very good rugby player. Tadhg Furlong was excellent too.

I'd come away from Soldier Field that day thinking there would be a group of guys who, no matter what happened when the sides met again in Dublin two weeks later, had created history by being part of the first Irish team to beat the All Blacks. And a number of them, I thought, were going to be on the Lions tour the following year.

You cannot coach that experience. That was just gold for me, as Lions Head Coach, and I was absolutely delighted for them.

### Friday, 11 November
### Munster v Maori All Blacks, Thomond Park, Cork

This was very touching. The ground was packed and the Maori laid down an All Blacks jersey on the halfway line with the late Anthony Foley's initials on it, before they performed the *haka*. Their captain Ash Dixon then presented the jersey to Anthony's sons, Tony and Dan, which was very emotional.

The weather was terrible and Munster put out mostly a second team, but as the game went on they became stronger and stronger, and they thoroughly deserved their 27–14 win.

### Saturday, 19 November
### Ireland v New Zealand, Aviva Stadium, Dublin

More air miles and more media stuff the day before the match in Dublin. At 11.30am on the Friday, we had a meeting of the Lions Heads of Department, and all of us, along with some of the sponsors, went to the game the next day. We had a box in the ground, and went out together that night.

We stayed in the Intercontinental, and I met Dr Eanna Falvey there at 10am to discuss appointments for the tour. Eanna was to be our Head of

Medical, having been an assistant doctor on the 2013 tour, but this time we decided to take one rather than two doctors, and a second masseuse, or a manipulative therapist, as well as three physios. Dr James Robson had done a great job in the past, but sometimes you want to freshen things up as well as provide continuity. I knew Eanna could do the job.

I also met Stuart Lancaster in the hotel for a good chat. He told me of his experiences with the Leinster players, and gave me some feedback on the English players. Some people clearly saw us talking, one and one became five, and rumours circulated that Stuart was to be part of the Lions coaching ticket.

As for the match, and being a New Zealander, this reminded me of what makes All Blacks players tick, especially after a kick up the backside. For example, Dane Coles had rarely played as poorly as he did in Chicago. He didn't throw that well or play well generally, like a few others, but he was a different player two weeks later. For the All Blacks, that day in Dublin wasn't about their performance. It was all about the result and making a statement. 'If we've got to do this the hard way, we'll do it the hard way. We don't care how we play once we win.'

*Saturday, 26 November*
*France v New Zealand, Stade de France, Paris*

I went to the match with Ger and Bobby, and France played really well that day, making plenty of offloads and line breaks, and dominating possession and territory.

I bumped into Wayne Smith, the All Blacks Assistant Coach, the following Christmas in New Zealand and said to him: 'I thought France played quite well and had a lot of offloads.' Wayne explained that they'd gone into that game with the specific intention of tackling lower due to World Rugby directives, as high tackles would be severely sanctioned. But as a consequence, France got quite a few offloads away.

Again, typical of the All Blacks, against the early run of play Israel Dagg scored off a Beauden Barrett cross-kick, and early in the second half the game turned on an intercept try by Barrett. Otherwise there wasn't much between the sides, with the final score 24–19 to the visitors. The strong message for me was that you just can't switch off against the All Blacks. You have to stay alive at all times.

Despite losing, France showed, as Ireland had done in Chicago, that you've got to take the game to the All Blacks and be positive. It's the only way you can do it. You've got to be bold, and take risks.

*Wednesday, 7 December*
*Announcement of coaches' appointments,*
*Carton House, Maynooth*

This was the unveiling of my core coaching team of Steve Borthwick, Andy Farrell and Rob Howley.

It was up to me to sound out prospective coaches. If they said yes, I'd inform John Feehan and he would take over the negotiations. My initial thoughts were to take two attack coaches. I was always taking Rob Howley. He understands the game and he understands me. We've worked together at Wasps, when he was a player, and at Wales, and I've a lot of time for him. He has a great work ethic, he's very, very loyal and had been on four Lions tours before, two as a player and two as coach. He cops plenty of criticism in Wales, but that doesn't bother me. It's similar to the criticism Sam Warburton gets in certain quarters in Wales.

I wanted Joe Schmidt on board as well, and spoke to him. He said he'd think about it, but rang me back the next day to say he wouldn't make himself available. He wanted to work with a young Irish squad in Japan on their summer tour in preparation for the 2019 World Cup. I was disappointed, but I respected his decision.

I also asked Gregor Townsend but as he was taking over from Vern Cotter as Scotland Head Coach, he had to go on their tour to Australia and Fiji. I thought it would have been a great opportunity for Gregor. Coaches can learn a lot from each other on a Lions tour, and it would have been beneficial for his development, but I understood his position.

A little later, I also spoke to Kieran Keane, the Chiefs' Assistant Coach, about coming on board to work with the attack. I thought it would have been a coup getting a well-regarded Kiwi coach. But by that time, he had agreed to take over at Connacht.

I spoke with another Kiwi coach, Jason O'Halloran, who was the Assistant Coach with Scotland. He'd played Super Rugby and coached in New Zealand. He was initially keen, but he had committed himself to working with Dave Rennie and Glasgow during pre-season.

So ultimately, four coaches had turned me down!

Faz (Andy Farrell) was always going to be my Defence Coach again. He understands teams and environments. He's been a professional from a young age in League, was a very successful League player and captained Great Britain at a very young age. He also understands the game and speaks well to the players. He has a great delivery, and can bring emotion and passion when it's required. I also figured he could do the job on his own.

I didn't know Steve Borthwick but England had been going well in the last couple of years. The people I'd spoken to about him had said that he was technically excellent, very organised and had a great work ethic. I rang him and said: 'Would you be available?' He was delighted to be asked and I told him: 'Everyone will have to work very hard, but I hope you enjoy the experience as well.'

It's also important to have all the nations represented if possible, which is why I was disappointed neither Gregor nor Jason could come on board. But with Rob, Faz and Steve, we had coaches from Wales, Ireland and England.

I didn't name Graham Rowntree as Scrum Coach then, but having worked with him in 2009 and 2013, he was another I was always going to ask on board, and the same with Neil Jenkins as Kicking Coach.

*Thursday, 5 January to Monday, 9 January 2017*
*Two-week recce to New Zealand*

There were eleven of us in the Lions party, and we still hadn't signed off on all the hotels, training venues and gyms. We were up at 7am every morning and also examined the changing rooms, coaches' boxes, the distances from the hotels to the ground and where the buses arrived. Basically, all the logistics of the tour.

There was continuity from 2013, but there were some new heads of department on board, so it was a good chance to get to know each other as well, before a pretty intensive six-week tour in New Zealand.

I returned to the UK on 20 January. With the Six Nations looming, the focus was now very much on the Lions squad.

## 2017 Six Nations

*Tuesday, 31 January*
*Visit to Irish squad training in Carton House*

This was the first of my four visits to each of the countries' training camps. Everyone gets a bit paranoid about me watching them train, that I might be analysing their calls and moves. My sole interest was the content, intensity and duration of their sessions and finding out from the coaches their weekly workload.

That information was more valuable than anything else; the structure of the day and the week, and getting a feel for how tough the training is, so that the Lions could tailor their weeks accordingly.

England and Wales are quite similar in how they plan their weeks, likewise Scotland and Ireland. Vern Cotter and Joe Schmidt have obviously coached together in the past with Bay of Plenty and Clermont Auvergne.

That morning, Joe showed a clip outlining the new tackle diktats from World Rugby before the Irish players went onto the pitch for a good session; accurate and intense. Funnily though, I'd heard from someone that the team meeting which they'd normally have on the Tuesday morning had been moved to the night before!

After training, I had lunch with them and caught up with some of the players. The following day, I visited Temple Street Hospital with Brian O'Driscoll. It's the Lions' chosen Irish charity partner and Brian has worked with them for over ten years. He gave me a guided tour as part of the Lions publicising a fundraising dinner at Mansion House on 3 March, where we would both be speaking.

Brian is a good lad and we get on well now. Time is a great healer, and a day like that puts rugby and everything else in perspective, visiting young kids in their wards with their parents. When you see kids who are severely ill, it underlines what's important in life.

*Saturday, 4 February*
*Scotland 27 Ireland 22, BT Murrayfield*

When Ireland came back from 21–8 down at half-time to dig themselves out of a hole to lead, I thought: 'They're going to win this.' But you had to give Scotland credit for hanging tough, and they showed a huge amount

WE REALLY ARE IN THIS TOGETHER'

of character. Stuart Hogg was excellent with two tries. Alex Dunbar also scored one, while two penalties by Greig Laidlaw in the last ten minutes sealed the match for Scotland.

## Sunday, 5 February
### Italy 7 Wales 33, Stadio Olimpico

This was the first weekend with the bonus point system and Wales probably left a bonus point behind. It was terribly wet, but I thought they played pretty well in the conditions.

## Saturday, 11 February
### Wales 16 England 21, Principality Stadium

The only away win outside of Rome in the Championship. Again I thought Wales played well and were a little unlucky not to win. Everyone talked about Jonathan Davies missing touch in the 77th minute, but I didn't think that was the issue. Alex Cuthbert made a defensive error and there were a couple of great passes by George Ford and Owen Farrell which led to Elliot Daly scoring in the corner.

It was an incredibly physical game and exactly what I was looking for. Daly was doing well and so too was Jamie George off the bench. I was also impressed by Maro Itoje.

Dan Biggar went well and I thought Ross Moriarty was sensational that day, but they took him off and brought on Toby Faletau. If Wales had won and Moriarty had stayed on, he definitely would have been awarded man of the match. He did a very good job defensively and carried well. The combination of Sam Warburton at number 6 and Justin Tipuric at number 7 either side of Moriarty was effective too.

*Sunday, 12 February*
*France 22 Scotland 16, Stade de France*

I actually thought both sides showed plenty of courage and character. The difference between them was the French scrum, and they got their driving maul going when they were under pressure. Finn Russell kept attacking the French with his running game, and I thought he came away from the game with a lot of credit.

*Saturday, 25 February*
*Scotland 29 Wales 13, BT Murrayfield*

Watching Wales dominate the first twenty minutes, I thought they were going to win comfortably, but they were terrible in the second half. In fairness to Scotland, they showed character again and scored a couple of nice tries. Finn Russell played with no fear, Stuart Hogg was good and Tim Visser made George North look pretty average.

I met Prince Albert of Monaco after the game. He's a big rugby fan and was staying at the Balmoral. He said: 'We're having a drink later in the Whisky Bar. Come and join us.'

So I joined them and while chatting with him asked: 'Are you coming on the tour?'

'I don't know if I can make the tour, but I'd like to see you train,' he said.

'Why don't you come over to one of our training camps in Wales or Ireland?' I said.

He would come to Carton House for a day. He watched training one morning and had lunch with the boys, helping himself to the buffet just like anyone else, and chatted with a few of the lads, which was pretty cool.

## Sunday, 26 February
### England 36 Italy 15, Twickenham

An interesting day. Italy's tactic of not contesting the tackle area and pouring around the English side of the ruck worked well. But even allowing for that, England were poor. Italy led at half-time and after an hour were still within a score.

Sitting in the stand, I was thinking that the weekend was turning into something of a disaster. Wales had been very poor at Murrayfield, Ireland could have lost at home to France, and it seemed Italy might beat England.

At least Conor Murray and Jonathan Sexton went well again, and one player who really impressed me when he came on for the last twenty-five minutes at Twickenham was Jack Nowell. He seemed to change the game. He had lots of touches, caused Italy plenty of problems and scored two tries.

## Friday, 10 March
### Wales 22 Ireland 9, Principality Stadium

I had spoken to George North's agent that week. He'd asked me what chances George had of getting on the plane to New Zealand. I said: 'Not many at the moment.' He asked me what George had to do and I said: 'Firstly, he has to defend better, and he needs more touches on the ball.'

Against Ireland, he had three touches in the first couple of minutes. George played well that night, scoring two tries, and so did Rhys Webb. The Welsh loose-forward trio were excellent again. CJ Stander made one early break and he had been man of the match a couple of times in the tournament, but Ross Moriarty decided there was no way he would be this time. He basically tackled CJ out of the game.

I had been watching the Irish scrum closely and was again impressed with their front-row. Rory Best had been captaining well and Tadhg Furlong seemed to be getting better and better. But Ireland tactically tried to play a bit too much rugby, and that played into Welsh hands.

## Saturday, 11 March
## England 61 Scotland 21, Twickenham

Having watched the two teams train that week, I thought England looked really sharp and intense. I didn't expect Scotland to win. But whether I was right or wrong, I thought this was the most important test of the season for their players, bearing in mind the Lions would be away in New Zealand.

So I thought beforehand that if they lost by ten or fifteen points, that might be a good result. They'd beaten Ireland and Wales at home, but now it was time to perform at Twickenham.

Not only were they beaten by forty points, but it could have been a lot more!

Jonathan Joseph was excellent, and it was reassuring to see Billy and Mako Vunipola back playing for England again.

*Saturday, 18 March*
*Ireland 13 England 9, Aviva Stadium*

Rob Howley had been vindicated in keeping the Welsh team unchanged for their win over Ireland, despite a barrage of criticism as usual in Wales. After that match, we decided to have a little wager on the Ireland–England game.

He'd seen the Irish players in the Principality Stadium and thought they looked battered and bruised. It had been a very physical game, and he didn't think they'd be able to fully recover in time for England, whereas I thought Ireland would win.

Apparently Ireland had a very light week and didn't train that much; just rested and recuperated. By all accounts, England tried to cover off too much and tick all the boxes, and it looked that way at the Aviva. Ireland thoroughly deserved to win.

Jamie Heaslip was injured in the warm-up, and Peter O'Mahony came in from the start to have a stormer. Sean O'Brien, CJ Stander, Iain Henderson, Tadhg Furlong, Rory Best, Jack McGrath, Johnny Sexton, Robbie Henshaw and Jared Payne all had big games, and all made the plane as well.

It was a little bit similar to the last game in 2013 when Wales played England, who were going for the Grand Slam away from home that day too. Another massive occasion, plenty of Lions head-to-heads, and you want players to step up when it really matters. I was still hugely conscious that the Lions would be away for six weeks and ten games in New Zealand, but apart from England winning in Wales there had been no significant away victory in the Six Nations.

That was a small concern, but it also reflected how competitive the tournament was, and how close the teams were. Wales, England and Ireland were all capable of beating each other, while France showed signs of a revival. it was also Scotland's best Six Nations for a long time. That's not a bad thing.

*Wednesday, 22 March*
*Coaches meeting, Petersham hotel, Richmond*

Myself, Rob, Faz, Steve, Graham Rowntree and Neil Jenkins were all there. For the first time this was purely about Lions squad selection, and analysing the players who were in contention. We were still thinking about thirty-seven or so.

Ironically, the players' harshest critics can sometimes be their own coaches, because we know their weaknesses as well as their strengths more than anyone else. It's not as if everyone was just batting for their own players. The coaches were fair and honest.

They know their players' mental make-up. Are they tough? What are they like in a team environment? Are they good people and characters? When considering a touring party from four different countries, it's not only about skill levels.

We went through every position. We didn't reach a ridiculously high number of players; we focussed more on the obvious contenders, and ones that we were still watching. There were a few areas still under consideration: second-row, hookers, and number 12. We were also a little bit concerned about the depth at tight-head.

We had a management get-together the next day in the Hilton Syon Park, meeting first as a group, then had breakout meetings, as coaches, medical teams, and so on, before a full get-together when John Spencer and I both spoke about the importance of everyone's role.

I also said to them: 'We're all heavily invested in this tour, and everyone's role is important, but the biggest thing I want from all the staff – and you may not appreciate how much of an impact this can have on the players – is that I need you emotionally involved. I need to see, and the players need to see, what it means to you when we win or lose. It shows that we really are all in this together.'

That was the most important message I delivered to all the management.

In the past, I've seen staff not show any emotion after a match because they are merely doing a job. But when you see a bagman or a physio disappointed after a loss, or elated after a win, it shows everyone is invested.

I needed to see that, and so would the players.

By this stage, my diary was pretty full. I had flown back to Cardiff the day after Ireland played England, to face a week like this:

| | |
|---|---|
| Monday: | London for an interview with SkySports |
| Tuesday: | Lions dinner |
| Wednesday: | Coaches meeting in London |
| Thursday: | Appearance for QBE (another of the Lions' main sponsors) in London |
| Friday: | Charity dinner in Bridgend |

There would be many other weeks like that one leading up to the tour. I knew I had to step back a little from rugby. I didn't go to any of the European quarter-finals on the first weekend in April. For me, going to matches is as much a PR job as anything else, because you can get them on your laptop afterwards, you can watch from different angles and you see more than you would when you're in the stands.

*Tuesday, 11 April – Thursday, 13 April*
*Planning meeting: Coaches, Strength and Conditioning,*
*Director of Operations and Analysts, Los Mas Pare, France*

Michael Holland and his wife Susan, good friends of mine when I was at Wasps, have a beautiful home in the south of France which they have fully renovated over the last ten years. They kindly hosted the Coaches, Strength and Conditioning staff and Analysts for three days of planning and selection.

This was a very fruitful time for the rugby staff to spend some quality time together and fine tune the tour preparations.

We also had an excellent selection meeting in which we were getting close to finalising the squad.

*Tuesday, 18 April*
*Coaches meeting to rubber-stamp 41-man squad,*
*Syon Park*

We were down to the final two or three names. There had been a media frenzy speculating about who was in the squad and who wasn't. I don't blame the coaches, and I don't believe any of them leaked any information, but maybe one or two people they spoke to had let a few things slip.

We were split on Jonathan Joseph, but I thought he was too good to leave out.

Our discussions brought up another issue. In taking thirty-seven players in 2013, with twenty-three involved in each match, this left us with only fourteen players for separate sessions. We usually had three or four injuries as well, so we were training with ten or eleven players. They weren't as productive as they could have been.

By bringing forty-one, there would potentially be eighteen players not involved in a twenty-three-man match-day squad. Even with three injuries, that would leave fifteen other players for a meaningful training session on the morning of a game who wouldn't be playing that night. Ultimately, that was the deciding factor in taking forty-one.

Although we were planning to call up some additional players a week before the first Test, if there were not too many injuries before then among the original forty-one there would be no need for any replacements. And that's exactly what happened.

One thing that concerned us, and that we knew would cause a stir, was that we had only two Scots, Stuart Hogg and Tommy Seymour, in that original forty-one-man squad, which was hard on Scotland. After all, they'd won three games in the Six Nations.

Even though we'd consciously tried to pick the best forty-one players regardless of nationality, we were still acutely aware that one of the four nations was not particularly well represented.

The way I operate, I like to leave scope for one or two changes overnight. I hate it when a selection is leaked, especially a Lions squad. I like it when no one forecasts it 100 per cent. It means we're still in some degree of control, but also it assures the players that at least the coaches aren't leaking the information.


*Wednesday, 19 April*
*Lions squad announcement, Syon Park*

I was pretty upset with SkySports, and I felt sorry for Jamie Roberts. The previous day they had reported: 'SkySports can reveal categorically that Jamie Roberts will be selected for the Lions tour.'

I approached one of the SkySports people before the squad announcement and said: 'Can I have a chat with you?'

I added: 'I think what you guys are doing is totally unacceptable.'

'What do you mean?'

'You've been saying that Jamie Roberts is in the squad. I can't see how you can do that. I can tell you now we have not picked Jamie Roberts in the squad.'

I felt for Jamie. SkySports are the major broadcaster, so everyone assumed that if they were reporting this, it must be correct. You can't make a statement like that unless you are 100 per cent sure. I don't know where they got that from but it was wrong, and it could only have built up Jamie's hopes. He'd been speaking to Rob Howley and didn't think he was going to be included, but all of a sudden he would have seen that or heard of it. He was gutted.

## Captain

The only player who knew he was in the squad was Sam Warburton as captain. I rang him only a week previously because I didn't want to place him in the position where he'd have to lie for a few weeks. He hadn't captained Wales in the Six Nations, but I think he enjoyed just being able to go out and play.

So when I rang him and asked if he'd like to captain the Lions, I left it a little open. I wanted to hear his reaction.

'Sam, if you were offered the captaincy, how would you feel about that?'

He just said: 'Oh, I'd love to do it. It would be the highlight of my career. It would be such an honour.'

'OK, do you want to do it?'

And he said: 'Yep, thanks very much.'

His response was exactly what I wanted to hear. If there had been any uncertainty or hesitation in his voice, I might have left it open and may even have gone for someone else. But his reaction confirmed he was the right person.

Knowing him as an individual, as well as a player and captain, I knew if we didn't select him for a Test he would take it on the chin. That's the kind of person he is.

Alun Wyn Jones was another option as captain, having done a great job in the third Test in 2013 and when leading Wales in the Six Nations, but the second-row was such a strong, competitive position. None of the five we chose were clear picks for the Tests.

Some players were unlucky not to make the squad. We spoke about Garry Ringrose at length, and had there been an injury he was the next in line. Andy spoke really highly of him, and said the tour could be the making of him. He still has things to work on in his game, and he was pretty quiet against Wales, but there's definitely something special about him. We also seriously discussed Simon Zebo, Keith Earls, John Barclay and Finn Russell. But, ultimately, we were stretching the Lions budget in taking forty-one, and some very good players were always going to miss out.

That was another sign that this was a stronger Lions squad than four years previously, and as coaches all of us truly believed that.

But we also knew that against the All Blacks, it would need to be.

# 5

## INJURIES, TRAINING CAMPS AND FAREWELLS

## Final countdown, Lions to New Zealand 2017

*Sunday, 7 May*
*Ben Youngs withdraws*

Ben rang me on the day after Leicester had won their last regular-season Premiership game away to Worcester, to inform me he was pulling out of the squad. His brother Tom's wife, Tiffany, had suffered from cancer before and it had returned. The prognosis wasn't positive and he just felt that it was more important to stay at home and support Tom and the family.

As a coach, the first thing I always say to the squad – and I would actually say it to the Lions players again when we came together the next day – is how lucky we are to be involved in the Lions but family comes first, and if there are any issues with family to come and talk to us. If things are right at home, then hopefully we will get the best out of them on the training pitch and on the playing field.

I think it's important for players to feel that they've got the support from the management if they have any issues individually and personally, because they're still young men and relatively inexperienced in the ways of life. It's not like someone with a nine-to-five job. This is different, and we've got to be there as a support mechanism.

I've got a huge amount of respect for both Ben and Tom, and know how close they are as a family. Ben said he'd love to have gone on tour and it was a big decision for him to make, but I fully understood and appreciated his circumstances.

We decided to call in Greig Laidlaw. On that Saturday we were relieved that Conor Murray had completed his first half-hour of rugby for Munster against Connacht after two months out with shoulder-related nerve damage.

*'Messy Monday', 8 May*
*Lions registration day, Hilton London, Syon Park*

Some players had known each other for years, others met up in the two mini-camps in Wales and Ireland, but most were meeting new teammates for the first time. Everyone was a little bit apprehensive but at the same time excited.

The players tried on their new Lions gear, completed all their relevant paperwork, underwent medical screening and took part in the first squad photo. This is also when we had our first full squad meeting during which everyone was introduced.

All the heads of department spoke: Bobby Stridgeon, (Strength and Conditioning), Dr Eanna Falvey (Medical), Rhodri Bown (Analysis), Charlie

McEwen (COO), Anna Voyce (Commercial), Dave Barton (Communications) John Feehan (CEO), John Spencer (Tour Manager), and myself.

I spoke to the guys about what to expect in New Zealand and I asked them to fill out answers to a few questions. 'How did you feel when you were named in the squad?' 'What are you going to bring to the squad?' 'List five strengths about you as a player.' It was all connected to positive affirmation.

Then we separated the players into their four country groups to nominate a song each in response to the *powhiris* we would receive in New Zealand. Laidlaw and the Scottish boys decided on *Highland Cathedral* and the English boys chose *Jerusalem*. At one stage they were talking about *Swing Low* but I said: 'I don't think that would be a good idea.' I'm not sure if they were joking or not.

The Welsh boys chose *Calon Lan* and the Irish lads went for *The Fields of Athenry*. I had suggested to the Irish players *Red is the Rose*, the song we adopted at Connacht in 1996 and 1997, but they had never heard of it, to my surprise. It's a lovely song. The boys from the north were a bit worried about having *The Fields of Athenry*, but that is what the Lions are all about – accepting differences and making compromises.

The players not chosen for the press conferences or interviews had obligations with the sponsors. It was a fairly full-on day for the players.

I did some online digital stuff as well as a round of media interviews. It wasn't as taxing as normal – or as it would become in the weeks ahead.

*Sunday, 14 May to Thursday, 18 May*
*First training camp, Vale of Glamorgan*

Two weeks beforehand we had agreed that if there was going to be fewer than ten players available, we would cancel the week. There just wouldn't have been any point in training with less than ten players for four days.

In the end, we had fourteen, and thirteen trained regularly, which was good – Sam Warburton, Rory Best, Kyle Sinckler, Joe Marler, Iain Henderson, Ross Moriarty, Toby Faletau, Greig Laidlaw, Ben Te'o, Jonathan Joseph, Anthony Watson, Tommy Seymour and Stuart Hogg. Jared Payne still had a calf muscle strain, which had been an ongoing problem.

One of the good things about that week was that there were only three Welsh players, Warburton, Faletau and Moriarty. That meant the rest were players who hadn't worked with us before. Four years ago, the first get-together in the Vale of Glamorgan consisted mostly of Welsh players because they'd been knocked out before the Pro12 semi-finals. It was like a glorified Welsh camp.

This week was very much about core skills and conditioning work. Some of them hadn't played for a little while, so from 7.30am we had them doing the altitude chamber, cryotherapy twice a day, and on the bikes. There were also weights and some units' work, where we split into smaller groups, before rugby in the afternoon. Monday and Tuesday were double sessions, and quite tough. Wednesday was a lighter day and then we worked really hard on the Thursday morning before they dispersed just after lunch.

We were looking for intensity in training, some recovery stuff, and it was also beneficial from a medical perspective as they could assess all the players.


*Saturday, 20 May*
*Billy Vunipola withdraws*


Saracens lost their Premiership semi-final against Exeter and that evening I got a phone call from Phil Morrow, their Performance Director, warning me that Billy would be calling me.

Billy rang to tell me that his shoulder was no good and that he wanted to pull out of the tour. It had been an ongoing issue for the last five months. In retrospect, I think he had it when he had his knee operation, and he probably should have had the shoulder done at the same time.

'I'm favouring it. It's popping out all the time,' he told me. It had popped out a couple of times in that Saracens–Exeter game.

I said: 'Why don't you come across on Sunday and get it scanned, talk to the medics and if there's a way to manage you during the tour, then we could potentially do that?'

He was going to come across to Carton House on the Sunday, but he rang me that morning and said: 'Look, I didn't sleep last night and my head's not in the right place. I'm not coming. I'm not playing on the tour.'

At that stage, I wasn't going to try and convince him otherwise. Once a player has made that decision, it's a done deal. The first conversation had been different. Then he had left the door open.

Ultimately, you've got to respect that a player knows his own body. When he rang me the second time, I thought: 'I'm not going to pursue this, because if he needs a pathway through the tour and he doesn't play well or he misses a tackle, or it pops out again, that's not fair on him.'

Billy made a massive call in his career, but I think he made it because he didn't want to let himself, or the Lions and the other players down. He didn't want to feel like we were carrying him.


*Sunday, 21 May to Thursday, 25 May*
*Carton House, County Kildare, Ireland*


This was more of a rugby week, and it helped us hugely that Saracens, Leinster and the Ospreys all lost their Premiership and Pro12 semi-finals, even if Munster and the Scarlets went through, as did Wasps and Exeter in the Premiership. We only had three players in the final at Twickenham, and six involved at the Aviva, including Ken Owens, who was injured, whereas we had six from Saracens, five from Leinster and three from the Ospreys available to us.

So we had a net gain that week, and it also meant our three outside-halves – Owen Farrell, Johnny Sexton and Dan Biggar – came into camp when we might have had none of them.

We had planned for anything between twenty-two to thirty players. So while it was disappointing for those clubs, for us to have thirty players in camp was a huge bonus, especially to have three number 10s, just from an organisational point of view. They are so important to the structure and the game plan, and they also bring the best out of each other. They're three spiky, feisty characters and that meant there was plenty of competition from that week onwards. Along with their club or provincial teammates, they also come from winning environments, and although they'd all lost semi-finals, they still came into the camp with a certain amount of confidence and expectation.

Johnny and Owen had been the two number 10s four years ago, and I could see a big change in Owen. In that time he'd gone from a youngster with potential to a world-class player. He was twenty-two then, and twenty-six now, which is a period of growth and maturity in most people's lives. As well as extra confidence, now he brought chat, leadership, belief and had more respect from the other players.

Four years ago in Dublin on the Wednesday night, Mike Phillips gave Owen a bit of gyp for something he did. 'You're only here because your father's a coach.' It was a bit of banter over a few drinks. But even if Mike had been with us again, I don't think he or anyone would dare say that four years on. No one would doubt that Owen is here on merit after all he's achieved.

In 2013, Johnny was very much the main man; talking, chatting and in charge of everything. This time he'd come into camp after an unusually poor game by his high standards in Leinster's semi-final defeat to the Scarlets. Players sometimes have little blips. It was going to be interesting to see how his tour would progress.

We didn't do the 7.30am starts, but we did some weights and unit sessions on the Monday and Tuesday mornings, with rugby in the afternoons on the pitch, and then we had a night out in Dublin on the Tuesday. All the staff and the players, sixty to seventy of us, went to Marco Pierre White's for a meal, and then filed into Kehoes pub afterwards. It was pretty packed, even though it was mostly just our group.

Every night in the Vale and in Carton House we'd had half-an-hour's choir practice, after bringing in Dr Haydn James, the Welsh choirmaster who does the games at the Principality Stadium. In the Vale, he brought in some of the singers from his choir, who sang our four adopted anthems. That was really valuable for us and he came across to Dublin on the Monday of the camp in Carton House as well.

So on the Tuesday night we trialled our songs for the first time in public, both in the restaurant and in Kehoes. Of course we thought we sounded brilliant. It's amazing what booze can do! In fact, some of them recorded the sing-song on their phones and it was actually shocking when we saw some of the videos the following day, but the boys had enjoyed themselves. We had two buses, one came back at 11.30pm, and the other at 1.30am. The guys who came back at 1.30 were a little bit the worse for wear, but it was a good night for us, players and staff.

As a result, the Wednesday session became more of an organisation day, and more of a walk-through. But that Tuesday night was quite important from a bonding perspective. You can't bring sixty or seventy people together, and not have a few nights out. It can't be all work. They have to mix socially.

It's a challenge. People talk about team building exercises and whatever, but you can never quantify the value of guys going out and having a couple of drinks together. They become a little bit less inhibited, reveal more of themselves, and get to know each other better. We also try to mix players up from different nationalities in the rooming lists.

For the Monday departure, we had sixty-four business-class seats and five first-class seats. At our Carton House camp, I told the players that the five first-class seats had been allocated to the staff, but that we'd decided to give them up to the players. So they put all the players' names into a hat and drew out five. It was ironic because four of those drawn were in that camp, Joe Marler, George Kruis, Jared Payne and Kyle Sinckler, but when George North's name was called out there were shouts of 'Re-draw! Re-draw!' because he wasn't there. He was the only one of the missing eleven drawn out of the hat. So there was a re-draw for one place, which went to Alun Wyn Jones.

We trained pretty hard on the Thursday morning before we had lunch and dispersed in the afternoon. I came away from that camp feeling like we'd covered quite a lot.

From a coaching perspective we had put our defensive strategies in place with Andy Farrell. Steve Borthwick had put the lineout structure in place – the lineout calling, full lineouts and short lineouts – and off the delivery from the lineout we'd organised some attacking plays as well.

We'd gone through kick-offs and exit plays with Neil Jenkins, and we'd done a lot of contact. One of the things I found useful from the previous tour was that in every training session we did some element of contact, because it's such an important aspect of the game. It doesn't even have to be full-on contact, just contact technique.

We made sure that we did that in those first two weeks, and would continue to do that on tour. Having thirty players in camp was going to put pressure on the other eleven players coming in on the Sunday after the Pro12 and Premiership finals, and the day before we travelled to New Zealand. They would be arriving cold. We felt we could repeat most of the same messages from week one into week two, but we didn't want to be repeating it all again for those eleven players. But everything had been recorded, and was on a server for those players to download and catch up on.

## Sunday, 28 May
### Lions Farewell Dinner, Roundhouse, London

The players arrived in dribs and drabs, but all were in the Royal Garden hotel in Kensington by lunchtime or early afternoon. All the Lions kit was there in one big room. Officials from our flying partner Qantas came to the hotel to take all the kit away and we just kept our carry-on bags and our suit carriers, which included our burgundy velvet dinner jackets for the Farewell Dinner.

We had another meeting and another choir practice, before changing and going to the dinner at the Roundhouse, a concert venue situated in a former railway engine shed in Chalk Farm, in north London. The dinner, basically a thank you to all the sponsors, commercial partners, the home unions and others who have supported the Lions, was in an upstairs auditorium and there were about 250 guests there.

Not long after we arrived, All Blacks Coach Steve Hansen said publicly that the Lions should have come out to New Zealand a week earlier, implying that we were more concerned with a farewell dinner than training and acclimatising.

We did discuss the viability of moving the dinner forward a week. In theory, we could have moved those thirty players in Carton House and the staff out to New Zealand a week earlier. But the logistics involved in changing flights for eighty-plus people that had been booked fifteen months previously, and given the preparation which had gone into the leaving dinner, made it too difficult. I also fully understand that you do things with the Lions that you would never do with your national team. Around seventy-five per cent of the Lions' revenue is driven by commercial sponsorship, and there have to be obligations that go with that. True, you sometimes feel like it's a commercial tour doing a bit of rugby, because you've got so many commitments to their principal partners, Standard Life, Canterbury, Qantas, Land Rover, QBE and EY. But it's fair enough that they are guaranteed a number of events involving players. You just try to frontload these as much as possible.

Furthermore, it is important that the Lions travel together, and splitting their departure in two goes against the Lions' ethos.

Gabby Logan hosted a couple of Q&As at the Farewell Dinner, the first with myself and Sam Warburton, and the second with Andy Farrell and Graham Rowntree.

Her final question to me was: 'What's the last thing you are going to say to the players as they go out of the changing room before the first Test?'

'Probably the last thing will be "just go out and beat those Kiwi bastards!"' I joked.

It's a kind of a Kiwi–Aussie thing. The guy who was there from Qantas was an Australian, and his wife a Kiwi, and he said to me later: 'My wife and I have just doubled up laughing because we understood the joke.'

When we were leaving, we decided to turn back and finish with a song, so we sang *Highland Cathedral* and *The Fields of Athenry*. That was our second venture into song, in public. Some of the eleven new arrivals were at the back reading the words on their phones. I don't think we were brilliant, but it had to be done.

I was hoping we would be more in tune on the pitch when it came to the All Blacks.

# LAND OF THE LONG WHITE CLOUD

**6**

## Lions to New Zealand 2017

*Monday, 29 May*
*Qantas flight to Melbourne*

We were finally on our way. The last few months had seemed to take forever but then the few weeks before departure just flashed by.

Our flight from Heathrow was at 1.30pm, but we had to be up at 9am, because we had to do our group photo on the stairway to the plane.

The first leg was six hours to Dubai, followed by a thirteen-hour second leg down to Melbourne. There we stayed in an airport hotel overnight – I managed about two or three hours' sleep – before rising at 4.45am for the three-hour flight across to Auckland.

I sat next to Bobby, Paul Stridgeon. He's been with me at Wasps and Wales, and is coming back to work with Wales after a stint with Toulon. I've known him a long time, ever since he came to Wasps in 2002. He's from Wigan and wrestled for England in the Commonwealth Games in 2002 before coming to Wasps to do a bit of fitness training and work with Craig White. We paid him a few quid, and then took him on full time at Wasps. He was a really important addition to the Strength and Conditioning team. When Paul left Wasps he had a year with Warrington Rugby League before being appointed to England for six years. For the last few years he has been with Toulon, becoming one of the top strength and conditioning coaches in world rugby.

He's nicknamed Bobby after the character in the Adam Sandler film *The Waterboy*, who carries drinks bottles for an American football team. He's mad really, an unbelievable energiser. He gets on well with the players, and lifts everyone's spirits. He strikes the right balance between hard work and fun, and knows when to put the thumb on people for some hard graft and when to pull back and let them enjoy themselves. That's a pretty special skill.

After speaking with Eanna Falvey, he suggested that we change our travel schedule to have a six-hour stopover in Melbourne and arrive in New Zealand around midday, although personally I would have preferred to carry on straight through from Dubai to Auckland. That would have meant landing in New Zealand at five in the morning. The medics felt that stopping off in Melbourne, getting a few hours' sleep, breaking up the trip, changing and arriving around midday would be a lot easier from a recovery point of view. It still took some of the players and staff four or five days to come to grips with the jet lag. But who's to know for sure whether it would have been any better going straight through. One good aspect of that schedule was that we could review training footage on our laptops.

When we landed, it began to feel more real. There was a welcome at the airport, where John Spencer spoke on our behalf, and we sang *Calon Lan*. The boys did a good job. At this stage of the tour, you're not entirely sure where else you're going to come across a welcome, but with four songs we were well prepared and ready for them. It gives you a lot of confidence. We'd done a lot of work on them and had some real fun practising them. It's taken a little from the rugby preparation, but the benefits for squad togetherness and bonding can't be measured.

When we came through arrivals, there were quite a few Lions fans there, and I had to do a few short interviews. Now it was happening. The Lions had landed, and as a Kiwi going home it was impossible not to be excited about it.

In between interviews, Luke Broadley, our Communications Manager, found Trudi in amongst the crowd and brought me over to her. It was the first time I'd seen her since the week after the Six Nations in March.

We arrived at our hotel and the rest of that first day was just a recovery session, with some pool work in the hotel and weights and spin cycling in the gym next door.

We had some choir practice again that night, which was partly to keep everyone awake. Dealing with jet lag, the fatal thing to do is to take a nap. That ruins sleep patterns. So you try to keep the guys up until ten or eleven o'clock at night, in order to get them into the time zone as quickly as possible.

## Thursday, 1 June

It was only two days into the tour when I began to see another side to New Zealand, or at least to some of the New Zealand media, and particularly Gregor Paul of the *NZ Herald*. My son Bryn had been picked for the Provincial Barbarians, our first opponents in Whangarei on the Saturday. I know journalists don't write the headlines, but when Paul insinuated that I was going to have our players target Bryn, I was furious.

He said that I had instructed Ben Te'o to run down Bryn's channel, and the headline was disgraceful: 'Gatland Finds Baa-Baas' Weakness – His Son.'

I don't know how you could deduce from my comment in the press conference that I had instructed Ben or anyone else to target Bryn, or that I felt he was the Barbarians' weakness.

My actual words had been: 'I spoke to him [Bryn] last night and he seems to be enjoying the week. We will catch up tomorrow. He probably expects to make a few tackles on the weekend, but we haven't spoken too much about the game.' As a result of this, somehow the article read: 'Lions coach Warren Gatland is targeting his son Bryn for tomorrow's tour opener against the New Zealand Barbarians.

'Gatland senior is going to instruct New Zealand-born second five-eighths Ben Te'o to angle back and target Bryn at number 10 – an unusual state of affairs for a proud father to be masterminding a game plan affecting his son.'

It was just an unbelievable leap in logic.

I went absolutely mental with our press guys, Dave Barton and Luke Broadley, and they rang Gregor Paul and the sports editor to get it changed. After several phone calls, the headline was eventually changed to: 'Gatland v Gatland: Warren Aiming at Bryn in Lions Opener.'

The opening line was changed to: 'Lions coach Warren Gatland says his son Bryn probably expects to make a few tackles against his side in tomorrow's tour opener.'

But the second paragraph remained untouched.

This was to be a special day for both of us, and for someone to twist that around and make it into some kind of family feud, with me targeting Bryn, was nasty.

It was part of what already seemed a deliberate campaign against me from the *NZ Herald*. I don't know why that was, but perhaps it emanated from those comments I'd made about the New Zealand–Australia game the previous autumn. Ever since then, it seemed, I was fair game.

New Zealand is a great country, with great people, and it's the number one rugby nation in the world, but it can be a hyper-sensitive country when it comes to taking criticism. Whatever else you do, you do not criticise New Zealand, especially its rugby. On one of my previous trips home, I said something along the lines of: 'Here in New Zealand we have a sense of self-importance, that you can make a difference to the rest of the world in terms of your opinion. Then you leave New Zealand to live abroad for a while and you realise no one gives a damn what we think. We don't make a huge difference financially in the world. We think that because we have had a nuclear-free policy since the 1970s it makes a difference to the Americans, but they don't give a damn.' It was just some comments along those lines.

Oh my God, I just got absolutely hammered.

Memo to brain: don't criticise New Zealand. I've learned my lesson once and for all.

That's why I always laugh when New Zealanders become so upset by critical comments from the *Sunday Times* journalist Stephen Jones, and how much they dislike him. When he writes columns or appears on New Zealand television, I've no doubt he doesn't believe everything he writes or says, yet the reaction he gets is unbelievable. I remember saying to some people: 'Do you not realise what he's doing? He knows exactly what he's doing. He's just playing the game. Yet every time he writes something you just bite.'

So, on this tour I've become a target for journalists, especially from the *NZ Herald*.

Steve Hansen has been feeding them too. He gave an interview to a couple of the English papers just before the Lions squad arrived, in which he said: 'Unless Gatland has an epiphany, we pretty much know what to expect.' That was a little bit derogatory towards me.

Steve has said before that they know what to expect from Wales, but the previous summer after our three-Test tour here, he admitted that we had played some rugby. But hey, I know the way it works in New Zealand,

and with the All Blacks and the *NZ Herald*. They get a little bit of inside info on the All Blacks and toe the party line as a result.

After our first breakfast in the Pullman hotel on that Thursday morning, all the players did some gym work, and after lunch we went for our first training session at the QBE Stadium in North Harbour. It was supposed to be a very light session but in fact we had to cut it short. The guys were supposed to be going at about sixty or seventy per cent, but some were putting in around ninety or 100. So I said: 'We've got to stop this. If someone pulls a hamstring, or does something because they're training too hard, they're not going to be too happy.' The players had just got too excited; running around feeling pretty good about themselves.

Almost all of the forty-one-man squad took part. Jared Payne did a little light training, but Sean O'Brien still wasn't fit. I was a little worried about them at that stage. We had Jared scanned, but nothing really showed on his calf even though it kept tightening up. Sean had been a little slow coming back with a calf problem, but Ken Owens was making good progress with the ankle injury that had kept him out of the Pro12 final.

Before the afternoon's training, I had my first main media session of the tour at lunchtime in the QBE. I was obliged to do one after each team announcement, and after each game, which meant I would be in front of the media four times most weeks. I didn't mind really. You got used to it.

We had named the team early that morning via social media on our Lions digital service. The players knew a week beforehand as we'd told them in Carton House. Yet it never came out. It never leaked. I was really pleased about that.

Thirteen of the side had trained in both the Vale and Carton House – Stuart Hogg, Anthony Watson, Jonathan Joseph, Ben Te'o, Tommy Seymour, Greig Laidlaw, Joe Marler, Rory Best, Kyle Sinckler, Iain Henderson, Ross Moriarty, Sam Warburton and Toby Faletau, with Sam as captain. We also included Johnny Sexton and Alun Wyn Jones, who had trained only in Ireland.

This meant we had a good blend of experience, including the captains of Ireland, Wales and Scotland, in Rory, Alun Wyn and Greig, as well as nine new Lions. I told the media what I had told the players. This was their chance and their responsibility to launch the tour with a good start.

## Friday, 2 June

After breakfast, I met Dr Eanna Falvey, who had news about Jared Payne. We'd picked Jared on the bench, but he had to withdraw when his calf tightened up again, so we replaced him with Elliot Daly. Jared knows the score; that he has to be fit to play in one of the first three games. Then if the calf goes, it goes.

We met at 10.30am before the whole squad went to the QBE for the Captain's Run, a tradition in our sport where the captain takes charge of the training session before a big game. We went through a bit more than we would normally do the day before a match, because we were still going through some organisational detail.

There was some contact work, some defence and a few attacking options, and then we left the rest of the Captain's Run to the match-day twenty-three. It was like a lull after the excitement of the first session in New Zealand the day before. Players felt a little jaded. Those outside the twenty-three trained for a further twenty minutes.

We had lunch at the QBE and from there fifteen Land Rovers took all the players and members of staff up to Whangarei, while the coaches travelled in the buses.

The match-day twenty-three didn't have the same commitments as the non-twenty-three. The non-twenty-three had more visits to hospitals and schools. But the twenty-three also had a few other tasks. They had to make a video of their trip; get a souvenir, and buy a pie. Six groups of players would later be judged on these tasks.

You'd never do those sorts of things the day before a game as a national team, but we felt there was merit in frontloading some of these obligations. We'd split the tour into two parts: the first being everything before the Maori game, the second everything after. We knew we had some bridges to build from 2005, so we wanted to get out there and try and win some hearts and minds. I think a big failing of 2005 was that the Lions committed to events which they then pulled out of, and that really upset people. So we vowed that anything we committed to we'd fulfil.

This road trip was also a little bit of fun, even though it wasn't the best preparation for the first match on tour.

That night after dinner in the Distinction hotel in Whangarei, we skipped choir practice! Instead the boys had a Captain's meeting, with just Sam and the players. The boys made their presentations and were judged on their videos, souvenirs and pies, and the video that James Haskell, Sean O'Brien, Jack Nowell and Luke Broadley made was unbelievable. It was hilarious.

At Whangarei Boys High School, they had met a couple of local cops, one of whom had played for Northland, Doug Te Puni. Doug was a hooker who scored a famous try for North Auckland against the Lions; the first try of the opening game of the 1993 tour, when he ran it in from about forty metres.

The boys asked them if would they take part in the video, and they agreed. 'Drive around to my local street,' Doug told them.

The boys filmed at low speed in a controlled area. Sean had taken his red shirt off and tied it around his neck, like it was a cape, and the boys held him out the window to make him look like he was Superman flying past in the Land Rover. Then the two cops, with their lights going and siren blaring, screeched past the Land Rover and stopped them. They arrested Sean, putting him in handcuffs, and he tried to do a runner.

The video was awesome, and just the thing to get the Lions party in good spirits before the more serious tasks ahead.

## 7

## BAA-BAAS NOT SO SHEEPISH

### Lions to New Zealand 2017

*Saturday, 3 June*
*Provincial Barbarians v Lions, Toll Stadium, Whangarei*

The rain had poured down on the Friday. The kickers had gone to Toll Stadium, the match venue, and there was loads of surface water on the pitch. We thought: 'We're going to have to change our play tactically, with some driving mauls, pick and go, and plenty of kicking for territory.'

It also rained heavily during the night, but the drainage at both Pohe Island, where we trained on the Friday, and at Toll Stadium, was superb.

On the morning of the game, sixteen of the non-twenty-three trained again at Pohe Island. Jared Payne and Sean O'Brien sat it out, but Ken Owens was fully involved. We trained them hard and the players were blowing like anything, which made me think we could find that evening's game pretty tough, especially as most of the boys still weren't sleeping well. A lot of the staff were struggling too, waking up early.

The jet lag has an impact, and yesterday it had taken five hours to get to Whangarei. You would never normally do that the day before a game, but the Lions are no normal team.

Even so, we're still expected to play some good rugby.

The match-day twenty-three had a walk-through in the afternoon before a pre-match meal. At the team meeting, myself and John Spencer spoke.

I'd borrowed a phrase from Paul O'Connell which I use regularly with Wales. It's probably one of the best I've heard anyone ever say in rugby. 'Right, let's be the best at everything that requires no talent.'

I spoke about that, and 'staying alive'. A big aspect of playing New Zealand teams, and especially All Blacks teams, is to be alert for quick taps or quick throw-ins.

I also spoke about 'getting back in the game' and a term Andy Farrell uses, 'the bounce' – showing energy and enthusiasm by bouncing on your feet. I said: 'No one out-talks us and no one is more physical than us.'

I mentioned the nine new caps in the starting fifteen: 'That's something that they can never take away from you, being a Lion, and you have the responsibility of getting this tour started and getting us off to a win.'

We made our way to the ground, and at the start of our warm-up I spotted Bryn, went over to him, gave him a hug and said: 'I hope you have a really good game tonight.' And I meant it. I wanted him to play well.

The rain had finally relented a couple of hours before kick-off and it's a sand-based pitch, so it had drained well, although it was slippery. Bryn kicked off and Iain Henderson went up a bit early for the catch and missed the ball. For the first seven minutes we didn't touch it. If we had taken that kick-off and exited, we would have been set and put them under pressure. Instead, we had to defend in our own 22 for what seemed like an age.

Then we probably tried to play a little bit too much. We needed to be a bit more direct and turn them a little bit. We didn't kick the ball in the first twenty-six minutes.

When we did move the ball we looked dangerous. It didn't feel like we were too far away. We started getting in behind them and Ben Te'o made a couple of nice breaks. We created a few chances and got over the goal-line four times. Stuart Hogg gave a poor pass when we made another opening. If he had put that waist-high to Anthony Watson it was a try, and that's normally one of his strengths. He's such a good passer of the ball. I spoke to him about it afterwards, and he was disappointed with himself. He probably should have put Tommy Seymour over as well in the same corner, but went for the line himself.

Right on half-time I thought JJ, Jonathan Joseph, had scored, but the referee didn't go to the TMO. That's three tries and a penalty we left behind. Instead of being ahead at half-time, we came in 7–3 down.

But everything was in our own hands. They had put us under a bit of pressure with their kicking game but we'd won most of the 50/50s, and I just said to the guys at half-time: 'I don't think we're too far away. Get a couple of scores and I think we'll win this game quite comfortably.'

We needed to be much more direct in the second half, which we were, and to turn them around with our kicking game. Defensively our line speed was much better. We squeezed them, and some of the guys off the bench gave us good impact: Owen Farrell, Justin Tipuric and Mako Vunipola.

We scrummaged really well with the first pack, but after the changes the scrums became messy. They also did the same in making changes and that had an impact on their scrum as well, which we didn't adapt to. But the most disappointing aspect was giving away eleven penalties and one free-kick, and looking back, seven or eight were avoidable. As a result they had eighteen lineouts and we only had six.

Ideally you want that to be the other way around, or at least that they have less than ten. Of our six lineouts, we won five and three of them were in our own 22. One was not straight, we had two drives which were going forward until we took them down ourselves, and another where we were penalised for leaving the lane – so no platform off the lineouts. Our breakdown work could have been better too.

We'd talked about 'ball carrying plus two' but we made guys redundant by, at times, putting too many numbers into the breakdown. We also weren't clinical enough in clearing paths, and as a result left ourselves short a few times. But we'll get better at that.

At the end, Owen hit the post with a penalty to push us two scores clear. JJ was penalised at the ruck for stupidly playing the ball in an offside position, and then Alun Wyn Jones was also penalised for going over the top at the next lineout. Suddenly, we were defending on our goal-line with two minutes left at 13–7 against the Provincial Barbarians.

I didn't feel like they were stressing us. All our troubles came from our own mistakes. The referee, Angus Gardner, missed a couple of things and a few knock-ons. But that happens. You have to put up with it.

I thought Anthony Watson played well. Stuart Hogg is criticised for his defending but he made some important tackles. Toby Faletau, for the first fifty minutes, was outstanding before he went into a bit of a hole. He wasn't seen much in the last twenty or thirty because he'd given everything. But he had made one fantastic try-saving tackle from behind, showed some nice footwork and carried well.

Our front-row was solid. Alun Wyn gave away two or three silly penalties, which were avoidable, but he hadn't played a lot of rugby up until then. He'll get better.

Iain Henderson didn't have his best game, and defensively at lineout time he wasn't great either. I'm not going to blame him, but he just needs more of a presence. George Kruis came on and immediately had a presence at lineout time, getting up in the air defensively.

Sam Warburton was blowing hard early in the second half, but he had some good carries. He's honest. He admitted at the press conference that he needs two or three games under his belt, and he definitely needed that one.

After the game, everyone was flat. They were disappointed, which is understandable, but I was thinking: 'Welcome to New Zealand.'

The preparation had been far from perfect and the boys still hadn't recovered from the jet lag. The Barbarians may have been a scratch team, but most of their players were knocking on the door of full-time contracts. Some had played Super Rugby, so it was by no means an average side.

Bryn had told me beforehand that the Barbarians were unbelievably pumped up, which we'd have to expect from every team. We would have to be the same for every match. We weren't quite there yet, but it was the first game.

I caught up with Bryn and the rest of our entourage on the side of the pitch after we'd finished our interviews. It was a little strange for me, because whenever I watch Bryn's games I really only watch him, but this time I wasn't watching him. I was watching our team. But I knew he had played well.

I went into the Barbarians' changing room after the game and spoke to their coaches, Clayton McMillan, Roger Randle and Joe Maddock. Roger said to me how good Bryn had been as a leader for the week. Bryn had made it easier for him to give them a framework and he really wanted the players to take ownership for the last two or three days.

When I looked at the tape I saw a few more of his tackles. He challenged the line and both his kicking game and his skill level were excellent. You could see he was vocal. The boy did play well.

Later, the bus trip took us an hour to the Copthorne hotel in Waitangi, beside the Treaty Grounds where the official *powhiri* was to take place the next day.

As the following day was a day off, this was an opportunity for the squad to have a few beers in the changing room. But no one really did. Everyone pretty much went to bed when we got to the Copthorne. They were all knackered from the travel and Friday's road trip, as well as the game.

That night in Whangarei had been special. All the family were there supporting Bryn, and I sourced about thirty tickets for that game. They wanted him to do well of course, but after that Saturday night they switched allegiances. They put their Lions gear on for the rest of the tour, as Bryn would do after the Blues game.

## Bryn Gatland

*'I was told I'd be in the Barbarians squad about six weeks before the game. In the week of the game, a few of us in the leadership group had an idea that we'd be in the team, and we were told on the Tuesday.*

*'I didn't have many dealings with Dad that week. I went over to the Lions team hotel at around 7pm the night before the match for a chat. We sat in the restaurant of the hotel for about forty-five minutes. He told me it was going to be a tough game! I remember that, but we didn't really talk about rugby much.*

*'I told him we'd had a full-on week because we were trying to cram so much into it, but I said we hadn't really focused on the Lions, because they hadn't played any games yet. We just did our own stuff, but Dad told me they had clips on every single player in the Barbarians team, including me, which was pretty cool.*

*'Mum had rung me on Thursday night to tell me about the piece in the NZ Herald saying that Dad was going to target "the Barbarians' weakest link, his son." I hadn't seen it. I laughed. I knew he hadn't said it, but if he had it would have motivated me even more.*

*'All the coverage had been pretty positive leading up to the game, but eventually I knew there had to be one article which was going to be somewhat controversial and focus on us. But it didn't faze me at all.*

*'There was no pressure going into it. I wanted to perform well, but as a team we knew everyone expected us to be beaten by fifty points. I've played*

in finals when the result has probably been more important but in terms of history, it was up there. You're not going to play against the Lions ever again.

'Before the match, I was goal-kicking and turned around and saw Dad was standing nearby, so we walked over to each other. He said that he really hoped that it went well.

'I said: "Thanks" and, of course, wished him luck.

'The coaches left it to five of us in the leadership group to run things. Because it was a one-off game, players were allowed to express themselves. We had quite a lot of freedom.

'The policy going out was not to take any shots at goal, to go for tries. But we also talked about something we might do when we were awarded a penalty. I'd walk up to the referee, point at the posts and say: "I don't want a shot at goal." And so the Lions players might think we were taking a shot at goal and hopefully they'd turn around. Then I'd take a quick tap or kick to the corner, or something.

'There were a few other things we didn't get to use as well, but one thing we knew was that we were not going to get many chances against them, so when we did get the ball we wanted to use our moves straight away. Like that bomb I did on their 22, or that cross-kick, and chips over their defensive line.

'We started pretty well. They dropped the kick-off, and we were straight into attack for the first five or ten minutes. We got a couple of early penalties, and after fifteen minutes it was still nil-nil. We kept going, got a couple of lucky bounces, I had a couple of kicks that worked and then we scored a try. We were loving it. We defended for the last five or ten minutes of the first half, held them up over our line a few times, and went in at half-time 7–3 up.

'Going in at the break ahead was massive. In the changing room the boys actually believed that we could win. I was thinking: "Whatever happens now we're already in bonus territory. We've done a pretty good job so far."

'Their line speed improved in the second half, and they were so big and heavy in the contact area. I found myself kicking at times for the sake of it. We ended up just holding on for most of the second half, but with ten minutes to go we were still only six points behind.

'We had a scrum near the end and if the pass had gone to the right person we probably could have scored. We also had an attacking lineout with a few minutes left.

'At the end of the game, we were in a huddle and heads were down. The boys actually looked disappointed, which to me was a good thing. While we hadn't won, we had earned the respect that we were after. That was the main thing. After we realised how well we'd done, we enjoyed the night.

'A bar in Whangarei was kept open for us, and a few of the boys went there, but most of us just stayed up and talked all night. We had only met that week, but now I'd say we're all good mates.

'After the game, I swapped jerseys with Johnny Sexton. A couple of our boys were actually a little bit shy of going into the Lions changing room. Sevu Reece, a Fijian who went to Hamilton Boys High, had been up against Anthony Watson. He still had his own jersey after the game, and I said to him: "Would you not go in and swap it?"

'He said: "I couldn't. I opened the changing room door, to go in there, but saw them and went 'Oh no', and walked out again."

'So I went to their changing room and got Anthony to come and swap jerseys with him. Sevu said he had a good chat with him, and as well as swapping jerseys, Anthony also gave him some shorts and stuff, so Sevu was stoked.

'We wanted to keep our jerseys, as they were pretty special to us. Thankfully, the Barbarians said they were going to make us another set, so we were able to swap with the Lions. That was huge. Some of our guys wouldn't have played against anyone at that level.

'Dad and I were both doing interviews for quite a while and he went over to the family before I could. Then we were on the field talking with all the family and a few friends.

'Dad said he hadn't been able to watch me too closely but that I'd put them under pressure with my kicking game. He also said he hadn't seen me make one tackle the whole game! When he watched it afterwards, he realised I'd made thirteen tackles.

'I didn't really know what to say to Dad. I knew he would have been relieved to get the win but at the same time disappointed by some aspects of their performance and that they hadn't won by more.

'On my Instagram and Facebook pages I had messages, even from the UK Lions Supporters, which were really positive, both before and after the game. That was pretty cool. We hadn't thought about it, or discussed it, until someone told me beforehand that there would be an estimated audience of 22 million people watching the game.

'And I didn't get any negative feedback whatsoever about Dad.'


## Trudi Gatland

'It was nice for my whole family because we were bringing thirty-five to that Barbarians match as soon as there was some media speculation that he [Bryn] would be in the Barbarians squad. As soon as he was named, everyone confirmed that they wanted tickets. Bryn had mates who drove up and down on the day from Hamilton. That's a four-hour trip. We all had a chance to catch up with Bryn and Warren on the sideline after the game and we have a couple of great photos to mark the occasion as a family.

'The powhiri the next day was wonderful, the sun shone over the Bay of Islands and the views were spectacular. We felt very privileged to be a part of the welcome onto Waitangi. That alone is a once-in-a-lifetime experience. Overall, it was a huge weekend for us.'

## Sunday, 4 June

One benefit from that opening game was that I was able to have a good chat with their outside-half afterwards and he gave us some good feedback about where he thought some of our threats were.

I spoke with Bryn the next day, and he felt that the wet pitch gave them a massive advantage. Had it been drier, some of our pace and footwork, and passing, would have given them more trouble. Bryn said that a couple of times when we hadn't had options out the back they were able to come really hard defensively, and he felt Johnny needed to be a bit more connected out the back. That is normally one of his main strengths, but he was playing a little too deeply.

At this point I was thinking: 'I'm not sure he's 100% certain about what game he should be playing or wants to play'. Coming into the tour, Johnny didn't seem to have quite the same level of self-belief and confidence of four years ago. He's working his way back into form. Against the Barbarians, I thought Johnny played a little bit deep, and wasn't attacking the line like he normally does.

I don't know whether he's just forcing things at the moment, whether it's a Leinster thing or not, but it's almost like his attitude is play, play, play, and the balance of his game isn't quite there at the moment. He should also be thinking: 'How do I pressure teams by turning them around?' He needs to have that balance between a running game and a kicking game, between taking it to the line and sitting back and getting us on the front foot by playing a bit of territory and squeezing teams. He's not doing that at the moment. He's just playing a little too much rugby, perhaps because that's what they want him to do at Leinster.

Even though the weather had dried, the pitch was still wet, and yet we didn't kick the ball until the twenty-sixth minute of the game. You can't go into modern rugby these days without having that variation in your game. The opposition keeps getting onto the front line and keeps coming hard at you because you're not chipping over the top, kicking it across field or banging it into a corner to make them turn and chase back.

We did that in the second half when Owen Farrell came on and put a little kick into the corner. We squeezed them and we ended up scoring.

So at the moment we have a few things to work on with Johnny. But there's no doubting his quality as a player.

The guy who is growing a lot out here at the moment is Dan Biggar. Some are writing him off. He probably hasn't got the same attacking ability as Johnny and Owen in terms of taking the ball to the line, but he's been training really well.

Bryn also said he didn't feel the pace of the game was as quick as some Super Rugby games he'd played in. The conditions dictated that to some degree, and they slowed the game down. Quite a few times early on their players were going down for a little treatment. They obviously wanted to control the pace of the game.

But Bryn also felt it was more physical than the Super Rugby games he had played in. I thought that was interesting, and encouraging.

The boys had pool recovery in the morning, hot and cold, as we'd run the non-twenty-three pretty hard on Saturday, before we had a Cultural Briefing at 10.30 in the Copthorne, outlining what to expect at the *powhiri*. We were told that there would be three challenges, and we agreed that John Spencer would do the first one, I'd do the second, and Sam the third.

After all the waiting, that welcome was something anyone who witnessed it won't forget for a long, long time. As we came up the grass at the bottom of the hill, the first line of Maori greeted us, and you could see a huge crowd along the side watching it.

The weather and the setting were perfect. It made the hairs on the back of my neck stand up. It epitomised what New Zealand is about, that isolation at the end of the earth, but at the same time and within the cultural mix, how everyone can understand and speak to each other.

The Maori culture in New Zealand is pretty important and it's been synonymous with the All Blacks for over 100 years, especially how the *haka* reflects the Maori warrior spirit.

As we began to walk up the hill, the sound of the conch shell was followed by the first *taki*, or challenge. A *taua*, or warrior contingent, descended towards us displaying traditional battle formations and performed a *haka*. The first warrior lay down on the ground a *taonga*, or offering, that was accepted by John Spencer.

We were led up the hill to the second challenge, which followed the same format as the first. I had to accept it. We were asked: 'Do you come in peace? You look like a warrior party coming into battle.' The first warrior lay down a *taonga* and I had to step forward, pick it up then step back, while always maintaining eye contact. That means you come in peace.

I'd never done that before. Normally there's only one challenge and Sam has invariably done it. This was the first time I'd been part of a visiting squad which accepted three challenges. This *powhiri* was on another level.

I thought it was spectacular and incredibly powerful, but there was one amusing moment. Amongst the Maori warriors was a guy with long hair and a musket, who was covered in tattoos and dancing around. One of the local community who led our delegation said to me: 'That's my brother.' Then he said one of the funniest things I've ever heard: 'I feel safe when he's there; but he does love showing his black arse to everyone.' It's a typical Kiwi thing to say: perhaps not the most politically correct, but the guy was talking about his own brother.

Next we were led to the third challenge, in which most of the 400-500 Maori performed an extraordinary *haka*. They had been rehearsing it for days, and had travelled there from all over New Zealand, some from as far as Sydney.

Then we were invited into the Meeting House. We had to remove our footwear on the veranda, and everyone's shoes were tagged with Lions logos so we could more easily find them afterwards.

After each warrior leader spoke, they broke into song. Then we responded. After Luke Broadley spoke we sang *Highland Cathedral*. John Spencer spoke and we sang *Jerusalem*. Then Robbie Henshaw spoke in Irish and we sang *The Fields of Athenry*, before Ken Owens spoke in Welsh and we sang *Calon Lan*.

That welcome was the Full Monty. All the other coaches were blown away by it: they told me the next day that Sam and the players thought it was pretty amazing. They'll never get to experience that again.

We boarded the bus to Kerikeri airport, flew to Auckland, and took another bus back up to the Pullman hotel. I said goodbye to Trudi, Bryn and Gabby. Trudi drove to Auckland to drop Bryn off, as he lives there now, before driving home to Hamilton.

The coaches met to review the opening game on our laptops: Rob Howley, from an attack perspective; Andy Farrell, from defence; Steve Borthwick, from the lineout; Graham Rowntree, from the scrum; Jenks looked at the kicking; Steve, Wig and myself also looked at the contact stuff. Collectively we studied all the stats and the numbers.

What really disappointed me was our game management, as well as other things that we can control, such as giving away twelve penalties. We'd only kicked the ball fifteen times in the game which is half the total Super Rugby sides are kicking on a regular basis. As well as only having six lineouts, and giving them eighteen in the game, defensively there were a few things to work on as well. But these were all fixable.

Today in the *Herald* (where else?) Chris Rattue wrote an article saying I was the wrong person to be Head Coach of the Lions, and described me as 'just a journeyman coach'. He didn't back that up. How can you be a journeyman coach with a fifteen-year record of trophies and success?

**2009 tour, South Africa**
*Left:* Working as Ian McGeechan's Assistant Coach at a squad training session.

*Right:* With Graham Rowntree, Ian McGeechan, Rob Howley, Shaun Edwards and Neil Jenkins.

**2013 tour, Australia**
*Left:* Now as Head Coach, enjoying the jubilant atmosphere in the changing room after winning the Third Test 41-16, and the series 2-1.

*Right:* After the Third Test in Sydney, enjoying the series win with my staff: Neil Jenkins, Rob Howley, Graham Rowntree and Andy Farrell.

**2017 Player Administration Day**

*Above:* The official squad photograph.

*Left:* A different kind of line-up: this time, it's the players' kit.

*Below:* Sam Warburton addresses the players.

**Squad Training**
*Right:* Sam Warburton, Ross Moriarty and Greig Laidlaw prepare for the cryotherapy chamber.

**Farewell**
*Right:* With John Feehan (CEO) and John Spencer (Tour Manager) before the Lions' Farewell Dinner.

*Left:* The players gather on the steps of our plane bound for New Zealand.

*Right:* Courtney Lawes and James Haskell settle in for the flight.

**Arrival**

*Right:* Greeting my wife Trudi at the airport in Auckland.

*Left:* Meeting the press for the first time on the tour.

*Right:* Undertaking the all-important *hongi* as part of the welcome ritual.

*Left:* Receiving a full Maori welcome is such an important part of any tour to New Zealand.

**Respecting a great nation**
*Above:* Attending a reception in the *marae* (Maori meeting house) at the Waitangi Treaty Grounds.
*Below:* Accepting the Maori challenge outside at the Waitangi Treaty Grounds.

*Above:* The Lions pay our respects at the Canterbury Earthquake National Memorial.

*Above:* Sam Warburton lays a wreath on our visit to the Pukeahu National War Memorial.

**New Zealand Provincial Barbarians, Toll Stadium, Whangarei, 3 June**
*Left:* Anthony Watson goes over for our only try.

*Left:* With Bryn, Gabby and Trudi after the game.

**Blues, Eden Park, Auckland, 7 June**
*Right:* Rieko Ioane scores the Blues' first try.

*Left:* The boys were pretty down after losing the game.

**Crusaders, AMI Stadium,
Christchurch, 10 June**

*Right:* Stuart Hogg has to leave the field
after an accidental collision with Conor
Murray. That was the end of his tour.

*Below:* Owen Farrell kicks one of his four
penalties to give us a 12-3 victory.

**Highlanders, Forsyth Barr Stadium, Dunedin, 13 June**

*Left:* Getting my messages across ahead of the game.

*Below:* Captain Sam Warburton speaks to his players before the game.

*Above:* Tommy Seymour grabs the second of our three tries, but we agonisingly lost 23-22.

*Left:* There's a stark contrast in emotions as the Highlanders celebrate a famous victory.

# A DOSE OF THE BLUES

# 8

## Lions to New Zealand 2017

*Monday, 5 June*

I woke up at 8am after a good night's sleep, showered, had breakfast and went to the coaches' room to review the Barbarians game some more and also to look at some stuff which the video analysts had put together on the Blues.

They didn't have the line speed of the other Super Rugby teams, which might give our attacking game more space, but they had a real quality team on paper, with players who could turn a game in a moment, and they had an offloading game.

The pool recovery and weights were optional before an early lunch at midday as we were meeting up at 1.30 before taking the bus to the QBE Stadium. The full squad trained there. The priority was the team for Wednesday.

We had an hour's session, splitting at the end for fifteen minutes of unit drills with the non-twenty-three and some conditioning.

Rob Howley has introduced a term called 'chaos' in 15 v 15 training sessions, at a high tempo and unstructured. The way the All Blacks play, you've got to stay alive. If you switch off for a moment, Aaron Smith will tap and go. What Rob means by 'chaos' is turnover situations. It's unstructured and the emphasis is on getting back into defensive shape by communicating and doing the same in attack when we have turnover ball.

We're trying to get the players to problem solve on the move. Following that transition from attack to defence, or vice versa, we're making the players react, and communicate. We're trying to do this in all aspects of the training, in units as well as fifteen-a-side, with limited time. The more you do it, the better they get.

You can't run training sessions where everything is structured and organised. You've got to maintain a high tempo, and make them uncomfortable, because that's what's going to happen, especially against the All Blacks. The more we do this in training, the less likely we'll be caught off guard by a quick tap or throw in.

Can this be achieved in the short period of time that we've got? Well, we've already seen an improvement, and this is the way you have to prepare for the All Blacks. No disrespect, but South Africa are much more structured and set-piece orientated. They are less likely to take quick taps and throw-ins, or run the ball from behind their own goal-line. With all New Zealand teams, you've got to expect the unexpected.

To a degree, we're going to have to take them on at their own game. We're not going to grind them down purely with a forward-orientated, kicking game. We will need tempo at lineouts, not allowing them to get organised, and keep the ball on the pitch. We need to turn around those lineout numbers from last Saturday.

It looks as if there will be a reasonable platform at scrum time. A good few scrums went down last Saturday, and the referee said 'play'.

I think we have the ability to play what is seen as traditional, northern hemisphere rugby; plenty of mauling, one-off runners, or pick and go. At training we've placed a big emphasis on a strong set-piece and our driving game. If we need to exploit that and be direct, we will.

We had a snack at the ground before taking a bus back to the Pullman hotel. We announced the team at 5pm, giving fifteen more players their first start of the tour. Given the lack of preparation, as coaches we tried to select as many established combinations as possible: Rhys Webb and Dan Biggar at half-back, Robbie Henshaw and Jared Payne in midfield, Maro Itoje and Courtney Lawes in the second-row.

We also went with Elliot Daly and Jack Nowell on the wings, and Leigh Halfpenny at full-back. The front-row was Jack McGrath, Ken Owens and Dan Cole, with James Haskell, Justin Tipuric and CJ Stander in the back-row.

The front-row, along with Iain Henderson, and the halves from the Barbarians game were on the bench, along with Liam Williams and Peter O'Mahony. Liam and Peter will start against the Crusaders on Saturday, and we decided to keep Sean O'Brien, Conor Murray, Jonathan Davies and George North back for that game, as well as Mako Vunipola, Jamie George, Tadhg Furlong, George Kruis and Owen Farrell, who had all been on the bench in Whangarei.

We named Ken as captain, so he was alongside me for the press conference in the Pullman. It was at the end of that press conference that I became a little angry about a reference to 'Warrenball', which would lead to a few headlines over the next few days.

That evening all the coaches and management were at the media quiz, a tradition in the early stages of the tour. I had a few beers with some of the media guys afterwards.

Another of the mistakes made in 2005 when bringing in Alastair Campbell as the head of a large communications department was the heavy handed approach to the travelling media. They were kept at arm's length and the players had been schooled in what to say, giving the journalists bland quotes. The Lions communications team and management also overplayed 'Speargate', when Tana Umaga spear-tackled Brian O'Driscoll in the opening Test, and by the end they'd alienated much of the travelling media as well as the New Zealand media.

Ian McGeechan restored much of the relationship between the Lions and the media in 2009. As both a player and a coach, Geech had been on tours where only a handful of writers had travelled with the Lions, and though the numbers have multiplied in recent times, he saw the value in having a good rapport with them, both professionally and socially.

I had a similar view. I enjoyed having the occasional drink with the journalists who I could trust with off the record conversations. There was no harm in giving them some ideas of how I was going about my work. Like Geech, I was fully aware that, just like us, they were a long way from home.

Ironically, as the tour progressed, I think the campaign against me personally, and the Lions, by some of the New Zealand media, probably unified the UK and Irish media boys behind us even more.

## Tuesday, 6 June

An early start, as the non-twenty-three had weights at 9.15 before we met at 10.30 and took the bus to the QBE Stadium for the Captain's Run. The non-twenty-three arrived after us for a light run-out, an organisational session. We knew we'd be running them hard the next day, so that those players would be in the same cycle as the twenty-three involved in the Blues game. Thursday is a travel day for the whole squad and no one will train. Then there's another Captain's Run on Friday.

At the team meeting, I told the players that on Saturday we didn't earn the right to go wide. You earned that right through the speed of the ball and generating front-foot ball. It could also be from the variation that came with a positive kicking strategy; little kicks over the top and cross-kicks to the winger, to slow down the opposition's line speed. This gets them thinking, which eventually creates space.

We could also be direct if necessary, depending on weather conditions. That might be a message from the box: 'OK, we need to squeeze these guys. We need to pick and go.' Or we might send on the message: 'Get in behind them. There's some space there.'

We looked at Argentina, and they had a bit of success against the All Blacks attacking around the fringes with pick and go, or by making Aaron Smith tackle, getting offloads away and bringing their wingers up the insides. They used this tactic effectively in Hamilton last year, even though they were well beaten in the end.

Many of the players facing the Blues come from some of the strongest club sides in Europe. There's a good pedigree there. I'm looking forward to it. I'm excited about seeing Maro Itoje play. He's probably been the 'winningest' player in northern hemisphere rugby in the last two or three years. I love his energy at training; his chatting and enthusiasm. Even though he's young, he's vocal. He has an absolute raw energy about him. I knew from speaking to Andy Farrell, Graham Rowntree and Steve Borthwick that Itoje is that sort of personality. He played in the England Under-20 side that won the World Cup in 2014, and he's gone from success with Saracens to success with England.

There's a bit of competition in that second-row. Courtney Lawes played well for Northampton in their last few games and had a pretty good Six Nations. He's aggressive and abrasive. He's been prone to giving away penalties, but he has become more disciplined. He'll be looking for a good lineout performance and a big work-rate defensively and in his carrying.

There's also plenty of competition at loose-head. We've been impressed by Tadhg Furlong. He's a very good athlete. There's competition too at hooker and in the second-row. There are different options in the back-row, where we need to match some lineout ability with physicality to get that balance right. On Saturday, the half-backs, midfield and back three will be interesting as well.

The thing about a Lions tour is that a player might only get one or two chances before we pick the Test side, and they have to make the most of those opportunities. The next couple of performances may tip the balance in selection. This is what we've been saying in coaches meetings. We're open-minded about it. We have to be, for our sakes as well as the players.

For sure, we need to be getting the match-day twenty-three for the first Test into a Saturday cycle. It reduces the risk of them having to back-up games twice in a week. At the same time, you don't want to show your full hand against the Maori a week before the first Test, so not everyone will get into a Saturday cycle, and some players who won't play against the Maori will still be involved in the Test side. They might play against the Highlanders and then not play for ten days. So be it. The thinking is still fluid.

## Wednesday, 7 June
## Blues v Lions, Eden Park, Auckland

The *NZ Herald* had picked up on a back-page headline in the *Sun* the day before which read: 'Censored Gatland's Foul-Mouthed Rant.'

They had reported a comment I'd made under my breath to Ken Owens after the press conference on Monday evening while some of the dictaphones were still running.

'F*** it. I don't know why I have to keep f***ing defending myself.'

So today's back-page sports lead in the *NZ Herald* was a picture of me taken from a training session where I'm pointing in the direction of the camera, and I'm not smiling, with the headline: 'Grumpy Gatland.'

They reported that: 'Gatland muttered expletives as he left, according to the Sun!' The piece inside was headlined: 'It Could All Turn To Custard.' That was implying if we lost to the Blues, then there was a distinct likelihood we would lose to the Crusaders as well next Saturday, in which case we'd be one from three and the tour would have 'turned to custard' already.

As for the cursing, it doesn't bother me. I wouldn't like to be quoted every day like that, but it shows I'm human.

It had followed the last question of that Monday press conference, when Nick Purewall of the Press Association had referred to 'Warrenball'. In fairness, Nick only suggested the Lions were capable of playing more than one way, and, being a Kiwi, I may have been a bit sensitive with my answer.

'What do you mean by one way? When did that way start? You don't know the answer to that, do you?' I stared at him and said: 'Was it when we were successful at Wasps or when I was coaching Waikato in the Air New Zealand Cup? I don't know, when did a certain style change? If you can tell me the answer to that, I will answer the question when the timeframe is appropriate – then I can potentially give you an answer.'

After one more answer, I muttered those expletives. Yes, maybe I over-reacted a bit, but some people have become fixated with the phrase 'Warrenball'. When you ask someone directly: 'What is Warrenball?' they can't really answer it. It's a phrase that has been lazily picked up on. I don't really know what it means myself. But I know it insinuates a direct, physical and unimaginative brand of rugby.

It was Brian Smith, the former Australia and Ireland Coach, who coined that phrase before the 2013 Lions tour. Interestingly, Smith was contacted in Sydney by the *Daily Telegraph* that week and said: 'It was certainly not meant to be derogatory, that Wasps and Wales approach of massive blitz defence and a crash-ball centre such as Jamie Roberts taking you over the gain line.' He also pointed to 'the number of trophies Warren has won with club and country. That's why the Lions appointed him in the first place.'

But the term still seems simplistic and less than flattering.

I would like to think that any team I've been involved with has been innovative, tried to do things differently and think outside the box. I've always wanted players to express themselves on the pitch. If you talk to anyone I've worked with, it's not about playing by numbers. It's the ability to express skill levels, and play what's in front of you when the opportunity arises.

Rugby is a sport where you need a certain amount of structure. That's the modern game. There's a limited amount of space on the field, so how do you manipulate the space? How do you try and create mismatches in the game, and get players to play heads-up rugby when they have the opportunities to do so?

With the Celtic nations especially, you don't have a huge pool of players. You have to play with what you've got. We happened to have a group of Welsh players that came through together who were quite big and physical, like George North, Alex Cuthbert, Mike Phillips, and Jamie Roberts. Sometimes you've got to adapt and use the skill sets at your disposal.

Jamie is a fine defender and good at getting across the gain line; giving you some front-foot ball to play off. Why wouldn't you utilise that? But we also had Shane Williams, who's not exactly the biggest man in the world, and Leigh Halfpenny, who is not a man mountain either.

On this tour, we intend to be very positive in the way we play. We've had that discussion with the players. We can't just try to bash New Zealand teams and the All Blacks up front. We will need a bit of that X-factor every now and then, someone to get a special offload away or a pass over the top. We will have to match them, not just bash them.

Clearly, I'm going to be in the firing line pretty much every day. It's taken me by surprise really. It's obviously a planned strategy, and they are getting some traction out of it. Whether it's an instruction from up top or not, I don't know. But you've just got to carry on regardless. Anyone who knows me also knows that criticism motivates me. Like any Kiwi, when your back's to the wall, it brings out the best in you. We like a challenge.

I had a lot of Kiwi mates texting me and encouraging me to 'ignore the crap' and 'you don't have to prove yourself to anyone, because your record speaks for itself'. One example was a text from Glenn Ross. He coached me at school, in the First XV at Hamilton Old Boys and at Waikato. I've known him a long time. He's still teaching and is the rowing coordinator at Hamilton Boys, rowing being another of his passions.

'Gatty, stick to your guns and don't get distracted by the propaganda machine! Stay on the front foot like you always have and make them realise what you do works! The current media take, I am sure, will be driven by people who want you to fail.'

Wednesday was another long day. The non-twenty-three went to the gym and were on the bus at 10.15am for training at the QBE Stadium. We had a meeting at 11am to outline what we were doing. This was the core of the side that would be playing the Crusaders.

They were having relatively more time together and it showed in training. The session was just over an hour, including the warm-up – some unit sessions and then game-related stuff. Again, because it was a match-day, we wanted to work these players hard, as Thursday would be a travel/recovery day for all the squad.

So although it wasn't a very long session, it was a good blowout. We did some contact work as well, some defensive blocks with Faz and split for about fifteen minutes. Rob took the backs, and Steve and Graham took the forwards for lineout drives, contact work and scrummaging.

Unfortunately, Sam Warburton strained his calf about twenty minutes into the session. The physio examined him and it looks like he won't be right for Saturday which is a bit annoying. He needs rugby.

Ross Moriarty has a strained back from the weekend, but apart from that Jared is OK, and Sean O'Brien trained fully, although he dropped a few passes and wasn't too happy with himself. A little bit rusty. It happens. Even experienced players get a bit anxious when they haven't been training or playing for a while. You can get pissed off with them for dropping the ball because they haven't been concentrating, but Sean is on his way back and you can see his frustration, so you don't bollock him for that.

The match-day twenty-three had a walk-through in the gym at 3.40pm. The pre-match meal was at 4.15, and the team meeting at 5.45pm. The bus journey to Eden Park was fairly short. The Lions supporters began to make their presence heard and seen at this game, and the stadium was packed.

We were a little apprehensive, unsure of what we would be facing. This would give us our first clear idea as to what the opposition would be like and how we'd compare. The Blues were the only one of New Zealand's five Super Rugby sides out of contention for the play-offs, but we were conscious that this was their cup final of the season. They'd also beaten every Australian side they'd faced and had a good record at Eden Park.

Of course, because of Bryn's involvement with the Blues, he knows all their calls and all their moves. It was hard on Bryn, because I'm his dad, but I wouldn't ask him anything that might compromise him. So, like the Barbarians, that Blues game was another one we couldn't talk about beforehand.

I think it was important for our relationship. He could have told me anything and no one would have known, but you'd like to think there's still some integrity in the sport even though certain parts of the media aren't demonstrating that.

The Blues had plenty of players with X-factor, and one of them was Rieko

Ioane, who scored after seven minutes. Their scrum-half fed a pod of three players and James Haskell got drawn in, which isn't like him, for Charlie Faumuina to pull the ball back. They'd given a full debut to their outside-half Stephen Perofeta, and he passed wide to Ioane, who had space outside Jack Nowell as a result of our defence being pulled in. But the fault line was infield.

We responded well. CJ Stander scored off a maul and Leigh Halfpenny kicked us ahead. At 10–5, we conceded a penalty after the siren, and myself and the other coaches left the box for the changing room, expecting it to be 10–8.

We were waiting there for five or six minutes wondering what the hell was going on. There were no TVs. Eanna Falvey came in to tell us that the referee had gone to the TMO to see if the Blues had scored a try.

'What the f***!' I said. 'Did they tap it or something?'

'No, it rebounded off the post.'

When they all came in, I was told we were 12–10 down. The players didn't think it was a try, but we couldn't change it. So we focussed on what we needed to do in the second half.

I didn't see the try until we went back up to the box for the start of the second half and viewed it on a laptop. The penalty hit the upright. Jack Nowell and TJ Faiane contested the rebound. The ball was then deflected over our line and Sonny Bill Williams touched it down. I don't know how the officials could be sure that Jack tapped it back, and that TJ Faiane hadn't touched it, but that's what they decided. Try awarded.

From 15–10 down, we came back well and Leigh's two penalties nudged us in front. It had been a good test of our character and we responded well. CJ made some really good carries. Had we won, it would have been something solid to build on. But with six minutes to go, Steven Luatua popped a little ball out the back of the tackle for Sonny Bill to break through as Maro stepped up. That was a pre-called move. The Chiefs had scored against the Blues with the same move in a pre-season game. We needed to stay on Sonny Bill, and then Liam Williams has to tackle ball and all. You can't go low on Sonny Bill. He offloaded to Ihaia West coming through at pace, and there was no stopping him.

I didn't think Sonny Bill had been having a great season up until then, but he played bloody well against us. That was by far his best game. It was a big game for him. He needed to perform if he was going to be selected for the All Blacks in the Test series.

We still had a chance to win it with a lineout in the corner, but Rory Best overcooked the throw. Final score was 22–16 to the Blues.

It was a quiet coaches' box. I was gutted. We'd had chances to nail big moments which we didn't do. That was disappointing.

Due to my round of media duties, I wasn't able to see Trudi or the kids at the ground. It was late when we got back to the Pullman, where the boys had a meal. The coaches and I had a beer back at the hotel, where I finally caught up with Trudi for the first time. I wouldn't say I was good company that night.

It's hard to go to bed at a reasonable hour after a night-time game, especially when you've lost and you're charged up with adrenalin, emotion and now disappointment. It's the same for the players. I called in on the video analysts, who were into their night-time shift cutting up the game for us. I felt for them.

I talked with them and the other coaches. I didn't get to bed until after 2am. But if I'd gone to bed any earlier, I wouldn't have slept anyway.

## Bryn Gatland

'Earlier that afternoon I had met my agent, Dan Kane of Esportif, to see what options he might have for next season. There were a few possibilities, including overseas, but nothing concrete. Only twenty minutes after that meeting, he called and gave me the news regarding the Blues next year that I had been hoping to hear.

'The family were thrilled of course. Mum does this thing where she jumps up and down, and claps, like a seal. She was also delighted because she didn't want me going overseas.

'Dad was getting a hard time in the media, so when he hooked up with us a bit later, it was nice for Mum to able to cheer him up.

"Has your day got any better?" Mum asked Dad.

"No, not really."

"Well, Bryn might have some news that might pick you up."

"Oh, what's that?"

'I told him. "The Blues want me in their full squad next year."'

## Trudi Gatland

'Warren was so happy. His face just changed. I wish I'd videoed it. His whole mood just lifted. He gave Bryn a hug and said: "That's great news. Well done." As a start to the tour, it couldn't have been better for us as a family.'

## Bryn Gatland

'Of course Dad has been a huge influence on my rugby career, but in a subtle way. He's never wanted to be a coach of any teams that I've played in, and I would be the same. I didn't really want that. Some dads love it. Some kids love it. But we didn't do that. He'd just watch a game and ask me straight after how did I think I played. I'd say if I was rubbish, or if I was OK or if I thought I was alright, and he'd say a few things here and there. You don't want to overload someone with information, because they only take in a few things.

'He'd give me little pointers: Play a little flatter. Or a little wider. Keep my hands up. Look for a second touch. I needed to kick a bit more in the first or second half, or use cross-kicks more. Defensively get up in someone's face. All of that has been important.

'I also listen to him when he talks about how he ran a team or why they do certain things. Then I'd take that into teams that I play for, especially at school level.

'I get a few comments every now and then from other players. "It's like playing against a thirty-year-old man." They think I play a different style of first-five (outside-half) from most twenty-year-olds. That probably comes down to the way that Dad thinks of the game. We actually think quite similarly.'

## Trudi Gatland

'There was a lot of trust involved over those two weeks. Tana [Umaga, the Blues Coach] would have had Bryn in there with the Blues on and off all season.'

## Bryn Gatland

'I had been an injury replacement with the Blues, but I ended up being in there longer than expected. I was stripped for five games and played in four. I went to South Africa, Australia, the Brisbane tens, so I ended up spending at least two months there in total.

'Then the week they didn't need me anymore, because they had their player back from injury, the Crusaders called me in as an injury replacement. I went down to Crusaders for two weeks, and in the first week I was there they played the Blues in Christchurch. I rang Dad and said to him: "It's weird, I know the calls for both teams!"

'When I was watching, I was thinking: "This is how the Crusaders are going to move it." And I knew how the Blues were going to defend it. Then I knew how the Blues were going to run a move and how the Crusaders were going to defend it! I've never had such an insight into a game in my life.

'But the Crusaders coaches were the same as the Blues had been. They said: "Look, we're not going to ask you to say anything. We don't think that's ethical and we're not going to compromise you." So I could stay at the Crusaders for another week which was good, but the Blues boys were giving me a bit of stick after the game. "Did you tell them our calls?" It's been an odd few months.

'So watching the Blues play the Lions, I wanted Dad's team to do well, but I also wanted the Blues to do well. During the game I stayed quiet. After it was over, I pretty much went home straight away. I was thinking to myself: "Dad might need cheering up all over again."'

# 'DON'T WORRY GATS,
WE'VE GOT YOUR BACK'

9

## Lions to New Zealand 2017

*Thursday, 8 June*

After breakfast, the players had a pool recovery in the hotel and I reviewed the Blues' game with the other coaches on our laptops. At midday we checked out, grabbed some lunch and headed to the airport for our 3pm charter direct to Christchurch. I continued to look at the Blues game on the bus and the plane.

There were some positives, as well as plenty to work on, and as a coach I always try to concentrate on the easy things to fix. Even if you lose by twenty-one points, you can turn things round quite quickly in a week.

You look at things like territory and possession, and they were pretty close. We created some five-on-three opportunities but we need to be a bit squarer and flatter in attack. We conceded some soft penalties, and the yellow card against Liam Williams for his second challenge in the air put us in a bit of a hole for a while. We even had a chance with a lineout at the end of the game and we didn't nail it. There were other moments we didn't nail. But these are fixable, and there were some good things as well.

At 5.30pm, myself, Sam, John Spencer, John Feehan and Charlie McEwen went to the Earthquake Memorial, which was completed last February on the sixth anniversary of the 2011 quake which claimed 185 lives.

That was quite special. We were welcomed by the Christchurch Deputy Mayor, Andrew Turner, in the park area on the north bank of the Avon River and were led to the marble Memorial Wall. It was a nice, dusky evening, and it was beautifully lit up. They've done a lovely job in the way the names of the victims are carved into the marble.

John Spencer spoke and thanked everyone on behalf of the Lions for 'the privilege of sharing these moments with you, and of allowing us to express our respect.' Sam Warburton laid a wreath at the Memorial Wall.

We met some of the survivors and also relatives of those who had lost their lives, including the Quake Families Trust Chair Bruce McEachen and his wife Jeanette, whose son Matthew was one of the victims. We also met Summer Olliver, who was trapped in the PGC building that collapsed and as a result suffered serious injuries, as well as her mum Trish and her fiancé Ricky Shalders. We spoke to first responders including Mark Elstone and Steve Rule from the New Zealand Fire Service, and Tony McCormick, a member of the public who helped to rescue people from the building. Some were trapped there for five hours.

One of the victims was an Irishman, John O'Connor, who died in the PGC building where he worked. We met his Kiwi wife Sarah, and their sons Dan, eight, and Sean, six, who was born three months after the quake. Sam presented the boys with cuddly Lions and signed their Lions caps, and we arranged tickets for them to go to Saturday's game against the Crusaders at the AMI Stadium, even though it was a sell-out. Sarah told us that John would have supported the Lions. One of the boys decided he'd be cheering for the Lions and the other for the New Zealand sides and the All Blacks.

I played plenty of games in Christchurch during my time with Waikato, and I've been back a couple of times since the earthquake. Obviously, it's harder to get your bearings in the city now. Many of the traditional landmarks are gone. They've been through a terribly hard time but they're recovering. Some of the people we met spoke about the opportunity that comes with rebuilding the city to fix some of the planning mistakes from the past.

It's always been one of the hotbeds of New Zealand rugby, where the supporters have been referred to as 'one-eyed Cantabs', because they are very parochial and passionate about Canterbury and the Crusaders. Maybe this is one reason why this region has always been so successful. I'd expect Saturday to be absolutely no different. That visit, although it made us a little late for our press conference to announce the team to play the Crusaders, was a thoroughly worthwhile occasion.

● ● ●

Alun Wyn, as captain, was alongside me for the press conference, when I was asked if this selection for the Crusaders match indicated a shadow Test team.

'Not that we have spoken about,' I said. 'I gave one of the coaches a piece of paper and said "write down your Test team" and he couldn't get anywhere near it at the moment. Players are going to get one or two chances to make an impact before we start thinking about the Test team. We haven't spoken about Test combinations.'

Believe it or not, that was the truth.

*Friday, 9 June*

The non-twenty-three went to the gym in Christchurch, while we met with the match-day twenty-three at 10.30am before taking the bus for the Captain's Run at Linwood Rugby Club. It was another new team, with George North, Jonathan Davies, Conor Murray and Sean O'Brien all making their first appearances of the tour. It was also a first start for Jamie George, Mako Vunipola, Tadhg Furlong, George Kruis, Owen Farrell, Liam Williams and Peter O'Mahony. That meant, as promised, every one of the forty-one had been given a start in the first three games.

This group had trained a bit longer than anyone else, because we'd run them hard on the Wednesday and they'd met together again on the Thursday. That night they'd had a players' meeting, first with forwards and backs separately, and then together, to get some clarity. You could see the benefits in the Captain's Run.

After the warm-up, Andy Farrell ran a couple of defensive drills. Then we did a few exit plays and kick-offs, before the players ran through their attacking options. I came away from that session thinking 'we're sharp here'. Andy and Graham Rowntree said the same thing.

The players stayed on and did a few lineout spotters. A few calls had been stuffed up in the first two matches, so George Kruis wanted to make sure that everything was right. That was meant to be about ten minutes but it went on for about twenty, which was a bit longer than I would have liked but we were still working through calls.

The coaching staff went for a meal that night in a restaurant called the Twenty-Seven Steps, which is, as you might imagine, upstairs. The analysts and the strength and conditioning team also came along, as did Frank Endacott, a former New Zealand Kiwi rugby league coach who had also coached Andy at Wigan. He'd been to training, where he had a good chat with Andy. He's now a players' agent and it was great having him with the group that night.

We were a little late heading out, because I had gone to meet the referee for the match, Mathieu Raynal. When I caught up with the coaches at the hotel, they asked me how it went and I said: 'I don't like it when a meeting goes that well.'

I went there with about five points which I wanted to raise, and he had already picked up on all five. One was the angle of the Crusaders scrum, about their loose-head, Joe Moody, staying square, and their tight-head, Owen Franks, not coming in at an angle. We also spoke about their blocking close to the tryline at lineout drives, where they tend to put someone in front of the ball-carrier. When you meet with the ref, you are asking him to sometimes look at a few points which may come up during the game, because as coaches we are always trying to push to the limits the laws of the game.

*Saturday, 10 June*
*Crusaders v Lions, AMI Stadium, Christchurch*

In the pre-match interviews, I'd been reminded that I'd said dropping a couple of games in the build-up to playing the All Blacks wouldn't be the end of the world, once we were gelling as a team. Was that still the case?

I couldn't hide behind that one. Sometimes it's about winning too, and building momentum and self-belief. 'To be honest, the result of this game is really important.' We needed a win, and I said it straight out. I knew it as well as anyone. A win – and preferably a big performance to go with it.

I genuinely felt that the Maori game a week later, although billed as 'the fourth Test', would be easier than playing the Super Rugby teams. Not that I didn't believe the Maori had plenty of talent individually, but the Super

Rugby teams had been together for seven or eight months, whereas the Maori would only have ten days together. We would actually have a couple of weeks and games on them. Also, if we could beat the Crusaders, the Highlanders and the Maori, we'd be in a strong position going into that first Test.

The night-time kick-offs make for long match-days, and after breakfast we had to focus on the non-twenty-three, which would mostly be the team to play the Highlanders in Dunedin the following Tuesday.

At 9.15am, the non-twenty-three went to the gym before taking the bus at 10.20 to Linwood Rugby Club for training. The Manager of the club is Aaron Flynn, brother of the former All Blacks hooker Corey, who played scrum-half for the Crusaders. The night before, John Spencer had spoken at a fundraising dinner at the club.

We ran the boys pretty hard because Sunday was going to be another recovery/travel day for the entire squad. This only left them Monday for a light Captain's Run, and we wanted everyone to continue on the same cycle.

The hardest thing about this tour is that, unlike Australia, we've been on the move so much that the guys haven't had a day off, or if it's been a day off, it's still been a travel day.

In South Africa and Australia, we often stayed in one city for an entire week. Not doing that in New Zealand was a mistake in the schedule. After the first game, we should have played the Chiefs the following Wednesday and not played the Blues until the Tuesday of the first Test. Then we could have spent that whole first week in Auckland. Instead, we've effectively been travelling twice a week.

We're heading to Auckland after the Chiefs game next Tuesday night, and taking the Wednesday off. Everyone needs to switch off for a day. A Lions tour to New Zealand is a pressure-cooker. Mentally it's quite draining. We need to remember that the players are not machines.

That session at Linwood was private, and all the club's under-age teams had been training across the road. After we finished, they were invited over and our players signed pictures of the squad, posed for photos and gave out a few balls and other bits and pieces.

Ger Carmody would later inform me that Aaron Flynn told him that he'd received a call from the NZ Herald. They wanted to know if it was true that our security guys had been heavy-handed in turning kids away, and that our players had refused to sign autographs.

Nothing could have been further from the truth. The players couldn't have been more accommodating, and Aaron told them as much. But it made me think: 'What's going on here? What sort of negativity are some of the media trying to create?'

We'd taken plenty of criticism for our first performance and for losing to the Blues; we were being written off against the Crusaders and now this.

We were fully aware of the negativity in 2005 and we had spoken about making a conscious effort to engage with the community. We'd done that en route to Whangarei when visiting hospitals and schools the day before the first game, which we would never normally do, but we felt it was very important. We wanted to set a tone from early on.

But when Ger told me about that phone call, I was a little surprised. It really put me on my guard.

In the meantime, I caught up with some good friends from Christchurch, Alan and Tracy Steel, to give them tickets. I went to school with Alan at Hamilton Boys. I have a very close group of friends from my time at Hamilton Boys High and we celebrated our 50th birthdays together in France a few summers ago, at the home of my friends Michael and Sue Holland. Whenever I come back, they have a laugh with me, and bring me down to earth.

Before the tour, they wanted me to employ them as 'the laughing men'. They'd come to every press conference and any time I said something remotely funny, they would burst into laughter. Alan said to me: 'You definitely need the laughing men now!' I had been thinking of mentioning them at one or two press conferences – 'I wish the laughing men were here' – except that no one would have got the joke.

Trudi arrived down from Hamilton at about 3pm, so I had a quick coffee with her and then we did a walk-through in the park across the road at 3.45, before a pre-match meal. We held our team meeting in the hotel at 5.45 before taking the bus to the ground.

At the meeting, I was tempted to say nothing at all, and in the end kept it to a few seconds. 'You boys looked sharp yesterday. We know how important today is. We're ready to go.'

• • •

It's a short drive to the AMI Stadium from the hotel. It was a cold, dewy night. The AMI is the old rugby league ground, with temporary stands to increase the capacity as a new home for Canterbury and the Crusaders, after the old Jade Stadium, or Lancaster Park, was damaged by the 2011 earthquake.

The changing rooms are portakabins, through a tunnel at the end of the ground. It still feels temporary rather than permanent. The ground was packed and as atmospheric as usual.

The players were still getting to know the warm-up. That can require two or three games before everyone feels comfortable with it. But, even with another new team and four players playing their first game, this was the slickest warm-up so far.

There was good voice from the staff, Alun Wyn, Sean and the rest of the players, but not too much. I could feel the tension and anticipation.

The Crusaders fans love their pre-match ritual: six knights on horseback doing laps of the pitch. But then you have to dodge the horse poo as you walk along the sideline, which is a little disconcerting before a match!

Aside from the result, the biggest kick I got out of that night was coming out of the tunnel from the changing rooms for the warm-up. In the front row there were about six guys all in Waikato jerseys. In the AMI Stadium. Home to the Crusaders.

As I was walking past, what was I hearing? 'Come on Gats! Come on Gats!' They were shaking their fists and one of them said: 'Don't worry Gats, we've got your back!'

How cool is that? I got such a kick out of it because Waikato people are so loyal. That was one of the highlights of the tour for me. We always joke that it doesn't matter where in the world you go, you'll see someone wearing a Waikato jersey. When we lived in London, occasionally you'd see someone walking along the street in one, and the kids would see it. They'd go: 'No, Dad. Don't Dad.' I'd roll the window down and as we were going past, I'd shout at the top of my voice: 'Come on Waikato!' and carry on driving. The guy would look around wondering where that came from. The kids would duck down with embarrassment.

That night, we also knew what we were up against; a team with nine All Blacks in it, including six in the forward pack, and the best team in Super Rugby, with fourteen wins from fourteen. You couldn't ask for a better challenge and I thought the way our boys responded was the most impressive thing about the night.

The players set the tone from the start, and when we needed it our defence was outstanding. We had chances. There had been plenty of criticism about us only scoring two tries in three games, but we had been creating chances and, in my opinion, coaches are required to provide a framework that creates opportunities. It's up to the players to finish them. If you create a two-on-one, it's not a coach's job to finish it off, to make the right pass or catch the ball. In any case, it would be more worrying if we weren't creating chances.

Our set-pieces were strong, and Peter O'Mahony put big pressure on their throw. That led to one penalty, and a scrum to another, both of which Owen Farrell kicked. Against an All Blacks' front-row, our scrum was really strong. Conor Murray's kicking game was brilliant. Owen attacked the line, and the length of his penalties to touch put them under more pressure.

But then we had a tricky ten minutes or so, on the pitch and in the coaches' box. First Stuart Hogg went off after his face caught Conor's elbow, a freakish accident. We had a few options at full-back, Liam Williams and, conceivably, Owen or Johnny Sexton. But at that stage of the tour we were still looking at alternatives. Anthony Watson had played on the wing for England but had looked good at full-back for Bath, so we brought him on as a straight swap. He did exceptionally well.

Tadhg Furlong got caught out at one scrum, they made it 6–3 and then Jonathan Davies went off for an HIA, which he failed. OK, this was a chance to bring on Johnny Sexton, shift Owen out and look at that 10-12 combination.

I was so pleased that Johnny played well. I honestly feared until that point that he might be gone. He hadn't played well in the Pro12 semi-final against the Scarlets, or in the opening tour game against the Barbarians. I appreciate no one else had done; they were all still suffering from jet lag. But his body language wasn't positive. Not that he struts around anyway, but his shoulders seemed a little hunched. Even the way he was speaking to the media, saying that Owen was in the position he'd been in four years ago as a European Cup and Six Nations winner, I thought the tour was proving a challenge for him mentally.

Johnny had rediscovered his mojo. He attacked the line better, was really physical in defence as usual, and also varied his game well. He and Owen mixed it up nicely, rotating between '10' and '12'.

Owen also kicked a third penalty to leave us 9–3 up at half-time. We made our way back from the coaches' box to the portakabin and I was struck by how composed the players were. Sometimes, when you're leading a game you're not expected to win, there can be a little flapping and excitability. But there was clarity. We'd handled the changes well. To me this demonstrated a confidence in our ability to win the match.

In the second half, at 9–3, Owen missed not the most difficult penalty to put us two scores ahead, but he was convinced he kicked it. Neil Jenkins thought it was over too, and he should know. We looked at the replay and we thought it was over. Afterwards, I spoke to Angus Gardner, the touch judge, and he disagreed.

Our bench was excellent; it wasn't just Johnny and Anthony. The front-row, Jack McGrath, Ken Owens and Dan Cole, did well. Maro Itoje and CJ Stander each made a good impact too.

Our game management helped us control the game and Owen's fourth penalty made it 12–3 and meant we could see it out quite comfortably. At the end, there were a few shouts and a few f-words in the coaches' box before we shook hands. We enjoyed that one. We needed that one.

The entire squad came into the changing room. Greig Laidlaw led us in a rendition of *Highland Cathedral*. Our singing was improving too! We really pumped that out.

We left the ground after 11.30, and were back in the hotel by midnight. Bus trips are always nicer when you've won a game. People are a little more animated and jovial.

I had a few beers and a chat with the other coaches and analysts. We went down to the bar, and Ronan Keating was there with his son Jack, whom he'd brought over for the Blues and Crusaders games as a birthday present. He approached me and said: 'Congratulations. Would you mind me taking a photo?'

'No problem at all.'

Ger then organised a few drinks in the team room upstairs for the boys, who invited Ronan to join us. They played some Boyzone songs along with a couple of Ronan's solo ones, and gave him some banter. After about forty-five minutes of this, he stood up and sang a few songs for us. It was fantastic.

I went to bed at about 2am. Some of them stayed on for another hour or two. Ronan and Jack had an early flight home the next day, and I believe Jack definitely had a good night.

All in all, we came away from that game feeling pretty good about ourselves. That was more like the Lions.

## 10

## A HIGHLANDER LOW

### Lions to New Zealand 2017

*Sunday, 11 June*

The *Sunday Star-Times* did player ratings for Saturday's Crusaders game, and the combined total for the Crusaders' starting team came to ninety-four. The Lions' total amounted to eighty-six, and yet we had deservedly won the game 12–3. Both their flankers got a seven, while Sean O'Brien and Peter O'Mahony got a six. At least Toby Faletau got a seven: I thought his footwork had been excellent.

I was a little surprised that the whole focus the next day was on the referee's performance and his interpretation of the scrum. Some people had even referred to him as the 'new Wayne Barnes'. But for me, Mathieu Raynal is one of the best scrummaging referees in the game, and we had just followed his instructions and what is normal practice in the northern hemisphere, with a slight gap before engagement. We'd also prepared for a scenario of full engagement without a gap, as had been happening in Super Rugby.

There should also have been a couple of penalties against the Crusaders for blocking.

Clearly it was going to be quite difficult, in certain quarters, to earn any credit for the way that we played but that's life. You're only here for a few weeks, you just put that to one side, and you start thinking and preparing for the next game.

Conor Murray's box-kicking had really been on the money. We didn't always get up in the air to compete, but the Crusaders didn't handle the box-kicking very well, perhaps because against the Blues we had kicked longer. We knew there was a risk in doing that against the Blues given their counter-attacking game, but we were consciously trying to show the New Zealand sides and the All Blacks different pictures, mixing and matching our kicking game a little to keep them guessing.

After the game and the press conferences, Brad Mooar, the Crusaders' Assistant Coach, had come into our changing room and said to me: 'You threw a couple of things at us differently, things we weren't expecting.'

'Well, we're trying to change things up,' I said.

The most telling comment he made, for me, was that they had learned a big lesson in game management. That was a tribute to Conor and Owen Farrell, and also to Johnny Sexton when he came on. We had never really run Johnny and Owen together as a 10-12 in training before. Genuinely.

● ● ●

We announced the team to play the Highlanders at 10am, with fifteen changes again. After the boys had their medicals, massage and a pool recovery, we checked out of our hotel at midday, had some lunch, and a meeting at 1.15pm.

If there are any organisational changes you can cover them off in a short, five or ten-minute meeting. We usually did this before travelling. John Spencer would thank the local liaison guys or hotel staff. Ger, the medics, the commercial staff and myself would raise a few things about what was ahead of us. The aim was to cover a lot off for the week, and reduce the amount of meetings.

Then we took the bus to the airport for our 2pm flight to Dunedin, and checked into the Southern Cross Scenic hotel. Dunedin is known as a very traditional student city and a party town. It's where doctors and lawyers study for their degrees, the city where the future leaders of society are developed. They get the wildness out of their systems for three or four years in Dunedin, and then become pillars of society. But the students were on holidays while we were there, so it was very quiet until match-day, when all the Highlanders and Lions fans would roll into town.

After dinner I had a press conference with Sam Warburton, who was captain against the Highlanders.

## Monday, 12 June

We didn't have a full review on the Sunday, as it was a travel day, so the players could watch the Crusaders game on their own time. This morning we had a squad meeting at 9.30, which began with the backs and forwards having separate reviews.

This led to a fifteen-minute review by the full squad. With reviews, we try to be concise. Steve Borthwick had said that some of the earlier meetings were too long, and I agreed. There was some healthy debate and Andy Farrell pointed out that in the early stages of the tour we needed to cover the information in more detail to ensure clarity. Andy also emphasised that not all teams are the same and the Irish players were comfortable with longer review meetings. Thereafter, the unit reviews were kept to a maximum of fifteen minutes and the same with the team reviews.

The match-day twenty-three for the Highlanders game were on the bus at 10.15 for training, and the non-twenty-three at 10.45, as we decided to make the most of the closed roof at the Forsyth Barr Stadium by bringing the entire squad there. It's the hardest pitch in New Zealand by a long way. Opposition players often struggle and cramp up, because they're not used to such a firm surface.

That evening, following an afternoon off, we had the first presentation of the Bobby Cup. That's when Paul Stridgeon, aka Bobby, picks his man of the match. When he was at Wasps, Bobby found a plastic cup one day in the Academy changing room and came upon Alex King in the ice bath.

'Kingy, you're my Player of the Day from yesterday, here's the cup.'

'Why don't you give it to me at a meeting?' said Alex. 'And say a few words and stuff.'

This was in September 2002. I had joined Wasps the previous season and I had just taken over from Nigel Melville as Wasps' Director of Rugby at the start of the 2002–03 season. When Bobby told me about this, I liked the sound of that idea, and it became the Bobby Cup. He'd present it to his man of the match, a day or two after every game we won, and he'd tell a few jokes. This progressed to him also making a video every time he presented the cup.

Bobby went around London in a Wasps outfit called 'Sting', coming across people, getting up to mischief, going into bars, restaurants and nightclubs, and Tony Hanks, in the club's analysis department, helped edit the videos.

For two seasons in a row we had runs of fourteen wins in fifteen matches, and Bobby started to run out of ideas.

'Gats, what the f*** am I going to do this week?'

'Just get it done mate,' I said to him. 'Just get it done.' And he did, every time.

When Bobby became the Head Fitness Coach he passed it on to others, but has revived it whenever he's been with Wales or the Lions.

On this tour, rather than do it after every game we won, we opted to do it after every two wins, and we'd beaten the Barbarians and the Crusaders.

As part of the build-up to this, Bobby had put together one of his videos, 'Bringing Rala Back From The Dead' for the tour. That was hilarious. Patrick O'Reilly, the infamous Rala, had retired as Baggage Master with Ireland, and the video began with Ger Carmody explaining that I'd only have Rala on tour on the condition that he passed a fitness test. They scoured the world for a doctor, and found one in Verona by the name of Aineo Falvarinio, played by Bobby of course.

Ben Uttley, who produced and put together the official Lions documentary, superimposed Rala into different movies. First there was *Clash of the Titans*, where the line 'Our temples are burning. . .' prompts Rala to say: 'So, call the fire brigade.' Then he was standing in for Joaquim Phoenix in *Gladiator*, before it cuts to Rala in *Jurassic Park*.

The camera then cuts to Rala in the cryotherapy chamber (filmed at the Welsh training centre in the Vale), before there's a close-up of him doing some altitude training, in which he says: 'Bobby, this is killing me.' When the camera pans back, Rala is crawling on all fours on the treadmill.

There's a scene played out to *The Godfather* soundtrack where Rala is imitating Michael Corleone puffing on a cigar before finally they checked his kidney function. This required a urine sample, after which Rala says: 'How's that Bob?'

It's a pint of Guinness!

Then the video cuts to Ronan Keating, whom we had invited up to the team room two nights before, to announce the winner to the camera. He was good at that too.

'I've been asked to announce the winner of the Bobby Cup,' says Ronan.

'Who is it?' someone asks off camera.

'It doesn't really matter who it is, right? Nobody cares.'

'No, no. I care.'

'No, no. People don't care who the winner of the Bobby Cup is. No. No. Nobody cares.'

'Say it.'

'Nobody cares,' says Ronan, walking away.

'Say it.'

Ronan turns back and shouts: 'Toby Faletauuuuuuu!'

The whole video was brilliant, and the boys loved it.

After that extravaganza, myself, Ger and the coaches had a meal out together that night in the Octagon, whereas Trudi went out with her parents and auntie. Trudi had hired a car and they'd done some sightseeing. They went up the peninsula to visit Larnarch Castle and the gannet colony, where they ran into quite a few Lions fans.

As we were preparing two teams for the next two games, I didn't have much time to see them. While I was happy with the Crusaders game, by that Monday night I was already a little stressed again before the Highlanders.

Our hotel was attached to the casino, and a few of us dropped in there for some downtime. One of our analysts Vinny Hammond, who likes to bet, seemed to be doing alright. I played at a couple of tables, blackjack and roulette, but I didn't make my fortune.

*Tuesday, 13 June*
*Highlanders v Lions, Forsyth Barr Stadium, Dunedin*

Our first casualty of the tour. Eanna Falvey met me at breakfast and informed me that Stuart Hogg had suffered a facial fracture against the Crusaders.

He's been desperately unlucky since we arrived. Although he defended well against the Barbarians, things didn't happen for him in attack, and then to be ruled out of the rest of the tour after accidentally colliding with Conor Murray's elbow was cruel.

I went up to Hoggy and said: 'Look mate, I know it's no consolation at the moment, but our thoughts at the start of the tour were that we were probably looking to start you in the first Test at 15.' His attacking strengths are so good that we most likely would have done that and I thought it was only fair to tell him. Fortunately, we were well stocked at full-back, with Leigh Halfpenny, Liam Williams, Anthony Watson and Jared Payne, so there was no need to call up a replacement.

After breakfast and monitoring, the non-twenty-three worked in the gym and then trained at the University Oval. It was freezing cold and raining heavily, with a huge puddle on the pitch. What did Bobby do? He dived straight into it at the start of the session. Twice. The madman. We planned a session of about thirty-six minutes. Conor Murray's hand was still sore and Johnny Sexton had a stinger on his calf from the Crusaders match, so we were limited in what we could achieve.

Conor and Johnny took part in a walk-through at the start of the session, but due to the conditions I said to the players: 'Look, we've planned for a thirty-six-minute training session, with fifteen minutes for unit work at the end for some scrums and lineouts.

'But here's the deal. Give us lots of voice and intensity, and we'll cut the session in half and just do fifteen minutes at the end. But the deal is you've got to be vocal, you've got to be accurate, you've got to give a lot of positive energy to everything you do.'

'Yea, yea,' they said.

We wanted to reward them for doing something in unappealing conditions, and try to get something positive out of the session rather than doing it for the sake of it. It worked. When we went back to the hotel, Jonathan Davies said it was the coldest training session he'd ever taken part in – and he's from Wales!

We then turned our attention to the twenty-three to play the Highlanders, with a walk-through at 3.50pm, before the pre-match meal.

We met at six o'clock for a quick team meeting before getting on the bus. The message to the players was about bringing some physicality to the game, working hard off the ball, working harder than the opposition, trying to out-talk them, and, our well-worn mantra about 'staying alive'; that we react to anything that's a little bit different, not just a quick tap or throw in, but other things, such as whether they'd compete at lineouts or stand off. We needed to do that in a pro-active way, so that they didn't catch us out.

Only I spoke at that meeting, because when it's an hour and a half before kick-off, you don't want the players too wound up, or to overload them with points.

It was a short enough journey to the ground, about ten minutes. It was raining hard, so it was a relief to be playing indoors. Of course, we also have a roof in Cardiff, but unfortunately we don't have the final say on whether it's closed or not.

The players were composed. The messages had been clear. They were aware of how important the game was for them individually too. We couldn't con them into thinking there would be loads of Test places up for grabs. This group of players was also well aware of the significance of the win over the Crusaders, and we all wanted to maintain that momentum.

Having been down to the pitch the day before, we knew how hard it was going to be. Literally. We'd heard that they wanted to throw the ball around and try to run us off our feet. We also knew that they kicked a lot, but with attacking kicks.

The Highlanders made a blistering start. The little grubbers, the attacking kicks that we knew were coming, got Waisake Naholo in behind us, and they butchered a try. We were stretched at that point but a positive in the last two games has been our scrambling defence. The players were working hard for each other and we weathered a bit of a storm before playing some good rugby ourselves.

But we played too much rugby between the 22 and the opposition 10-metre line. We needed more variation to turn them around, some kicks to stop their line speed and get them thinking, and to regain possession as well.

We kicked to compete, but again we didn't do that effectively. We have players that are normally pretty good in the air, so we were going to have to do some work on that over the next couple of weeks. There were a couple of cross-field kicks from Dan Biggar to Tommy Seymour which he probably should have taken. Generally, that's one of Tommy's strengths.

We left a try behind too before Naholo scored the game's first try, when Robbie Henshaw was clearly blocked by their lock Alex Ainley. When you look at it from behind, it's clear and obvious to me that Robbie would have had a great opportunity to effect that tackle on Naholo, and it should have been a penalty to us.

That was a massive decision, and what disappointed me was that the TMO said to the referee: 'Do you want to have another look at it?'

Angus Gardner said to the TMO: 'What do you think?'

He said: 'Oh, I think it's a slight obstruction but I don't think he would have got there.'

The referee then said: 'I'm happy to go with your call.'

They were too quick to decide it wasn't worth looking at from another angle, and I think when they see the replay from behind the goal-line they'll be embarrassed. That was a massive call when there was so much at stake.

It was too dismissive. Gardner only went to the TMO once in the Barbarians game and it seemed he was quite reluctant to have the TMO help him out. If it had been a penalty to us, that would have put a completely different complexion on the game.

Soon after, Robbie got back to make a try-saving tackle. He'll be a little bit disappointed with some of his attacking options, but defensively he's been really sound.

We pulled level when Dan Biggar worked a loop around CJ Stander, and drew in Naholo before giving the pass to Jonathan Joseph. JJ showed some real pace to score. We're trying to get him into some space because he is dangerous then, but it's a balancing act.

CJ's offload took out two of their players. We've been encouraging our players to offload, but it's about picking the right time. That was the right moment.

You've got to encourage players to back their skills, to back their ability, to get a pass away or an offload at the right times, particularly in New Zealand. But there were a couple of occasions in this game when we tried to offload and put ourselves under pressure. We didn't go forward and then we were just shovelling horrible stuff.

We need to improve this in training, because some of the teams in the northern hemisphere don't always encourage players to play what's in front of them. But that's the way that the game is going at the moment; reacting to the speed of ball and to line speed, being able to read when guys are coming off the line defensively and change the play.

We've also been working hard on staying square. There were a couple of times when the backs were just a little bit lateral. We need to stay square to stop players drifting off us. That's something else to work on.

Still, we came in at half-time at 10–10. We hadn't played as well as we could have, but we were happy enough with where we were. I said to them: 'If we kick on in the second half, get a couple of tries, we can win this game relatively comfortably.'

As well as the blocking on Robbie, we felt a few other calls hadn't gone our way. The New Zealand media made a big thing of us getting a few decisions against the Crusaders, whereas I thought the referee had done a good job, but against the Highlanders nearly all the marginal calls went against us.

Early in the game Sam Warburton was clearly on the ball and it should have been a penalty to us, but Gardner didn't give it. Instead he said: 'Release it. Release it.' When Naholo then got on the ball, straight away he gave them a penalty.

We were also called offside a couple of times in midfield, yet after a break by Rhys Webb, the touch judge said: 'Angus, watch for that, they're offside coming back there. Be careful with that.'

Angus replied: 'Oh thanks.' But he didn't give us a penalty in front of the posts.

At half-time, initially we gave the guys a few minutes on their own, to rehydrate and have a bit of self-reflection, before we split as usual. The forwards and the backs had separate reviews. Then we came together. Andy Farrell noted a couple of defensive points, Rob Howley some on the attack and then I finished it off.

In this game, I just found that when we got down there, when we were direct in getting in behind them, and when we were making some pick and goes, or guys were coming off '9', we made some good yardage. We had to earn that right to go wide by getting front-foot ball. Then we were dangerous, but we looked to play when the ball was slow. So that was the message. Be more direct. Get front-foot ball, and then play in the wider channels.

That's what we saw in the second half. Tommy Seymour picked off a cross-kick by Lima Sopoaga, but at this level it's about taking every opportunity and Dan pulled the conversion to the left. Instead of 17–10 it was 15–10, and then they kicked a penalty to make it 15–13 when Kyle Sinckler was penalised for a no-arms tackle. Again, that was an avoidable one. That really grates with me, because it can be the difference between winning and losing.

But then we were nice and direct. Iain Henderson had a couple of good carries, and Sam picked up and went through. We kicked the conversion to make it 22–13. One more score and we were clear, but in that last quarter the penalty count was 7–2 against us.

That was very, very costly. We've got to be smarter. Again, there were some avoidable penalties. A general rule of thumb is to concede ten or less penalties in a game. On Saturday against the Crusaders it was seven, and against the Highlanders it was twelve.

Alun Wyn Jones came through at a lineout and was caught offside when trying to get after their scrum-half. A player of Alun Wyn's experience and ability would be well aware that this was an unnecessary penalty. They kicked to the five-metre line and scored off a driven lineout, bringing it to 22–20.

We got down to the other end a few minutes later. Owen Farrell had just replaced Dan Biggar and had a penalty just to the right of the upright, not too far out. You're thinking: 'OK, this is three points, 25–20 up.' But he pushed it slightly to the right, when nine times out of ten he kicks it.

That shot at goal was the first thing Owen did. But he had warmed up on the sidelines and I don't think he'd use that as an excuse. Neil Jenkins said he just pushed it.

Then they were awarded a scrum penalty. It was a really tough penalty against Dan Cole. It looked like their loose-head, Aki Seiuli, brought the scrum down, but the assistant referee said: 'Red, red, red.' So the referee penalised us. I think had Mathieu Raynal been on that side of the pitch, the penalty would have gone to us.

They went down the pitch and had another scrum. I felt for Dan. I felt for him a lot. At the previous scrum, you could see the reaction on the faces of the front-rows. The Highlanders' front-row were as surprised as anyone that the penalty had gone to them.

So for the next scrum, Dan feels a little compromised. 'I've just been penalised at the last one, so I've got to be squeaky clean here.' He's in a position where he feels he has to back off a little bit, he's penalised again, they kick the three points, and we're behind.

We still had one last chance off a lineout. Steve thinks we should have looked to drive it. But referees are often a little bit reluctant to award a penalty in a close game so near the end. We had earned a couple of lineout penalties, but I don't think attacking from off-the-top ball was the wrong option.

JJ ran a great line, and if he had caught Owen's pass, with his pace and footwork, he may have scored. Even if he was tackled, at the very least we then would have had a few options off the ruck. We also have variations off that move and we want to keep some of them up our sleeves for the Test matches. But he knocked on and that was it.

Still, it was important for our players to see how another New Zealand team celebrated at the full-time whistle and how significant that win was for them.

In the coaches' box, myself, Rob, Andy and Wig [Graham Rowntree] were all absolutely hacked off. In the changing room, I spoke with Robbie, and he was adamant he would have got to Naholo if he hadn't been blocked.

Much of the reason for this defeat was still down to us though, to not controlling the game when we were in a position to do so. We'd taken a massive step against the Crusaders and now lost. Was it a regression? I don't know. It's a little bit tough on this Lions team because they'd played on the previous Wednesday, and Thursday was another travel day. They didn't have much time together, and on Saturday they'd had the performance against the Crusaders.

This defeat leaves us with two wins from four games, and yet it could easily have been four from four, having been pipped in a couple of close games that could have gone our way. Instead, a second defeat could potentially have an impact on the squad's morale going forward. Six of the squad have now lost two from two.

There was bitter disappointment in the changing room afterwards. I just said: 'We shot ourselves in the foot.' There were some big moments which we didn't control, some penalties that were avoidable and we need to be better in that regard.

Dan Biggar said to the players that at 22–13 we were comfortable, but let it go. Alun Wyn Jones owned up to his error for the penalty.

I did my post-match interviews with SkySports UK, SkySports New Zealand, talkSPORT and RTE, and then the media conference. It's much easier when you've won, especially as the margins were so fine. If Dan had kicked that conversion or Owen that penalty, we probably would have won the game, and the line of questioning and everyone's perceptions would be so different. However, it still convinced me that playing these New Zealand Super Rugby sides, who are the best in the world below Test level, was ideal preparation for the All Blacks.

The All Blacks were going to be a slick machine. They were going to be unbelievably physical. But the teams we're playing are not that far away from the All Blacks. I have no doubt about that.

I went back to the changing room, where the opposition team came in and exchanged jerseys.

The players know that after the selection against the Maori next Saturday, the first Test will be a week later, and a few of them may be feeling that they've already missed out. They know that time is running out now, but for those who might not be involved in the first Test, they have to realise the series is not gone for them yet. As we've seen on so many occasions, between the first and the third Test players pick up injuries or lose a bit of form.

You can't drop your head and think: 'I haven't played that well', or 'I've been unlucky and I haven't had that much opportunity', or 'I've had a bit of a knock.'

Looking at their body language, it looks as if a few of them are starting to feel like that now.

For the first time we had a few beers in the changing room and a stand-up buffet reception in the ground before taking the bus back to the hotel.

Bryn had flown down to Dunedin for the game at the last minute as he didn't have training with his club. Trudi picked him up from the airport in the morning. Bryn, Trudi, her mum and dad and her Auntie Noeline plus Bryn's good mate Mitch East, who is down at Otago University doing Law, had piled into the rental car and gone to the game.

I met them briefly before the game when they had a quick dinner at the hotel, and again back at the hotel after the game. But I was annoyed with the result.

# 11

## Lions to New Zealand 2017

*Wednesday, 14 June*

Together with the Lions Analysts Rhodri Bown, Vinny Hammond and Mike Hughes, I took the opportunity this morning to review the Highlanders game. The ball had been in play for thirty-four minutes. Against New Zealand teams, you don't get a lot of ball-in-play time. Normally it's in the high thirties or low forties. They're just quite comfortable to kick the ball out and then go again, and wait for their moment. Then they come alive. That's when they're dangerous.

We had sixteen to seventeen minutes of possession ourselves and they had the same amount, but of that, we had over eight minutes' play time between our 22 and their 10-metre line. That's too much. Yes we want to encourage our guys to play, but it's a long way to score from. We need to be putting the opposition under more pressure by playing for more territory as well.

I spoke to Rob Howley and Neil Jenkins about our aerial game and inability to regain possession. It has been disappointing. We need to work on that. Ironically, when I met the referee the night before he told me he'd watched the video of the Crusaders game and said there were a couple of occasions where we should have been awarded penalties for blocking. The same thing happened against the Highlanders, but it wasn't picked up. Maybe we need to be a bit more vocal and let the referees know when someone does run a line and block us. It is hard for the touch judges and referees to spot that every time.

We then reviewed the Highlanders game with the whole squad. We were still disappointed. We'd been in control for most of that game and let it slip. I was particularly disappointed for those guys who had played in the two midweek games and lost both.

In each of them they'd been in front after seventy-odd minutes and didn't close it out. They were desperate to do so. We defended our line really well, cleared the ball, and then gave away an avoidable penalty. Alun Wyn came through the lineout and was caught offside. He's disappointed in himself. Then at the next lineout not everyone completed their roles and this allowed them to score.

Bobby had organised a trip on the bus to St Clair, a suburb five miles outside Dunedin on the Pacific Ocean, for a coffee and a bacon butty, or what he calls a 'banjo butty'. It's a North of England term. You have a bun with a piece of bacon and a really runny egg. So when you eat it, the egg runs down your top and you look like a banjo player.

The players were meant to do some recovery in the sea, but Bobby was worried about the size of the waves. It was raining, cold and pretty rough. The last thing we needed was for someone to drown while we were on tour.

The boys are still a bit downbeat too. The problem with rugby sometimes is that it's all about the result. It's either agony or ecstasy, with no in-between.

We went back to the hotel and checked out at 10.30am for our midday charter direct from Dunedin to Rotorua, which saved a stopover in Wellington or Auckland and halved the journey. As return flights were limited when we booked Bryn onto a one-way flight to Dunedin for the game, we found him a seat on the Lions' plane to Rotorua. After lunch at the Novotel, I borrowed one of the Land Rovers to take him back home to Hamilton.

The hour and a half journey gave us a good chance to have our first proper rugby chat since the tour began. As for the rest of the tour, and even when the Lions play the All Blacks, family comes first. As Bryn put it: 'It's funny, because you think it will be hard, but you can't help it. You root for the team coached by your dad.'

● ● ●

When we came to the first 'Welcome to Hamilton' sign, Bryn and I both shouted 'The Tron!' which started as a hashtag, #lovethetron, about six years ago. When we reached the house, no one was home. Luckily, we found the spare key in the usual place.

The garden backs onto the Waikato River. Trudi had made sure the decking and barbecue area were already spotless, in readiness for hosting all of the Lions management on the following Monday evening before the Chiefs game.

Trudi had flown to Auckland and then driven back to Hamilton, arriving home about an hour after us. We've been married 28 years. She's been the biggest part of my life and my career, always encouraging me, always supporting me. She's been a great mother, and we've been very lucky that Bryn and Gabby are fantastic kids. They've never given us any problems, they're very close to each other, and Trudi is very close to both of them. They're incredibly respectful of her.

She's been very supportive of the kids as well. I wouldn't say she's missed more than two games that Bryn has played over the course of his whole school, club and provincial rugby career. She's travelled all over New Zealand to see him play, even when he's been on the bench. This year also saw a quick trip to Canberra when he started for the Blues against the Brumbies. She said she wouldn't have missed it for the world.

We had a coffee and a chat for about an hour, during which time Gabby came back from the gym. Bryn had to get back to Auckland and they had a lengthy discussion about him getting a lift from Trudi, borrowing the car or taking the bus, not his favourite form of transport. I stayed out of that one.

In 2007 we had moved into town from Redbrook Drive, twenty minutes out of Hamilton, to this house in Awatere Avenue when I got the Wales job, as Trudi wanted to be closer to town if I was going to be away a lot. This was closer to the children's schools, the rowing club for early morning training and the children's friends, and generally made it easier for her to transport them around. Gabby was fourteen and Bryn twelve, and both were happy in their respective schools at the time, so we agreed that upping sticks and moving to the UK again was not a viable option. Hamilton is a great city to bring up kids. It's close to everything, be it Auckland, which is an hour and a half away, or the coast and our beach house at Waihi Beach.

## Trudi Gatland

'We are very lucky to have our lovely home on the river, only five minutes into the city and with space for friends and family to stay. Every weekend there would be extra teenagers staying over, especially the children's friends. They were boarders at Waikato Diocesan and Hamilton Boys High, so they could play their sports and go back and forth to rowing regattas.

'It was always great fun and there was a constant supply of food on the kitchen table. No one knocks on the door at our place, they can just stroll on *in and they all still do. God help the next people who live in our home as they will have people wandering in long after we have moved on! The neighbours and our kids' friends come over and swim in our pool in the summer even when they know we are probably at the beach. It's that kind of home.*

*'Warren is away for between twenty-five to thirty weeks of the year with about three trips home ranging from two to five weeks at a time, for Christmas, Easter and after the June tour. I get over to Wales for all seven weeks of the Six Nations and the four weeks of the Autumn series, and if the children are able then they come over as well.*

*'In the first five or six years they came with me most times, but more recently they have not always been able to. We were all at the 2015 World Cup in the UK and 2013 Lions tour to Australia, although Bryn only got over for the last two weeks of the World Cup and about two of the Lions games due to his own rugby commitments. They are very self-sufficient from being left at home at times and have learnt to cook and look after themselves from about seventeen years of age. My parents and friends have been a great support to me and the children.'*

## Gabby Gatland

*'Dad was playing for Waikato when I was born; and I was four, and Bryn was two, when he was coaching Connacht and we moved to Galway in 1997. So I started school in Ireland, at Scoil Íde. After Dad finished in Ireland and went to Wasps, we relocated to London. I had just turned nine.*

*'I was quite upset really, because I loved Galway, and it had always been assumed that once Dad was finished in Ireland we'd be going back to New Zealand. We used to come back every Christmas and I loved going home in the summer and seeing all my extended family. Then suddenly we were going*

to live in England, so that was a bit of a shock. But as soon as I started school, in St Augustine's Priory in Ealing, I made some friends and I loved it.

'We had been there three years when we moved back to New Zealand in 2005. At first I was quite excited, but as it got closer to actually having to say all the goodbyes, I was really upset again.

'But then it was the same again; once I started school in New Zealand, I loved it. I guess when you're young, you are easily adaptable, and it was easier still because I could pick up with my friends and also make new ones.

'I didn't think Dad being a coach and us moving around as a family was anything out of the ordinary, although every time I started a new school I was the new girl, especially back in New Zealand. One, I had an accent, and two, I started halfway through the school year, so that was quite different for me. But it wasn't too bad.

'When we were growing up in Ireland, after big matches Bryn and I would ask Mum: "Will we have happy Daddy today?" And if Dad's team had won, she'd say: "Yes, we have happy Daddy."

'The answers varied more in Ireland. One Sunday when Dad and Bryn went to the shops, Dad had bought a newspaper and started to read an article that annoyed him so much he snapped at Bryn. Dad felt so bad about it that when they come home he scrunched it up and said: "We're never buying the newspaper again."

'Mum says I'm the one that can best cheer him up after a defeat. Dad lives and works away from home so much, and has such a high profile, that when I do see him, I like to bring him back down to earth, and let him know who's boss!

'After a defeat, I also try to lighten his mood and make him realise it's not the end of the world. Even if I don't make a joke or do something silly, I'll talk about something other than rugby. For most of the people he encounters, rugby is all they want to talk about, the game and what went wrong, or what they think should have been done.

'I'm not really an expert. I don't think I am anyway. So I try to talk about other things, to help take his mind off it.

'In England it was different, because when he was coaching Wasps they very rarely lost. He was only in Waikato a short amount of time, but that was the same. Then when he coached Wales and we went over for the Six Nations, it was a different vibe again for the week after a win or a loss.

'I was fourteen when he moved to Wales. Over the next few years he might be away for up to six months. He'd come back and say something like: "Oh, we're letting her go to this party?" or: "We're letting her have a drink?" As time went on, it got easier, and we made the most of the time we had together as a family. Then we would try to do everything together and we still do. We like to think we're just as close as other families.

'When Dad is away and we're having dinner at home, we leave a space in the middle of the table for the house phone. The time difference is annoying, but he's pretty good at ringing at our night time because he knows that's when he can usually get us. Then we put him on speaker.

'One of the highlights was definitely when Wales beat England in their World Cup pool match at Twickenham in 2015. We were all there and I don't think I've ever seen him happier after a match, because whoever won that game was most likely going through. When the Lions won in Australia in 2013, that was pretty cool too.

'I'm continually asked how stoked am I to have Dad home as Head Coach of the Lions. No one here really knows what Wales are up to in the Six Nations. They only know Wales when they are playing the All Blacks. This is the first time when everyone knows exactly what he is doing and what a big deal it is.

'I didn't fully realise how cocky some New Zealanders are about the All Blacks until this tour, and there has been a negative spin in some of the media. I suppose people generally read a negative story rather than a

*positive one, although some of the headlines would have little relevance*
*to the article.*

*'We're extremely proud of Dad coming back to New Zealand as Head*
*Coach of the Lions to take on the All Blacks. I definitely think it's his greatest*
*achievement. He seems to keep taking on newer and bigger challenges. I've*
*noticed that people recognise him more and he's definitely made more of a*
*name for himself now. Yes, definitely proud, and I've a lot to live up to.'*

● ● ●

It has been tough being away from Trudi and the kids so much in the last
ten years. I signed a four-year contract with Wales in 2007, and the plan
was to come home then, but I've ended up signing two more four-year
contracts and will take them through to the World Cup in 2019. Then I'm
very open-minded as to what the future will hold.

All along we've had to balance my career as a coach and providing some
security for the family, then being able to retire and do what I want; follow
the kids and potentially grandkids.

When I'm in camp with Wales, it's not as bad. I can concentrate 100
per cent on rugby. It's different when we're not in camp, and I always find
Sundays the worst days, sitting in the apartment in Cardiff on my own.
Sundays have always been a family day.

I don't mind my own company, but when I'm ringing home and they're
all doing things, that's the hardest part. But the time we have been able to
spend together has been real quality time.

If it had been a club side, I wouldn't have been able to do it. In fairness to
the Welsh RFU, they have been brilliant. When I took on the job, they agreed
to let me have the off-season in July and August back in New Zealand, as
well as a couple of weeks over Christmas and at Easter after the Six Nations.

Before the last couple of years, when Gabby and Bryn have been busy, they were able to come over with Trudi for the November series and for the Six Nations.

Gabby's birthday is 22 July, so I've generally been there for all of them. Bryn's birthday is 10 May, so I've often missed his. I usually return to Wales in September, so I've rarely been in New Zealand for Trudi's birthday, which is on the 5th, and have been back in Wales for my own, on the 17th.

I also tend not to celebrate Father's Day, because they're usually not with me when it falls in the UK and I'm not usually at home when it's in New Zealand, but Trudi often gets two Mother's Days to celebrate, one in New Zealand and another in the UK.

This six-week tour is something of a bonus; not that I will have too much opportunity to spend time at our home in Hamilton. But at least I'll see more of them on this Lions tour than I did on the last two.

We still have a little family pre-match ritual which we've had a chance to repeat on this tour and will do for all the remaining games. It goes back to when I used to read Bryn a children's bedtime book called *Guess How Much I Love You*. It tells the story of two Nutbrown Hares, Big Nutbrown Hare and Little Nutbrown Hare who asks Big Nutbrown Hare the question in the title: 'Guess how much I love you?'

Big Nutbrown Hare tells Little Nutbrown Hare: 'I love you right up to the moon – and back.'

We would take our cue from that. Bryn, you see, is very competitive. One night he said: 'I love you to the moon and back.'

'Well Bryn, I love you all the way to the stars and back.'

He goes: 'Well, I love you all the way to the stars and back a million times.'

Every night I read him this story, and we would try to out-do each other.

One night, I spread my arms and said: 'I love you big much, and there's nothing bigger than that.'

Bryn had no answer, and so sometimes when I'm down on the pitch before a game, I look out for Trudi and the kids in the crowd and spread my arms. That means 'Big Much', which we also have written above one of the windows at the beach house.

● ● ●

On this visit home, I stayed until about 6.30pm, before I said goodbye to all three of them, and started up the Land Rover. I'd stayed in Hamilton longer than I expected. Tonight, all the players and management are going out for meals in about six mini-groups to half a dozen restaurants, just to get out of the hotel and spend a bit of time together.

On the drive back to Rotorua, I rang Bobby to have him take me off the list as I wouldn't be back in time for it. I arrived back at the Novotel Rotorua at about 8pm. A guard on duty opened a barrier for me to return the Land Rover to its slot alongside the others in the rear car park.

'Have a nice night,' he said. 'I hope you win a couple more games, Mr Gatland.'

'Thank you. Cheers.'

'I'm pleased to see you smiling,' he said.

I went to the bar, where Stuart Hogg was having his farewell last night with us. Four of the backroom staff (Gemma Crowley, Ben Uttley, Ellie Yeates and Belinda Armstrong) stayed up with him until around 5am, at which point John Spencer, Bobby, John Ashby, one of our Strength and Conditioning coaches, and Mark Savory, one of the security guys, got up and saw him off. They'd been singing in the bar, including the four songs that we'd learned. They all sang *Highland Cathedral* as he was leaving.

I told Stuart before I retired for the night that he was good enough and young enough to be on the Lions tour in 2021. And hopefully he will be.

## 12

## JOB DONE

## Lions to New Zealand 2017

*Thursday, 15 June*

Coming down to breakfast, the first thing I did was approach Peter O'Mahony. We'd picked him to captain the team to play the Maori All Blacks. Looking at the side, I thought he was the most logical person to do the job.

Sean O'Brien brings a lot of voice and X-factor to the team, but Peter has had that experience with Munster. He's a doer. He never takes a backward step. He doesn't say a heap though, and he was the same when I asked him to captain the side. He said yes, and that was about it.

We had put the team announcement back from the day before. Wednesday had been a travel day and we didn't want to call another meeting just to announce the team. The guys wanted some time on their own, so we deferred it.

Again we made fifteen changes, and reverted to eleven of the side that had beaten the Crusaders. Alun Wyn Jones and Owen Farrell were due a rest, so Maro Itoje came into the second-row and Johnny Sexton at number 10. We picked Anthony Watson instead of Liam Williams on the wing because he'd only started one game, and Leigh Halfpenny came in for Stuart Hogg.

We thought Jonathan Joseph played really well against the Highlanders and there was a discussion about picking him again against the Maori, but Jonathan Davies only played twenty-six minutes against the Crusaders so he got the vote this time.

Our initial thought with Mako Vunipola was to bring him off the bench in the Tests, as England do. He's very effective in this role. But he's been great starting, emptying the tank for an hour.

I'd thought of Joe Marler as the starting loose-head, but for some reason it hasn't worked out for him. As for the hookers, Jamie George has been in the right place at the right time, and his throwing has been good. Generally though, there's not much between the three hookers. I think any of them could do a good job.

Tadhg Furlong still has some things to work on with his scrummaging, and he knows that. He's been caught out a couple of times but he's working hard, while his energy around the pitch and his carrying have been exceptional. He also has skills, and we encourage that, even if he's also thrown a couple of 50/50 passes. He's a big man and more than a scrummager. He's a very good rugby player.

Maro deserved a start. He had great impact coming off the bench against the Crusaders. He has some things to work on as well, but his energy and work rate are absolutely phenomenal. There seems to be a nice balance between him and George Kruis, who's a more traditional English second-row.

We'd also stuck with the same back-row that played against the Crusaders – Peter, Sean and Toby – and picked Sam Warburton on the bench as CJ Stander needed a rest. Although Sam started against the Highlanders, we wanted to keep him involved and he still needs more rugby.

He's a little like Sean. They're both very, very powerful athletes. Before the hour mark against the Crusaders, Sean had nothing left in his legs. He'd run himself into the ground. That's what he does, and Sam is very similar. The more games he has under his belt the better he is and the longer he goes for.

One of the first things I did after breakfast was review the tape of the Highlanders match and send World Rugby's Referees' Chief Alain Rolland an email. I said we were very happy with the way Mathieu Raynal handled the Crusaders game, but there were a few things in the Highlanders game that were disappointing, particularly the first scrum penalty against Dan Cole. There was also some blocking which was not being picked up, the prime example being on Robbie Henshaw for the Waisake Naholo try. I asked Alain to have a look at the end-on view, and to listen to the discussion between the TMO and the referee.

Later that evening, Alain emailed me back to say he would be arriving in New Zealand on 22 June so we'd catch up the following day. He also said he'd had a look at it and that he agreed with the decision to award the try.

So I emailed him again and said: 'Alain, can you please listen to the discussion on the ref link and look at the view from behind the goal-line, and if it's still your opinion that it's a try then I'll accept that and just leave it.'

He came back to me and admitted that there was blocking by 'H4', meaning the Highlanders lock Alex Ainley, and as a result the try should not have been awarded. We've decided not to make an issue of it, because the New Zealand media will accuse us of whingeing. We're better off knowing that decision, and saying it quietly to a few people.

We had unit sessions in the morning, and a full rugby session in the afternoon. The big advantage for the team playing on Saturday is that they can have another full day's training, as well as a Captain's Run the day before. The other team has been getting one day, which is just a Captain's Run. They're effectively playing on the hoof, and that is not being taken into consideration. They are coming in for some criticism and I feel for them.

The session on the back pitch at Rotorua International Stadium was good. The forwards did scrums, mauls and lineouts, and the backs went through their attacking options.

Then we did about twenty minutes of 15 v 15, not full on, just running situations in one of our chaos sessions; reacting to turnovers, spilled ball, a lineout here and a scrum there. Stayin' Alive! We were still trying to drill that into the players.

● ● ●

This was also the day when Gregor Paul wrote a piece in the *NZ Herald* claiming there was a split in the camp. Our media guys, Dave and Luke, brought it to my attention. Under the headline 'Lions Tour Flirting With Disaster' he claimed: 'For a squad that came to New Zealand determined to avoid making the same mistakes as their 2005 predecessors, the 2017 British & Irish Lions seem to be meekly moving towards repeating that dark history all over again.

'Just as happened twelve years ago, the tour is starting to flirt with disaster. This time the Lions are in danger of splitting into two distinct parties with the midweek crew left to their own devices and the Test group firmly established as their own entity.'

He also wrote: 'According to All Blacks Coach Steve Hansen, the Lions have sent for five reinforcements. They already have forty players here and the extras are coming to enable the Lions to train as two full, separate squads.

'Well, that's what Hansen reckons, but the Lions, clearly surprised and no doubt massively irritated that the All Blacks coach knows their plans, have refused to say anything about the additions.

'Irritated because Gatland most likely hasn't sat the whole squad down yet and explained the move. It's never good when players read about major changes rather than hear them directly from their own coach. Looks bad. Looks sinister. Looks a lot like the coach might be losing it and in this case, it also looks a lot like Gatland has given up on at least half the squad.'

Steve Hansen had apparently said that we were bringing players in and was claiming that he had sources. I've worked with a lot of teams, and one thing I know for certain is that there's no split in our camp. They've been staying tight together and they've been behaving themselves impeccably.

It was obviously a campaign to try and unsettle us.

Losing the plot? The plan was always to bring in additional players a week before the first Test, to give as many of the match-day twenty-three as possible the best opportunity to prepare. We didn't want players to double up. We wanted to wait until after the Highlanders game before pulling the trigger.

That night we had dinner in the hotel, and afterwards the boys had a court session. If a player is fined, he has to roll the dice. Dan Sheridan, the photographer, rolled a four which meant he had to wear his burgundy velvet dinner jacket, all day, every day, no matter where we went, for the next few days.

If you throw a one, you get a free pass. If you throw a two, you can pass the dice to someone else, and if you roll a three, you have to entertain everyone for two minutes at some stage. A five means you're everyone's 'coffee bitch' and you don't want to throw a six. If you do, you've either got to get a tattoo of a lion or pay 500 dollars, which is a bit steep. One of the security guys rolled a six apparently, so they reduced the fine to 150 dollars. Sean O'Brien is chairman of the fines' committee and seems to enjoy the role hugely.

Then the boys put *Mike Bassett: England Manager* on the big screen in the team room, and bought in popcorn, Coke and chocolates. It's not to everyone's taste, as such, and some guys took it or left it. I left it.

## Friday, 16 June

I didn't sleep very well, which isn't like me. I was thinking about too many things, and maybe the pressure was getting to me.

The non-twenty-three had weights at 9.30am in a local gym before the whole squad met at 10.15am in the hotel prior to training. We'd heard that Rory Best had been awarded an OBE, so I mentioned that at the meeting and congratulated him. Rory got up and spoke to the players. It was a great achievement. Andy Farrell also spoke well about our defence and continuing to make little improvements.

Interestingly, that morning Johnny Sexton asked for another 15 v 15 session rather than a Captain's Run, which is very unusual. He felt the team needed to fine tune their calls under more pressure than running unopposed. We hadn't planned on doing that but we agreed. So we took the non-twenty-three, who were scheduled to train afterwards, to the Captain's Run.

The reason it's called a Captain's Run is because it's not coach-led, it's player-led. It's whatever they want to do, particularly the number 10 or the captain. Peter O'Mahony has known Johnny for a long time so he was quite happy to concede to his request. There's no point in arguing with Johnny anyway!

We began with some defensive drills, a few exit plays and then ten minutes of 15 v 15, which was the first time I'd done that as a coach the day before a game.

The match-day twenty-three returned to the hotel, and then we trained the non-twenty-three to begin their preparations for the Chiefs game.

Back at the Novotel, Eanna Falvey told me that Owen Farrell had suffered a slight strain, very high on his quad, at training. We had named him on the bench, and Eanna said if it was a Test match he could play, but we felt it wasn't worth the risk so early in the tour. We may have looked at that 10-12 combination with Owen and Johnny again for the last twenty or thirty minutes, but it was a good chance for Johnny to build on the confidence he gained from the Crusaders game.

Eanna had also organised a nerve test for Ross Moriarty by a specialist based in Auckland City Hospital. Co-incidentally, the nerve specialist was on his way to the game in Rotorua and had his equipment with him. So before he called into our hotel, I asked Ger: 'Is there any way you can get him a signed jersey?' And of course Ger did.

Eanna met the nerve specialist, and the news was bad. Ross had a trapped nerve, which is unusual for a lower limb, and he would probably require a minimum of six weeks to recover. He was out of the tour.

I didn't see Ross until Saturday morning. He was pretty gutted. His family had just arrived. He admitted to me: 'I thought it was a little bit more than just a slight injury. I felt it was worse than that.' He also said: 'Look, I'm young enough. Hopefully I can get an opportunity for a Lions tour again.'

It's hard to say anything to a player who's just received news like that. 'Just get yourself right and hopefully you won't be out for too long,' I told him.

He's a very, very honest player, Ross. What you see is what you get. He has a bit of an edge about him which I like. He's tough and he's very explosive, a good ball-carrier. It's hard on him that he didn't get more of an opportunity on this tour.

At 5pm, I went to meet Jaco Peyper and his two assistants, Jerome Garces and Mathieu Raynal, in the Sudima Lake Rotorua. Jaco has refereed games I've been involved in a good few times and I like him. We spoke about things that potentially might happen at lineout time, and whether they were going to compete at the lineout and maul.

We also spoke about the scrums, and pre-engagement. But the big thing for me after the Highlanders match and a few other games has been the blocking, whether it's stopping tacklers or runners off the ball. I mentioned the Highlanders try by Naholo, and that Alain Rolland had admitted that the try shouldn't have been awarded, although I also acknowledged that it wasn't an easy one for the officials to spot.

I came back to the hotel, and told the other coaches how the meeting went.

That evening, we watched the Wales–Tonga and New Zealand–Samoa games. We had looked into the possibility of flying to Auckland but that was too difficult, so the coaches and staff went to a little bar just beside the hotel called Ambrosia where we had some finger food and watched the games. John Spencer said he'd pick up the tab with his Lions card, but he went off and left it to me. So the Lions have a hefty bill coming on the credit card. I haven't told him yet.

I had a big interest in both games. I'm still the Welsh Coach, after all. I thought they deserved to win by more. A couple of calls didn't go their way, but it was a good win in the end. They'll be pleased with that, particularly with such a young team and three new caps in the starting fifteen.

The All Blacks looked a little rusty in the first twenty minutes. Samoa made a few breaks and were unlucky not to score a try or two. You'd also question whether the All Blacks' first two tries should have been awarded. But then they kicked into gear, Samoa just fell away and they romped home by 78–0. It became like a training run. It didn't alter my belief that we had to play some rugby and pressurise them, and there's no way our defence would be as generous. That's one area where we can bring more physicality.

*Saturday, 17 June*
*Maori All Blacks v Lions, Rotorua International Stadium*

As coaches we have to keep staying ahead of ourselves. The first item on the day's agenda was a coaches' meeting to discuss the Chiefs game next week after we'd each analysed it on our laptops.

Normally we'd train the non-twenty-three on the Saturday, but we didn't this time because we had trained them the day before. So, after the coaches' meeting, there was an opportunity for a little downtime.

Trudi, Bryn, Gabby and her boyfriend Sam drove down from Hamilton. Trudi's mum and dad came down too, so I caught up with them all for a while. They had lunch in the Lone Star across the road from the hotel, but I didn't join them. I stayed in the hotel. The presence of the Lions supporters had started to ramp up in the last few days.

At 1.30pm we had a management meeting, with all the coaches and heads of department, Eanna, Rhodri, Bobby, and Ger, to make some subtle changes to next week's schedule.

There'd been plenty of media talk about the six call-ups from outside, so we had a meeting at 2 o'clock to inform the squad of the players that were coming in and the reasons for this. They would be here to provide cover on the bench for the Chiefs and the Hurricanes games. This was all geared toward winning the Test series.

However, I reminded them that the players not involved against the Maori, and who play on Tuesday night, had a significant role to play. Even if they were not involved in the first Test, they still had a chance to be selected in the series. As we saw in 2013, there were nine changes between the first and third Tests. I added: 'And this is about everyone supporting each other.'

At 3.45pm we had our walk-through with the match-day twenty-three.

We were going to do it in the big park across the road where the music was already blaring for an attempt at the world record for the *haka*. A few of our staff would take part, including Andy Farrell. Apparently around 7,700 turned up, which was enough to break the world record.

But the players felt there were too many people around watching them. Sometimes I think that heightens the anticipation. It had happened in Christchurch, where we went to the park across from the hotel for our match-day walk-through. In any case, we went out to the car park at the rear of the hotel, where about twenty to thirty people ended up watching us anyway.

The players went for a pre-match meal at 4pm, and we met at 6pm before taking the bus to the ground. Only I spoke at the meeting, and briefly at that. It's an hour and a half before kick-off, so there's no need to wind them up too much. I wanted to keep things calm. Sometimes you get a feeling that 'these guys are ready', in which case, you don't want to say a lot.

We'd been training exceptionally well the last few days. The boys looked sharp, so I just said to go out there and give a performance, and maintain the momentum generated against the Crusaders.

At the ground, once again I was taken aback by how many Kiwis wanted to shake my hand and wish us well. There wasn't any animosity or negativity.

Soon after arrival, as before every game, I am obliged to do three pre-match interviews: SkySports New Zealand, SkySports UK and talkSPORT. After each game, I have to do all three again, including talkSPORT and RTE Radio together, and then the main press conference as well.

I was asked about the quality of opposition but I felt confident in the quality of our own team. I know we defended well against the Crusaders. We strangled the life out of them, and we were going into the Maori game with the same mindset.

After the warm-up, I looked into the stands and saw Trudi and the kids, and I extended both arms out wide. 'Big Much.' And they did it back to me.

In the changing room beforehand, I didn't say a lot. I just talked about our physicality and squeezing the opposition. It's all been said and by this stage you want to hand it over to the players. We went around the room, shook all the players' hands, wished them all the best and then let them be for the last few minutes.

Peter O'Mahony didn't say a lot either. When we asked him to be captain, I expected him to be more vocal. I was surprised. But he was like everyone else, still getting to know players. Compared with other squads that I've been involved with, this group are less inclined to shout and scream. There hasn't been rubbish talk. We've all been in changing rooms before where guys have been talking for the sake of it. They just want to hear their own voice, and no clear messages are being delivered. In saying that, Sean O'Brien and Sam Warburton were excellent. They spoke about being vocal, and positive, on the pitch.

Myself and the other coaches came out of the tunnel and walked up through the fans to sit in the coaches' box. It was next to the Maori coaches' box, where Carl Hoeft, Tana Umaga and Colin Cooper were sitting, so we shook their hands and said 'good luck'. I coached Carl at Thames Valley back in 1995–96 before he was signed by Otago and became an All Black.

We started the game well, but they got one opportunity with a speculative little kick through. We didn't gather it, and all of a sudden Liam Messam scored.

I wasn't worried. Then we started to put them under pressure defensively and really squeezed them. The back-row was good, Maro Itoje was outstanding and we dominated at scrum time. We'd worked hard on improving our scrum.

Leigh Halfpenny put us 6–0 up and then twice kicked us back in front, so we led 12–10 at half-time. But if we continued to have that kind of possession and territory in the second half, we were going to finish on top of them. We knew we had seventy-odd per cent territory and possession in that first half and, as it transpired, it was even higher in the second half.

At half-time we had twelve minutes together. Normally in the Six Nations it's fifteen minutes. So we gave the first two minutes to the players to rehydrate, and then split into units. The forwards talked about their lineouts and scrums, and the backs talked about their attacking and defensive shape. That generally takes two to four minutes, before Andy Farrell discusses the defence, and he was pleased with what we were doing. Rob Howley talked about the attack and as usual I finished off with one or two points.

A key message before the game had, again, been 'staying alive'. The Maori caught us out with a couple of throw-ins which they actually didn't take straight away, but then did so when we turned our backs. I told them to 'be prepared for that again'. I said our game management was good, our set-piece was strong, and if we kept doing this the scores would come.

In the second half, Leigh kicked another penalty, before he was caught with a high hit by their scrum-half, Tawera Kerr-Barlow. He led with his shoulder, and just dropped into Leigh. As the referee and TMO were looking at it again, I thought it might have merited a red card, but it was yellow and he was sin-binned.

We went to the corner and after the drive was held up, we were awarded a penalty from a scrum. We had a debate in the box about what should be done next. Steve Borthwick said we shouldn't go for another scrum. It rarely follows that you get a second scrum penalty. I thought maybe going to the corner for a drive would have been more effective too. But when a team is without their scrum-half, the loose-forwards tend not to scrummage quite so hard, as they're peering over the top. In any case, we took the scrum, our pack got the shove on, and we were awarded a penalty try.

We dominated territory and possession, but at this level it takes a while to break teams down. This match was another good example that these New

Zealand teams will play if they are allowed to. But we've been trying to take the legs from them, by squeezing them defensively and making them work really hard in the set-pieces. We're scrummaging hard on their ball, as well as trying to out-scrum them a little bit on our own ball. We're also trying to maul them a few times.

When a team has to really work their legs in the scrums and mauls, they become a little bit tired, and don't get around the park so much. We were getting a bit of success out of that.

It's an experience that I had a few times as a player. Waikato used to play Otago quite often, and they had probably one of the best hookers in the country in David Latta. He played for Otago over 160 times and captained them to a famous win over the Lions in 1993. He was unbelievably mobile and I used to say to our lads: 'I don't want him running around the park. I want us to scrummage him to death and take his legs from him.' And we were able to do that effectively on a few occasions.

Three years ago, Wales were in South Africa and, even given his age, Gethin Jenkins was still one of the best players around the pitch in world rugby. They mauled us and they scrummaged us, and he admitted to me afterwards: 'My legs had gone.'

So we have been trying to put some stuff in the bank, in terms of our scrum and maul, to go after these New Zealand sides. We did that pretty effectively against the Maori. There was less of a gap in the scrums, but we were prepared for that.

Again, our defence was dominant, getting up quite quickly, and so the Maori dropped deeper and deeper, which made it easier for us.

It will be interesting to see how the All Blacks go against that next Saturday. Ironically, the way to play against a blitz defence is for the '10s' to play flat. As soon as they start going deeper and deeper, it's happy days – you're going to get some reward.

We scored fourteen points during the sin-binning: the penalty try and then a pick and go, leading to a try for Itoje. That was pretty much game over. When we were awarded a penalty with ten minutes to go, we sent on the message to take the three, to put us more than three scores ahead. We didn't want them getting a sniff. With New Zealand sides, you never know. If they'd scored off an intercept or a turnover, then it's a thirteen point game.

Coming down through the crowd after the game, I had people saying 'well done', 'congratulations', 'good performance', and these were Kiwis more than Lions fans. I enjoyed standing on the sideline and seeing the reaction of the non-twenty-three players.

I did my various interviews and by the time I reached the changing room they'd already sung *The Fields of Athenry*, so I missed that one. The entire squad were there, and I told them it was a great performance. I said the defence was outstanding, that we strangled them and squeezed the life out of them. 'That was a fantastic result. Well done.'

I went into the press conference and said that claims of a split in the camp had, if anything, brought us even closer together.

The New Zealand media would be quite dismissive afterwards, saying the Maori hadn't had much time together and were a scratch side. Yet Luke Broadley told me after the game that it's the biggest loss the Maori have ever had against the Lions.

We've had two jerseys made for every game, so that the players can swap one with their opposing player. Some of our guys, not everyone, were really disappointed that the Maori players had official jerseys and another which was just a replica that you can buy in the shops. They hadn't been embroidered, or numbered. Most of their players came in and swapped their official jerseys, but four or five used the replicas, which were folded up and dampened to make it seem like it had been used in the match.

One of our players said to one of the boys who was going into the opposition changing room: 'Take that back into him. I don't want this. I can buy one of these in the shop.' In fairness to that Maori player, he saw our player at the after-match function and gave him the embroidered jersey he had played with in the match. Ben Te'o had also been given a replica. So he tracked down their player and asked for either his one back or to be given the real one, which is fair enough too.

It's not a big issue, but if the Maori wanted to swap jerseys then they should have made two of them for each of their players, like we did.

As it was our first post-match function since we'd arrived, everyone changed into their dinner suits in the changing room. At the Holiday Inn that evening, John Spencer and Peter O'Mahony spoke on our behalf, we sang *Calon Lan* and the Maori team responded with a *haka*. John spoke exceptionally well as usual, incorporating a number of Maori phrases he had learnt, and Peter was very good too. A few gifts were exchanged. The New Zealand and England Women's players were there, as they had played before our game. Trudi enjoyed wishing some of the Black Fern players well before the upcoming World Cup in Ireland, and a couple of them had a photo with me which was nice. Trudi stayed the night before going back to Hamilton the next morning.

There had been a bit of consternation the night before the game. Word had reached us that a woman who'd been in contact with some of the guys on social media had done kiss-and-tell stories in the past. On the bus back from the game we warned the players. We were now at that stage where someone could be looking for a story to sell.

By the time we finished the post-match function and were back in the hotel for a couple of drinks, it was late enough. I got to bed by around 2am. Job done.

## 13

# BACK TO MY ROOTS

## Lions to New Zealand 2017

### Sunday, 18 June

An early start for another travel day. The four Welsh boys we'd called up arrived before the Maori match and some of the Welsh party and management had come down to watch that game as well. The new boys had been kitted out and we were all on two buses by 11am to travel by road to the Novotel in Hamilton for the Chiefs match on Tuesday.

Dave Barton and Luke Broadley brought me up to speed on the media coverage of the Maori game. It was quite noticeable how everyone had billed this game as 'the fourth Test' beforehand, but there'd been no mention of it subsequently. All I've heard is how tough it was for the Maori to have only ten days together. Welcome to my world.

There was still no doubting the quality of that Maori backline, and most of their forward pack had been on tour to Ireland and the UK last year. But as I predicted all along, they weren't as cohesive as the Crusaders.

There was a nice moment in the game which I showed the boys in the review. Ben Te'o was giving Akira Ioane some verbals. He absolutely laid into him. It probably stems from his time in Australian Rugby League – they've got the biggest mouths of any players in any sport – so Ben's not shy about giving a little lip. Ioane walked towards Ben and said something. Out of nowhere Maro came over and I thought: 'This could be interesting.' But then Jaco Peyper interjected after the TMO said: 'You need to split those guys up.'

One of the first things we did was meet up as coaches after breakfast to select the side to play the Chiefs. We picked eleven players who hadn't been involved against the Maori and four who'd been on the bench, so it was pretty straightforward: Liam Williams, Jack Nowell, Jared Payne, Robbie Henshaw, Elliot Daly, Dan Biggar and Greig Laidlaw were the backline. The pack was Joe Marler, Rory Best, Dan Cole, Iain Henderson, Courtney Lawes, James Haskell, Justin Tipuric and CJ Stander.

We named the six call-ups on the bench – Welshmen Cory Hill, Kristian Dacey, Gareth Davies and Tomas Francis, and Scotland pair Allan Dell and Finn Russell – as well as Alun Wyn Jones and Tommy Seymour. We didn't want any of the loose-forwards having to back up, either from last Saturday or for next Saturday, and to freshen him up we'd rested Alun Wyn from the Maori game. Having lost Ross Moriarty, we only had seven loose-forwards, but Iain Henderson could cover the back-row.

We announced the team to the players in Rotorua before we hopped on the bus to Hamilton. After lunch we had a team meeting before training at Beetham Park. It was just a light, organisational run for the twenty players now with us who weren't involved in the Maori game. The two Scottish boys, Finn Russell and Allan Dell, weren't arriving until 9pm that night. There were about eighty people there from Lions Travel, who were watching the training. At times, you feel like you're on a commercial conveyor belt.

We had another meeting at 5.30pm with the players. One of the players' wives had said to Trudi that Father's Day in the UK and Ireland was that Sunday. So Trudi contacted as many of the wives and partners of the coaches, players and heads of department as she could to put together a Father's Day video. It was simply awesome. I know I had a tear in my eye, as did many others in the room. The clips were so funny, kids read little poems, and it was surprising how many of the players have children. At the end of it, Maro Itoje said: 'I have to get myself a baby!'

A split in the squad? That meeting demonstrated how tight they are as a group. We all know how hard a six-week tour is at the end of the season, but they've been so good. They've looked after themselves. There have been no issues at all.

It was nice to be home. We moved the press conference for the team announcement across the road to a room in the Ibis, which was pretty cramped. As I said at that press conference: 'If you cut me open, I probably bleed red, yellow and black [the Chiefs' colours]. I'm very proud of my roots. It's a great place to have grown up.'

The Chiefs didn't have any of their All Blacks, and four of their six Maori players were missing. They made Stephen Donald captain. I've coached 'Beaver', and I think he's a fine team man and a great guy.

Wales had been beaten 40–7 by the Chiefs here on our tour of New Zealand last year, and I recalled that match at the press conference. 'Twelve months ago I said: "Whatever you do, don't take a dummy from Stephen Donald," and the first thing he did was throw a dummy and score. So that will be the message again for Tuesday.'

Beaver doesn't do anything the traditional way, so I added: 'He's an icon around here, and I heard he just got engaged as well. I'd like to congratulate him on that. I think he was out whitebaiting [for fish] and the ring was offered out the back of the ute. That's typical Stephen Donald.'

Michael Corcoran of RTE said: 'You seem to have a lot of knowledge of this engagement?'

'Well, I do have my sources of information too!' I said.

After the main press conference, I did my briefing with the UK and Irish media, where I raised the issue of New Zealand teams using blockers off the ball. 'The frustrating thing for us is the amount that's going on, which makes it difficult to complete attacking opportunities because there is so much happening off the ball in terms of blocking players or subtly holding players.'

Although there had been a couple of penalties against the Maori, I said we would keep raising it. I was asked if we'd lost a number of try opportunities because of it.

'Absolutely, yes. When you go back and look at the tapes and all the stuff off the ball, where someone's run a line or stopped the opponent getting through.' I added: 'It's part of the game here. All New Zealand teams at the moment are doing it.'

Was I suggesting there was less of this in the northern hemisphere?

'I don't think it happens to the same extent, but I know how difficult it is to pick up for referees because it tends to happen away from the ball. Someone just changes the line and blocks. We clipped a lot of the situations. We have just got to be aware of it. For us, it's being smart and hopefully the officials are aware of it.

'If you look back at the very first kick-off in Chicago, the All Blacks were penalised for interference and blocking. All I am asking is the officials are aware of it and they were last night, so I was happy with it.'

After the briefing I had dinner at home to look forward to, but when Trudi came to collect me at the Novotel, she said: 'Come and say hello to these guys.'

One of them was Colin Bradley, the Financial Director for the Chiefs.

When he did my contract with Waikato, we talked about bonuses and I said to him: 'What if we win the Ranfurly Shield?'

'What do you want?' he asked.

'I want one of the old chairs in the stand.'

He agreed to it, and we won the Ranfurly Shield. Then he said he didn't have the authority to agree to the bonuses. So for the last ten years, whenever I've met him, I've asked: 'Where's my seat?'

This time, when Trudi brought me over to him, Colin had one made and presented it to me. Other mates of mine have been following the tour around in fancy dress, as sheep, and they were there as well. I sat down with them for a few photographs and a chat.

We lifted the chair into the back of Trudi's car and took it home. It's on the deck at the beach just metres from the water (fondly named 'Mooloolebar'), where we sit on summer evenings, light the fire and have a few beers or glasses of wine. It's a magical spot, but it's so popular with all the family and friends that we often run out of seating.

Finn Russell and Allan Dell arrived at the Novotel that evening. I was sitting in the foyer when they walked in. I shook hands with them and congratulated them on their result. Scotland had beaten Australia the day before, which was great.

## Monday, 19 June

We met at 10.45am with the team leaders, Rory Best, Iain Henderson, who was calling the lineouts, Justin Tipuric, Greig Laidlaw and Dan Biggar. We talked about the Chiefs and what they might bring: keeping the ball on the park, short lineouts, quick taps, quick throw-ins, trying to make the game unstructured with as few set-pieces as possible.

We then did a review of the Maori as well as a preview of the Chiefs with the whole squad. We showed them a clip of the last scrum of the game, on seventy-nine minutes, when you can hear Sam Warburton saying: 'Come on. Come on. Let's finish it off.' Then Sean O'Brien can be heard, in his squeaky Irish accent, shouting: 'Come on lads! Come on Jackie!' to Jack McGrath. We definitely out-talked them.

We spoke to the players about what we need to do in the last ten minutes. The bulk of this side had been ahead after seventy minutes against the Blues and the Highlanders.

We've been concentrating on four things on this tour. One is working hard, both off the ball and on the opposition. Another is being more physical. Another is out-talking the opposition. And lastly about 'staying alive' and not being caught out by the unexpected, which would be particularly relevant against the Chiefs.

Against the Maori we achieved the first three. We out-talked them. We were more physical. We worked really hard. But once or twice they caught us with a quick throw-in.

Rory spoke very well at the meeting, telling the players to 'have no regrets'. He added that 'this is the most important game because it's the next game.'

We were on the bus at 11am for the Captain's Run. That was mostly organisational, because we had the six new guys on the bench. We'd had Cory Hill in during the first camp in the Vale of Glamorgan, and even though there'd been some changes he was relatively up to speed. We ran a little bit of defence, did some kick-offs and exits, and brought the subs in.

Rory had asked if could they have a 15 v 15 session but it was just too late to change the schedule, because we had organised one in the afternoon for the other players. They were still in recovery mode from Saturday's game. So the afternoon session for the rest of the squad was fairly short and light. After an eight-minute warm-up we mixed in some short games by jogging through some attack options for two blocks of six minutes, and then condensed some defence, exits and kick-offs for six minutes. In total, we trained for thirty-two minutes, including the warm-up.

This week was also about making sure they were right for the first Test on Saturday. The message to the coaches was that we don't overcoach. I've been involved in teams when it's been easy enough to do another ten minutes here or there, and also to put another three, four or five kilometres on the distance the players cover in a week, or two or three hours of meetings.

The players also had a responsibility to limit what we did in the week, because as much as anything we need fresh legs and to have everyone sharp. So, at yesterday's full meeting, I said to them: 'You've got to monitor yourselves. You've got to monitor us. You've got to keep us in check as well. There's enough experience in this room.'

I had seen the Ireland players after they had been beaten by Wales in the Six Nations, and they were battered. I knew Ireland then spent the week recovering. Joe Schmidt backed off and gave the Irish boys a lighter week.

So this week I went to one of the Lions staff and said: 'Can I ask you a question? You know that last game of the Six Nations when England played Ireland? Did England do much that week?' And apparently they did heaps. They tried to cover everything. You can't do that.

I try to get a feel for it, and on that Monday night I asked the analysts to record every session, every walk-through and every meeting. But sometimes it's just a feel. As a coach, it's not about being prescriptive.

That night I also went to the Claudelands event centre to do a Q&A with the Chiefs' Coach Dave Rennie. There were 550 people there for a Chiefs' charity fundraiser. Stu Williams, the Chiefs' Manager, and Mils Muliaina picked me up at the hotel. We got there at about 5.45 and I went on stage with Dave at 6.30. I was back at the hotel by 7.30, and at 8pm a bus took all the management and backroom staff, more than forty of us, to our home in Hamilton for a drinks get-together.

The kids were there too. We all had some wine, beers and nibbles. Rala didn't come because he spends the night before every match in his room, for all the players to call in, have a little chat and clean their boots. He had called around in the afternoon to see Trudi. He said he just needed to see where Warren lived, and picture him there. Others arrived a little later. The analysts, as usual, had worked late, and they were on the first bus back as well.

It's surprising how much information you can gather from having some staff around for a drink. We haven't been quite as close as we had been in the past or as we are with Wales, where we might have a meal or a drink together. These socials are like informal management meetings. This particular management group is larger and the tour has been full-on. We haven't had the luxury of being in one venue for a whole week. Moving around from hotel to hotel has been logistically challenging. Even our days off have been travel days.

So it was a rare opportunity for all the staff to spend some social time together in an informal setting. They also organised some flowers for Trudi, and they'd written a card, thanking her for organising the Father's Day video.

Trudi likes being involved. She was awesome at Wasps. She'd do parents' lunches, players' lunches, and social events for players' wives. She's brilliant on names, and good with people.

Tomorrow, we will open our family room in the hotel, with couches, kids videos, snacks and a coffee machine. We did that in 2013 for the Tests. It is somewhere for the players to spend time with their wives or partners, kids and parents, who were beginning to arrive this week, without being pestered for photos. Trudi helped to coordinate that.

All the partners and wives also received gift boxes from the Lions, which is a gesture to acknowledge that the players are being taken away from them for a number of weeks. They're the sort of nice things that I feel are necessary. We also give a gift to the players. Normally the commercial team organise it, but this time I actually did. Thanks to a friend of mine, a guy called Steve Dalton from Sony, we gave all the players new Bluetooth headphones, with a little Lions logo on them. We try to give them something that's a little bit different and something they appreciate.

After the bus brought most of our guests home, I stayed a bit later with Graham Rowntree, Rob Howley and Andy Farrell for a bit of a chat. It can't have been that interesting though. Wig was quite tired and fell asleep on the kitchen table!

At around 11pm, Trudi drove us back to the hotel. She had played another stormer. She has been incredibly supportive. She is amazing.

## Tuesday, 20 June
### Chiefs v Lions, Waikato Stadium

I was down for breakfast by 8am as we had an early start. The non-twenty-three had weights at 10am before we met up to take the bus to Beetham Park for training.

The photographers had vision access as usual for the warm-up. I had a bit of a go at Luke Broadley as to why there has to be vision access at the start of every session. 'I don't think it's benefitting us,' I said to him. 'I think some of the journalists are writing negative stories and their desks are looking for the pictures to match the story.' Rather than a conversation, it was more a case of me letting off steam, which he probably didn't deserve. I was venting a little emotion because I desperately wanted the team to win that night, and Luke just happened to be in the line of fire.

After the warm-up, we did some contact work. We split for twenty minutes, for the forwards to focus on scrums and mauls, and then we jogged through some of our attack options. We also did some defence and finished off with some exits and kicking. Altogether it was about fifty-eight minutes, quite a long session. We wanted some clarity early in the week and I felt we'd achieved that.

Trudi came to the hotel at 12.30 to pick me up, and I went to Waikato Hospital to see my dad. When I arrived there, they were pushing him into a lift in a wheelchair to take him for an echo scan on his heart. He was puffy and didn't look that well. It put things in perspective.

My sisters have been up there and said his heart hasn't been good, and that he has high blood pressure. I'd last seen him after the Six Nations, when I came back to New Zealand for a week in April.

Trudi and I went for a little lunch across the road from the hospital. We discussed some options for my dad, such as organising Meals on Wheels for him. He doesn't want to go into a home. In April I had offered to buy him a mobility scooter, but he said: 'Oh, I wouldn't use that sort of thing.' I said OK. He just didn't want me to buy it for him.

It was during this lunch that Trudi asked me: 'How are you enjoying the tour?'

'I'm hating it,' I told her. 'I love being involved with teams and players and whatever, but it's the external stuff.'

Most of the time I can handle it, but on this tour it's felt like a constant drag. It's as if a needle has been put into me and is just slowly taking the blood out of me. I likened myself to a tree from which the sap is seeping out.

'The last few weeks have been tough.'

'Oh, I had no idea,' she said.

I said I'd been putting on a brave face. But, more and more, I was beginning to ask myself: 'Is this what sport has become like, where newspapers are looking for headlines, different stories, wanting to be critical, and wanting to be personal?'

I have been really disappointed with New Zealand journalism, and particularly the *NZ Herald*, whether it's been the personal attacks on me or the team, or slagging off the Lions. I think they've been quite derogatory.

As a Kiwi I was so excited about coming home again but the coverage has been a downer, although to put a balance on that, everywhere we've gone in New Zealand people have been so warm and welcoming. It's a completely different message to some of what is being written.

In fairness, SkySports have been very positive, whether it's John Kirwan, Stuart Barnes, Jeff Wilson, Justin Marshall, Miles Harrison, Scotty Stevenson or whoever, and I probably shouldn't be letting one newspaper get to me. However, you can only take so much of it. I really don't mind criticism, but it's the first time I've felt there's been an orchestrated campaign to unsettle me, and to split the squad.

Last week in the *NZ Herald*, Gregor Paul wrote about the All Blacks squad. He said that Malakai Fekitoa was going to miss out, that Dan Coles was going to be named as well as Kieran Read and Jerome Kaino. You don't have that information unless you're talking directly to someone in the All Blacks set-up.

I have heard of some things about the All Blacks that could be quite explosive if they were made public, and if it does get dirty then I will raise a couple of those things. At the moment I'm just keeping my counsel.

I look at all the supporters out here. There's been a great atmosphere in the grounds. You'd think all of the media would be excited about the first Lions visit in twelve years, and set the tempo for what could be a brilliant series, but there's a group out there that seemingly want this tour to be a failure.

The other day Gregor Paul also criticised the Lions for not embracing the midweek fixtures. The Lions have never, ever faced such quality midweek opposition. In the past there have been some easy games where you could rest players, or players could have a hit out and win games comfortably.

This tour hasn't been like that. He also made some comment along the lines that they'd rather have England here.

Trudi cheered me up, told me not to let it get to me, and dropped me back to the team hotel. She also came to my room to help me pack my bags, because they had to be down by 2pm for the trip to Auckland that night.

The match-day twenty-three and the coaches had a walk-through at 3.50pm, then had their pre-match meal, and at 5.45pm we met up before taking the bus to the ground. When I spoke to the players I was more animated than before any game so far. I said we'd had an excellent couple of days, and how well prepared they were. I said: 'We don't give a f*** about performance. Make sure you go out and win today, and the performance will come with that. We need to be physical against these guys. You've got to squeeze them, but you make sure you come off that pitch with a win.'

At the ground, we went to the changing room and one of the first people I bumped into in the tunnel was Stu Williams, and I gave him a hug. Before the Chiefs, he was Manager for Waikato when I was coaching them. I said to Stu: 'Mate, it's coming. We're not far away.'

Rory spoke very well again in the changing room before the game. You could see how much he'd learned from captaining Ireland in big games. The day before he had spoken about the honour of pulling on the Lions jersey, and that whatever the players' motivation was, whether it was for themselves, family, friends or whoever, to produce a performance to be proud of. Now, before the game, there was clarity in what he was saying, about people doing their own roles and their own jobs.

I could sense this team was hungry. A few of them had been involved in two defeats out of two, so this was payback time.

● ● ●

It had been a sunny and relatively warm day, and it was a perfect evening for playing rugby. The sand-based pitch at the Waikato Stadium, as ever, was like a snooker table, and the ground was packed.

Our set-pieces were strong, and our scrum and maul went to work from early on. We were 3–0 up and in control when Joe Marler was sin-binned for a shoulder charge off the ball on Nepo Laulala.

It was stupid and that's two games in which we've had yellow cards, which effectively puts you in lockdown mode, negotiating ten minutes of dead time. It was the same against the Blues when Liam Williams was sin-binned.

James Haskell had to be sacrificed when we brought on Allan Dell for the scrums, but we managed that ten minutes very well. When they went to the corner, CJ Stander came through their drive and forced a turnover. Even when they had a scrum, Jared Payne went into the back-row and we shunted them off their ball.

We drew that ten minutes 3–3 and then Jack Nowell scored a nice try. Liam Williams went outside to create space for Nowell, and then after CJ, Marler and Biggar took it up, Nowell was there to pick up and dive over. It was a good team try, because the clearing out at the breakdown was clinical, especially Rory and Iain Henderson, to create the chance for Jack.

I had spoken to both the wingers at the Captain's Run the day before, and said: 'This is an opportunity for you guys. Jack, for whatever reason in the first two games, it just hasn't happened for you.'

'Yea,' he said. 'I know. I'll make it happen tomorrow.'

I said to Elliot Daly: 'I'm telling you guys it's an opportunity for you. We haven't decided on the team and just go out there and make the most of it.'

I came on this tour thinking that if Jack Nowell plays the way he's capable of playing, he'll be in the Test team. I think he's a sensational player. He's not rapid quick like Anthony Watson but his work-rate, hands on ball and influence on a game is superb. I'd love to have him in my team every week. If he had played like he did in this game against the Blues and the Highlanders, he'd probably have been in the Test team.

With the last kick of the half, Stephen Donald's penalty left us 13–6 ahead at the break. Myself and the other coaches were down in the changing room by then, and I said to Graham Rowntree: 'I think we can put their scrum under a bit more pressure.'

After the players had their two minutes to rehydrate and refocus, we split into units and Wig conveyed that message to them. In the second half, we were much more aggressive at scrum time on their ball, and we got a few penalties from that.

We also spoke about maintaining the pressure and 'to keep taking the legs from them, keep working them and opportunities will come for us.' If we were smart, and didn't give anything soft away, we could control this game.

The second half wasn't dissimilar to the Maori match. We applied set-piece pressure, scored another penalty try off our maul, and then pulled away, although I felt last Saturday was more comfortable.

For these guys, it was more a confidence issue, as they'd let two games slip away, particularly against the Highlanders. When a team does that, their natural tendency is to say: 'Let's not do anything stupid. Let's not give away a soft try with an intercept or something.'

But with that 20–6 lead, their confidence soared. Five minutes later came the best try of the tour so far. There was some skill in that score and really nice running. It was like watching New Zealand teams. They score tries like that week-in, week-out.

We had been criticised for not scoring tries. We were seen as being dour and boring. We hadn't conceded a lot of tries, but we hadn't converted our chances. Now, all of a sudden, in the last couple of weeks teams can't score against us, but we're starting to score tries ourselves.

Justin Tipuric latched onto an overthrow and Dan Biggar, Robbie Henshaw, and Jared Payne attacked from our own line. Liam Williams released Elliot Daly up the left. He passed inside to Jared. Not many players could have made that left to right pass across his body. Then Robbie was on his inside for the offload. From the ruck, Jack took Iain's pass and showed good footwork and pace to score again. I enjoyed that one.

James Haskell didn't touch the ball in the move but it was his try as much as anybody's. He worked his butt off to cover sixty metres and smashed into the ruck to make the clear-out. If he'd been a couple of yards behind and not worked quite so hard then it would have been a turnover or a penalty for holding on. You look at that and go: 'Wow, that's the sort of effort you want.'

Our wingers had covered the Chiefs' little dinks well all night, and when Jack read one, Liam steamed onto the ball. It was a lovely bit of footwork by Liam. Jared ran a great support trailer for the offload and it was nice for him, a Hamilton Old Boy and former Waikato boy, to score.

It's been a tough tour for Jared, because he had the calf problem early on and hadn't been able to train. Against the Highlanders he didn't play that well, so I was pleased for him.

When I met Stu again in the tunnel after the match, we had a laugh about what I had said to him earlier. Stu admitted: 'When you said to me you weren't far away, I knew we would be hanging in there.'

As a group, the boys were desperate to win and I was delighted for them. Two days before the game James Haskell, who I think played really well, said: 'I just want to win. It's so important for us to win. I don't want to be known as a Lion who was never on a winning team.'

I was delighted for Rory. He captained the team four years ago against the Brumbies and things didn't work out for him. He was excellent tonight.

The non-twenty-three created a tunnel on the way back into the changing room and they made some noise. They were delighted for the players; whooping and yelling and clapping their hands. I thought it was just awesome.

We don't have a lot of extroverts; people who talk a lot in meetings or are generally vocal. I often give them opportunities to say something but not many take up the offer, although in smaller groups or on the training pitch, they talk or contribute, which has been good.

If they were a club side, I'd probably be getting the players to make more presentations and to contribute more, but it's hard to organise that given the time constraints.

The Chiefs had offered us their changing rooms to use their recovery pools. I'm not sure if any players did actually use them, and I stayed a little bit longer before going out to do the post-match interviews.

Melodie Robinson interviewed me for SkySports New Zealand and I left her with a parting comment: 'Let's hope from now on the rugby does the talking.'

I'm trying to send positive messages about the tour through SkySports New Zealand: the quality of teams faced, it's the best rugby country in the world, we're learning from playing these teams, we think we're getting better, highlighting the welcome and the hospitality in New Zealand. Even the weather has been great.

That's the one time I'm guaranteed to get those messages across, and in fairness SkySports have been good. I know it's in their interests, but they are genuinely excited about this tour and the upcoming series, and more people watch the coverage than read the *NZ Herald*. I think the *NZ Herald* has missed a trick there.

Our starting team had over 700 Test caps between them. They should be able to beat a Chiefs team missing their All Blacks. But then again the strength and depth of New Zealand rugby are like nowhere else in the world. I often get asked: 'What's the key to being a good coach?' So much of it depends on the players at your disposal. Good competitions, which New Zealand players take part in, make good players, and good players make good coaches.

I was also criticised for suggesting that the step up from the other games to playing the All Blacks would not be as big as some people expect. I genuinely believe that. Several of their forward pack will come from the Crusaders and it will be interesting to see what other combinations the All Blacks come up with for Saturday's first Test.

I'd expect them to bring Kieran Read back and put Ardie Savea on the bench when they announce their side. Kieran is such an important player for them and it's a settled team.

In terms of 'staying alive' the performance against the Chiefs was the best yet and a pointer to the first Test team. We were excellent in achieving our four targets, the most important of which was best demonstrated in the closing stages.

In the seventy-fifth minute, the game was won, we were 34–6 ahead, and the ball had been in play for ages, up and down the pitch. Their full-back, Shaun Stevenson, took a quick throw to himself and Rory absolutely nailed him. If he hadn't done so, Robbie Henshaw or James Haskell would have. It was brilliant.

There was a bit of controversy during the match warm-ups. I know that some teams film opposing warm-ups. We don't at Wales, although the Lions got caught doing it ahead of the Chiefs game. One of our analysts, Mike Hughes, had been asked by Steve Borthwick to video the Chiefs' warm-up. We were fortunate that it was against the Chiefs because their Manager Stu Williams came to see me about it. I said: 'Sorry, I didn't know this was going on.' I just tried to dumb it down, but I genuinely didn't know anything about it.

I made a big issue out of it within our camp. I said to Mike: 'Look, New Zealand aren't happy. They've made an official complaint and they want you sent home from the tour.' I was disappointed we had done this and wanted to give him a fright. I don't know why he was filming the Chiefs' warm-up anyway. What exactly were we going to learn?

Apparently England do it too. I said: 'If you're going to video someone's warm-up, you don't do it from the side of the pitch, you do it from the coaches' box or somewhere like that. At least be a bit subtle!' He didn't do it again.

When I went back to the changing room, Stephen Donald was there and we had a beer together. He said to me: 'You should be my publicist! Keep talking about me and saying nice things about me. When are you going to come back here and coach?'

'I don't know. Maybe after the World Cup.'

'I could be your Manager,' he said.

'Yea, you could do.' Stephen would be a great Team Manager too.

I told the players that we would need a good training session tomorrow, with our units in the morning and then the full session in the afternoon, and that we needed to keep a time limit on that.

If some of the non-twenty-three wanted to go out for a few drinks, I told them tomorrow night would be the night to do it. Tonight's not the night, because we would need everyone fresh and sharp for training tomorrow.

We haven't had a chance for a really good session yet, because some of the guys have been preparing for the next game. And that's the way it's gone. That's the way sport is nowadays.

## 14

## LET'S BE BOLD

# Lions to New Zealand 2017

*Wednesday, 21 June*

The announcement of the first Test team is a seminal day on any Lions tour. This was also the squad's first day off without any travel, so it was worth driving to Auckland the night before even though we didn't reach the Pullman hotel again until 1am. As for myself and the coaches, we still had a meeting that evening to name the team.

Although it was a light enough day, we all spent some time reviewing the Chiefs' game. Ironically, the possession and territory stats for the Wales game twelve months ago were almost identical to this match. But Wales missed out on three tries early on. We could have been twenty-one points ahead but after that the Chiefs took all their chances, and that's the way the game of rugby can be.

The players involved against the Chiefs had a pool recovery in the hotel in the morning, and some had medicals, but otherwise that was it.

I met up with the other coaches at 5pm in the hotel. We had a lengthy debate, an hour and twenty minutes, which is very long for us. We had to pick a team to beat the All Blacks, and to beat the All Blacks our set-piece has to be good and we will have to defend well, but we've also got to score points. I know the All Blacks don't acknowledge it, but the way Ireland kept playing until the end of the game in Chicago and kept scoring was critical.

To beat the All Blacks, you can't stop playing. You have to keep the scoreboard ticking over. So, we thought: 'Let's be bold and pick a team that can score tries.'

I can see us winning on Saturday and then, knowing what's to come a week later, picking a different team because you've got to prepare for a different All Blacks side, like we saw in Dublin following their defeat in Chicago.

The big calls, the ones that people perhaps didn't generally expect, were Liam Williams at full-back, Elliot Daly on the left wing, Peter O'Mahony as captain and Alun Wyn Jones in the second-row alongside George Kruis, with Sam Warburton and Maro Itoje on the bench.

We had a long discussion about the second-row and the back-row, where we debated having Sam at '6'. He'd done well there in the Six Nations, but we felt that Peter O'Mahony added balance, a bit of that glue you need in the back-row, and his numbers up until then were really good.

Peter's not a massive ball-carrier, or a big, physical rugby player, but he's very good at lineouts and he's experienced. We also thought that if we did play Sam, and he and Sean O'Brien ran themselves into the ground, they might have nothing left in the last fifteen minutes. This was a real concern for us, because both are quite capable of doing that.

We knew the quality of our '7s' coming out here and Justin Tipuric had a good game last night as well. But Sean's carrying has been outstanding and his voice on the park has been good. He brings leadership, experience, and his body's holding together. He's also been over the ball a lot.

That's one of Sam's strengths too. He's probably one of the best in the world at this, and we discussed whether we'd use them both in tandem, but the feeling was that Peter's exceptional lineout ability gave us a better combination for this game.

Toby Faletau was always in line to be our first-choice '8' on this tour after Billy Vunipola pulled out, and we felt he complemented the skills of Sean and Peter in the back-row.

Sometimes when you're picking a side, you look for balance. You look for impact players, players who are powerful and strong, but you also need the glue – the grafters. George Kruis is like that. As well as being a lineout technician, he's a typical old style English second-row. He'll carry the ball up. He'll hit rucks. But he's not going to have many offloads in the game, or carry and bust through people as Alun Wyn, Maro, Iain Henderson or Courtney Lawes have been doing.

We had a long debate about starting Alun Wyn, with Maro on the bench. Alun Wyn played well against the Crusaders, while Maro made an obvious impact when coming on. Maro was also outstanding against the Maori, but we felt for this game that we could get the best out of Alun Wyn, with Maro in reserve.

We could also have gone with Alun Wyn as captain. He captained the side in the third Test four years ago, and the team against the Crusaders. But it's one of those where you just feel it's the right call at the right time. Alun Wyn is under a lot of pressure from the other second-rows and he knows it, so we want him just to concentrate on playing his own game and being accurate.

We were disappointed with that penalty he gave away against the High-landers at the lineout. He knows that's avoidable, and at that maul where they scored, he didn't complete his role. That's the difference between winning and losing games. We've spoken to the players about the number of penalties we've conceded, yet the games we've lost have largely been down to one area. Our lowest penalty counts were in our two wins, against the Maori and the Crusaders.

I still expected Alun Wyn to give us a big voice. I don't think the captaincy would have been a burden on him, but we said to him: 'Go out and play your own game and give us some leadership as well.' Other players will support Peter. Peter was pretty quiet last week against the Maori. People who know him were surprised that he wasn't more vocal. Whether it was captaining the Lions or the occasion, I don't know. Maybe it's because suddenly you're dealing with players from other countries, but he spoke well beforehand in the changing room, and the players really supported him.

Leigh Halfpenny's had a bit of a groin strain, so he hasn't trained this week. Even allowing for Leigh's experience, we probably would have gone for Liam Williams anyway. We know that Liam is an exciting, talented player but every now and then he makes a poor decision which has resulted in a penalty or yellow card as we saw in the Blues game. This has been costly in the past. I spoke to him about an incident in the Crusaders game where it appears he has put a forearm into the back of a Crusaders' player on the ground after slipping off a tackle. I told him: 'If the TMO sees that, it's a yellow card.' Liam was adamant that it was unintentional but it didn't appear that way to me or anyone else I showed the clip to.

So I said to him: 'Look, we've picked you, but you've got to keep a cool head. You've got to be calm and your decision-making has got to be right.' I highlighted a chipped kick he opted for last night off a turnover, when he hadn't scanned the pitch. He should have put the ball through the hands, gone himself or kicked long. I said: 'You're better than that.'

But he caused the Chiefs problems with his footwork and we just feel that if we're going to beat the All Blacks we have to unlock them with a bit of magic from our players.

We preferred Elliot Daly on the left wing to George North. It just hasn't happened for George, and he's had a couple of chances. Elliot's been really, really accurate and hasn't made a mistake. He's an intelligent rugby player. What's more, his big left boot gives us a second left-footed kicker along with Jonathan Davies. That helps our exit strategy, keeps them guessing, and increases our chances of potentially finding grass, as well as giving us a long-range kicking option.

For the length of the pitch try which Jack finished off against the Chiefs, Elliot put the gas on and made the inside pass to Jared Payne. He's very skilful, classy and I like his work-rate. He can also cover centre and full-back if required.

Later that night, there was a headline in the *Express* online which read: 'North To Be Axed For Daly', so that didn't take long to get out – even before we publicly announced the team the next day. I know there are a few agents out here at the moment. They talk to the players. They ring them up and say: 'How are you getting on? Are you playing?' They piece things together and they contact journalists for favours.

It's funny how your thinking from the start of the tour changes over a short time, but that's the way it should be. I'd like to think, looking at it now, that this team has been picked on form. As we keep telling the players, sometimes you get one or two chances. That's just the way it is. As a coach of one of the Celtic nations competing with the best teams in the world, you have to play a certain way or pick certain players. You can then be pigeonholed as a coach. But at times you don't have a choice. With the Lions, you've got choices; you've got so much more strength and depth in the squad to pick from.

Anthony Watson is the other form winger, and we went with Ben T'eo alongside Jonathan Davies, with Conor Murray and Owen Farrell at half-back. Conor has been huge for us. His understanding, his vision, his kicking – no one gets close to him. It's almost like he sells a bit of a shimmy to get opponents half offside. Then they have to step back, and that gives him more room for his kicks which have been on the money. He's clearing the ball well. We also have Rhys Webb to give us an impact off the bench.

I like the place that we're in with the '10s'. I was pleased to see Johnny Sexton doing well in the last couple of games. I thought he played flatter against the Maori and we've spoken about going to Sexton-Farrell at some stage on Saturday. There's a big possibility that this may happen.

Things didn't go well for Johnny at the start of the tour and he looked a little miserable. He was probably disappointed with his form. He's such a confidence player, and I had never seen him like that. It was almost as if he was resigned to not being number one. But he's world-class when he's confident.

Dan Biggar is not going to go away. He'll push the other guys right to the limit, and I've been pleased with him as well. He's transferring what he does on the training field onto the playing pitch.

Owen Farrell's vision and ability to play what's in front of him has turned him into a world-class player. The way the game is going, I think you need more than structured rugby. We all put structure in place, but depending on the speed of ball and the width that you're creating, you then need communication from outside to give playmakers options. This can be to go through the hands or out the back, a little chip across the field, or kicking into space. Owen has the ability to play all these options.

Someone like George Ford is really good at that as well, but occasionally defence is the weakest part of his game. All our '10s' have defended really well, and they've given us defensive line speed.

At the moment, Owen's understanding of the game is excellent. He's got presence, as have the other '10s', but he's been a key figure for Saracens and England. What Owen has achieved already in his career is extraordinary, especially in the last four years, and with that comes confidence and a belief in your own ability. He has a leadership role and players respect him. Like Johnny, he's not afraid to give a few verbals to teammates.

At the start of the tour, we probably didn't envisage Ben being our inside-centre for the first Test, but he has taken his opportunity and he deserves to start. He's caused the New Zealand teams a lot of problems taking the ball up, with his footwork and his offloading, and he's made more busts and beaten more defenders than any of our backs by a long, long way. He's run over a few people as well. Ben brings a lot to the table but I can see us going for Sexton and Farrell together at some stage in the game, whether we're chasing it or looking to control it.

Interestingly this is only Ben's second Test start, and Jamie George's first. People speak really highly of Jamie and, having watched him, I was surprised he didn't start in the Six Nations against Italy. He's an outstanding rugby player and he's only going to get better. I spoke to him about having confidence and belief in himself. We picked him because we know how good he is.

Actually, all the hookers have been good. Ken Owens has been excellent off the bench and I thought Rory Best led the team exceptionally well against the Chiefs. A couple of crooked throws were disappointing but his work-rate is outstanding, particularly the amount of rucks he hits, and he's very good over the ball.

Our thinking at the outset of the tour was that Joe Marler might start and we'd spring Mako Vunipola or Jack McGrath from the bench, but Mako has been outstanding. We don't think we will get eighty minutes out of him, but fifty or sixty would be fine, with Jack then coming on. Jack's work-rate and scrummaging have been strong, while Tadhg Furlong has been one of the players of the tour. He's a genuine modern-day Test prop.

The Test fifteen has worked out to be seven English players and four each from Ireland and Wales, but I don't consider the make-up of Englishmen, Welshmen, Irishmen or Scotsmen. We just pick what we believe to be the strongest team.

There was a lengthy debate about the bench too. We see some talent in Kyle Sinckler. He came on against the Maori, and he scrummaged well again. He knows his role but sometimes it's about getting the balance right; hitting rucks and not looking to carry the ball all the time. Against the Maori he didn't carry that much, but he was always looking to do so. Then again, when they made a break, he worked really hard to get back and saved us with a turnover.

We also debated the bench, and whether it would be George North, Jonathan Joseph, Leigh or Jack Nowell as the reserve back. We went with the experience of Halfpenny. He probably doesn't give us as much in attack as the others, but he doesn't make mistakes. Leigh could be a good option if we're looking to control the game in the last twenty minutes. Our bench against the All Blacks is going to be very important, and we think we have real impact there.

People will debate the selection and disagree with it, but if we win the first Test we will probably start Maro next week, and we might also start Warburton, to bring in their physicality, because we would know what's coming down the line.

After agreeing on the selection, we immediately went to a squad meeting at 6.30pm in the hotel to announce the team to the players. We knew how tense they would be, so we decided that we'd begin proceedings with the second presentation of the Bobby Cup and Paul Stridgeon's man of the match from the wins over the Maori and the Chiefs.

First was his latest video, 'A Day In The Life Of A Lion' in which Bobby dressed himself up in a big lion suit which he'd hired in Rotorua from a Lions fan on tour. As the squad's youngest player, Maro is trusted with looking after our mascot, Billy the Lion. The video begins with Maro stroking Billy at the end of the bed. 'I love you Bill. I wish you were a real Lion,' says Maro, before lying back on the pillow and drifting off to sleep. The video fades away to a dream sequence.

The dream pans to Bobby as a lion getting up from bed beside Maro. He tucks Maro in, has a shower and heads out to drive one of the Land Rovers.

He visits the Lions Foundation House, goes to the stadium, does a warm-up, some tackling and kicks a few goals. He goes to the gym, runs on the treadmill, rows on the rowing machine, does some exercises with Phil Pask, one of the Lions physios, and some weights.

He goes out and becomes captain of a boat, which he pilots, then goes to the steam room before heading out again. By coincidence, there was a circus near the ground for Bobby to do some acrobatics on a pole, in front of a live audience of kids and some parents.

He returns to the hotel, goes up to his room and climbs back into bed beside Maro. The dream ends, and Maro sits up in the bed. He looks at Billy, strokes his head and says: 'Ah, maybe next time, eh?'

Finally the video cuts to Prince Harry, who James Haskell had asked to say to camera 'and the winner of the Bobby Cup is ...' Bobby then announced Jack Nowell as the winner, which I agreed with. It was only five minutes long but the whole thing was brilliant, and Ben Uttley's production is of a really high quality. The boys enjoyed that.

Then I read out the team and replacements. You understand there are going to be some very disappointed players, but you try to deliver the message that those who will play on Tuesday against the Hurricanes are still in the mix for the series. Just because we've picked this team doesn't mean we won't change our thinking for the second and third Tests.

I began by telling them we had a long discussion and some lively debate about several positions in the twenty-three. A couple of guys have forced their way in on the back of last night, and that's exactly how we wanted it.

I had wanted to protect the first Test match-day twenty-three, but as it's transpired Elliot and Liam played against the Chiefs and so didn't train with this group on Monday or Tuesday. Alun Wyn trained with the team to play the Chiefs on Monday, but we brought him to the afternoon session as well because we thought he'd be part of the Test twenty-three at least.

As a result, twenty or twenty-one of this first Test squad have trained together since the start of the week and that's been massively important.

I know plenty has been made of those six call-ups, and it's been tough on them. They're here as cover and we didn't put them on last night. We didn't need to. But their presence has enabled us to protect pretty much all of the first Test squad, and that's why we did it.

I told the players that tomorrow will be a really important training day for us. We'll have units in the morning, the rugby session in the afternoon and then everyone in the squad is going out for dinner.

I told the boys who are not involved in the first Test that if they want go out for a couple of beers, tomorrow night is the night to do it, not tonight, and not on Friday either. We've all been involved in teams when someone has woken up on the Saturday having been sick overnight or they've a back spasm, their hamstring is gone, something like that.

Plenty of them shook hands when the meeting broke up. The dynamics of the squad seem really, really tight. I'd like to think so anyway.

Back at the hotel that night I spoke with George North about his non-inclusion, telling him: 'Things haven't happened for you at the moment, and you've had a few injuries. Next time you get the opportunity you need to make the most of it.'

I've known George a long time. When he burst on the scene he was an absolute superstar and sometimes you want him to be under more pressure, especially in Wales, where we don't have a huge amount of depth. As a result, we have sometimes picked him even though his form has not been up to our high expectations.

George is a fantastic bloke, and it's worth stressing that there are no issues with him. He was our main match-winner in the series four years ago, and was very disappointed not to be picked for this first Test. In his career he's rarely experienced the disappointment of being left out of a side.

It was not an easy conversation. But that's what being a Lions coach is all about.

# 15

## Lions to New Zealand 2017

*Thursday, 22 June*

We announced the team for the first Test on the Lions' digital channels at 7am and I was down in the team room half an hour later. All the staff are usually there between 7 and 8am every day, studying their laptops, reviewing and previewing games. It's tough on the coaches and the analysts, because we're preparing two teams a week.

The All Blacks announced their side earlier that morning, and I was a little bit surprised, especially Julian Savea being left out, and Ryan Crotty at '13'. As expected Kieran Read was back.

I spoke to Shane Whelan, who is our Head of Digital, and he was very excited by the pretty positive online reaction to all things surrounding the tour. The numbers on the Lions' digital platforms have been massive.

Vinny Hammond also came over to me and told me that CJ Stander's grandmother had died. Vinny's girlfriend is good friends with CJ's wife, Jean-Marie, so Vinny actually knew this before CJ did. CJ's family were going to ring him and tell him the sad news. Vinny was just giving me a heads up.

I had a chat with Maro Itoje as well. I told him that we'd had a long debate about the second-row selection, and whether we'd stick with him or not. 'Don't read too much into it. We felt that coming off the bench, you'll make a big impact.' He was disappointed but he accepted it. He's a young man and he's got a hell of a lot more rugby ahead of him, including the rest of this tour.

The players assembled for a brief squad meeting at 9.45am in the hotel. The match-day twenty-three for the first Test went to the gym on the first bus at 9.50, and the rest of the squad and management went to the QBE Stadium, where we were joined by the first Test squad, for unit meetings and sessions at 11.25.

I spoke to CJ before the units about his grandmother's passing. He knew by then. I said to him: 'Sorry to hear about your grandmother. Is there anything we need to do, or anything you want to do? Do you want to go back home to South Africa?'

'No. No.'

'Are you sure? Even if you want forty-eight hours off for the funeral, just let us know.'

He said he'd stay. She was in her nineties but he was pretty close to her and he welled up a little. Our principle all along has been that family comes first, so we would have done whatever it took to make sure he was right. That is very important for us.

The forwards went with Steve Borthwick and Graham Rowntree to one end of the main pitch, and the backs with Rob Howley and Andy Farrell to the other end. As I normally do, I joined the forwards. With a full squad session in the afternoon, it was a 'double day', which is not ideal. The English and Welsh players are used to it, but the Scottish and Irish players aren't, so we tried to keep the unit sessions short.

The forwards did some lineouts, mauls and scrums, both with a machine and live, because it was a Thursday. The guys from the Chiefs game fronted up, which was really encouraging. Scrummaging against a machine is more for timing, and the same for non-contact lineouts. You want some organisation and accuracy, but then you want to test them with some live stuff as well.

The backs went through moves unopposed and then against the backs who had played against the Chiefs. We felt that our units had been good and the win against the Chiefs had been a real positive for the mood in the camp. We kept the unit sessions to a maximum of thirty-five minutes.

We had lunch out there, and did our media session, with me and Peter O'Mahony sitting at the top table. I was asked when this team came into my mind.

It may appear blunt, but I was being 100 per cent honest when I answered: 'It came into our minds on Wednesday when we picked the team.' Some people just don't seem to get that. I added: 'There was some good healthy debate and obviously there was the issue of the back three. The message to the players before we came out to New Zealand was that to play the All Blacks you have to be bold and take risks. Yes, we are playing to a structure as every team does, but we have been giving the confidence to the players to bring in an offloading game when it's appropriate.

'We feel our set-piece is getting better from game to game and we've improved defensively. We just need to bring that other element into the game, which is playing with some flair.'

After that the coaches and I held a meeting with the core leadership group before our team meeting in the afternoon. This comprised of Jamie George, George Kruis, Peter, Conor Murray, Owen Farrell, Sam Warburton and Johnny Sexton, and we spent about ten minutes talking about what they wanted in terms of structure and organisation, and how they wanted to play the game. These guys were very much the spine of the team, and we wanted them to have an input.

We kept the afternoon session to forty-five minutes. We were looking to run basically the same session that we ran last Thursday before the Maori game because we got so much out of that.

The whole squad trained pretty well. The intensity was exactly what we were looking for. We warmed up for eight minutes then did some short games (two minutes), contact (four minutes), and offloads (four minutes), before doing six minutes of attack drills and six minutes of defence. We finished off with what we called our 15 v 15 'chaos' sessions, building in transitioning from attack to defence and defence to attack. In total we trained for forty-five minutes, including the eight-minute warm-up. The 15 v 15 'chaos' was not full-on all the way through, but we upped the tempo for a couple of minutes at the end. We felt we were in good shape. There was a lot of chat and communication in reacting to things like a quick throw, a turn-over, or a quick tap.

We were back at the hotel by 4.30pm, where the players had a recovery session and a snack.

Months ago, I agreed to go to an event in Skycity. So I went there before joining the squad for our dinner in the Soul Bar & Bistro. About sixty players and staff made it out, but the first people I bumped into were Graeme Bachop, Richard Loe and Andy Earl. They had all come up to Auckland the night before for an All Blacks reunion dinner, and they were there with their wives. I had played with these guys for the All Blacks. It was great to see them all.

After the meal, I joined them for a drink and we reminisced a little. We shared a few old stories, including one I remembered from when I was playing for the All Blacks against Swansea in 1989. I actually scored a try that day before getting knocked out in the first half.

I had no idea where I was. Our second-row Alan Whetton went off injured, but I hadn't even noticed. There was a lineout to us and a call was made. I thought I was throwing to Alan but when I looked up it was Andy Earl standing there. I got through to half-time and Richard Loe said: 'He's not right. He's definitely not right, get him off.'

Andy came over to me and said: 'If you're not right, get off.'

'F*** off,' I replied. 'The only way I'm coming off this field is on a f***ing stretcher.'

'Fair enough,' said Andy. He respected that.

That's the way it was back then, but of course you would never get away with that sort of thing these days, and rightly so.

I walked back to the hotel with Anna Voyce, Charlie McEwen and Dave Barton. One of them said: 'Do you want to have a drink on the way back?' We found this little bar in the middle of nowhere, but when we walked in there were Lions fans everywhere. So I had one drink, did quite a few photos and said: 'OK, I'm going back to the hotel.'

Quiet nights were now a thing of the past.

## Friday, 23 June

This morning I talked with some of the team leaders about the Captain's Run. For me, it is completely about what the players want. We've done the coaching for the week. Now it's what does Peter want? What does Owen want? It's up to them. We want a little bit of intensity, but as coaches we try to take a backward step, leaving the players in control.

At our squad meeting Rob Howley showed some footage of the All Blacks, highlighting the changes they had made, especially bringing in Rieko Ioane for Julian Savea. I had already spoken to a couple of the players about this, and the need to put pressure on Ioane, to drop the ball on him, because he's not great in the air.

After the Captain's Run, the kickers had gone with Neil Jenkins to Eden Park – Owen, Leigh, Johnny and Elliot, as well as Conor and Rhys. Paul Stridgeon went with them too.

Rob Howley did the lunchtime press conference, with Conor alongside. We chose Conor because he's comfortable in front of the media and is a good talker, without giving too much away.

Everyone had the afternoon off, and then at 6pm we had the traditional handing out of the Lions jerseys. Rob and I had discussed this and narrowed it down to three players – Martin Johnson, Brian O'Driscoll and Paul O'Connell – who we thought were relevant to do the presentation. All three were modern-day Lions icons.

In the end, I decided we'd ask Brian. We knew Brian was coming in that day. Ger Carmody had got in touch with him while he was en route to New Zealand the day before, and he said he'd be delighted.

Normally when the jerseys are presented, it's only the match-day twenty-three in the room. Owen Farrell came to me and said: 'Is it OK if some of the other players come?' For example, Joe Marler wanted to shake Mako Vunipola's hand after the jerseys were presented.

I thought: 'That's fair enough.' So we sent out a message to the other players that if any of them wanted to attend they were welcome. I thought we should try to be inclusive. I also asked Ger to send a message to the staff, to see if any of them wanted to be there as well. Several of them took up the invitation.

I started the meeting and then I got John Spencer to say a few words. He finished by saying: 'We've got someone very special to present the jerseys, and I would like to introduce Brian O'Driscoll.'

Brian had only landed in Auckland that day, and he spoke brilliantly. He immediately got a bit of a laugh when he started with: 'Look, I'm absolutely delighted to be here to present the jerseys, but I would have preferred it if four years ago Gats had picked me for the third Test.'

I thought that was brilliant. People still try to make a big thing out of what happened, but I think both of us understand professional sport. I laughed. Fair play to him.

His speech was awesome. He talked about the opportunity they all had, the need to take their chances, and big players stepping up on the day. That was the key message for me: big players making the most of those opportunities and the big moments. He spoke for five minutes or so before calling up each player in turn to present them with their jersey. He started with number one, Mako Vunipola, and continued in numerical order except for Peter O'Mahony, who was called up last as the captain.

I hadn't realised the impact it would have on the other staff, but a lot of them approached me afterwards and said they were blown away by it. It made me think of one of our core messages: that it's all for one, and that we're all in this together. But if you are going to preach it, you have to live it. Sometimes you have to separate the players, but with the Lions it's not all about them. This has been a collective, of staff and players, working for a common goal.

That evening there was a function on the top floor of the Pullman hotel. All of the VIPs had arrived, such as the commercial sponsors, as well as the CEOs and the chairmen of the four home unions. It's not compulsory but we were asked to attend, so myself and the other coaches mixed and mingled for an hour or so.

Trudi had arrived in Auckland on the Thursday, and came to the hotel to check on the family room. This was located on the ground floor and was for relatives or partners who were now beginning to arrive in bigger numbers. It's a nice space for the boys to hang out with family and friends without being intruded upon. There was security on the door and you had to have ID to get in.

Owen Farrell's fiancée and Jamie George's partner had been among the first to arrive on the Thursday. Others came and went. Trudi's good friend, Julie, who was her bridesmaid, was there tonight and we spent most of the evening in that room chatting and having a relaxed time.

Afterwards, I went with some of the staff for a drink in the bar. It was very low-key. I was a bit drained. Then again, I was drained every day.

It's been like no tour I've ever been on – a massive learning curve and so tough for the coaches. It's just relentless. In 2009 and 2013 we could have the occasional easier day and a lighter training session, knowing we were going to win the next game reasonably comfortably. This tour hasn't been like that at all. Every game has been full-on and we have tried to give the players the best chance to prepare for each one.

Has that been the right approach? I am not entirely sure, because you don't want to do too much, but you also want the players to enjoy themselves. We've covered a huge amount in the last few weeks and from now on we have to make sure we don't overdo it.

I turned in around 1am. I always feel both apprehensive and excited the night before a match, but this time I was very positive.

We're going to win this game.

## 16

**THE AGONY**

## Lions to New Zealand 2017

*Saturday, 24 June*
*First Test: New Zealand v Lions, Eden Park, Auckland*

After nine months of planning and preparations, the first Test against the All Blacks was finally here. Normally, and ideally, on match-day I can focus exclusively on the game that night, but not this day.

Time management is one of the most difficult tasks on tour because, on the day of such a big match, coaches also need a little downtime, but it's hard to find even a spare half-hour. After breakfast, I was in and out of the team room all morning.

The non-twenty-three, those players not involved in the Test, went on the bus to the gym to do weights and then the management departed at 10.20 to join them in the QBE Stadium for training. We held a brief meeting with them at 11am, before training the guys for Tuesday's game against the

Hurricanes. It was hard to preview the Hurricanes, because without their All Blacks players they would have a few personnel changes. So there was a little pre-match 'prep' on video, but not a huge amount.

It was a reasonably tough training session because everyone would have the Sunday off, in theory, even though it's still a recovery and travel day. Meanwhile the kickers in the Test-twenty-three went to Eden Park again. Yesterday the weather had been perfect, but now the wind had picked up so they decided to go back there to practise their place-kicks, re-starts and box-kicks in match conditions.

At 2.30pm, Leigh Halfpenny and Neil Jenkins also went kicking at St Peter's College next to Auckland Grammar School. At the same time we had a meeting between the coaches and Eanna, Rhodri, Bobby and Ger to discuss our itinerary for the following week.

At 3.15pm the guys who were involved in the game had an optional weights session, what they call 'primers'. Then at 3.45 all of us met to get on the bus to go down to the gym for a walk-through.

We had brought in extra players from the non-twenty-three for our warm-up, to help us with scrums and defensive drills – Iain Henderson, CJ Stander, James Haskell, Greig Laidlaw, Dan Biggar and Jonathan Joseph. So they joined us for our pre-match meal at 4.10. I didn't have anything to eat. I was too nervous. I went back to my room.

A little later I called into the family room to say hello to Trudi. Bryn had played for his club, Takapuna, that morning but it was lashing rain, so Trudi decided not to go. All the families were there, along with the other coaches and players, and Trudi was talking with my sister Micharn and her husband Neihana. They live in Brisbane and I had got them tickets for the game. Micharn is twenty-one years younger than me but we are very close, and she was thrilled to be there. My other sister, Kim, had been at the Chiefs game but I wasn't able to catch up with her. Trudi's parents, along with

Gabby and Bryn, and Sam and Teegan, were all in the family room as well. Trudi's brothers, Clif and Paddy, also went with her to the game.

As the team room was close by, and the team meeting was scheduled for 5.50pm, the family room was emptied beforehand and the Lions security staff brought all the families out onto the footpath, which was cordoned off, so that they could cheer the boys onto the bus which was taking us to Eden Park.

Andy Farrell and I had a conversation before the leadership meeting. He said to me: 'I think they might try to play a high tempo game, ball on the front foot, not allow us to defend, play out on the edges and run us off our feet.'

However, a big part of the New Zealand psyche is to focus on the opposition's strengths. So I said: 'Andy, as a Kiwi, I think they will try and attack our strengths. And so they will have a crack at our lineout drive. They will try to stop our line speed. How will they do that? They will try and be physical. They will see our scrum as a strength too, and they'll have a go at our scrum at some stage.'

The leadership meeting ran on a bit, so by the time we went into the team room, the rest of the squad was already there, humming along to *Jerusalem*. About halfway through it, they all started singing it – quietly, not loudly. It was a cool moment. I thought: 'This is a group of guys who are pretty united.'

I told the players about my conversation with Andy, and as a Kiwi, my understanding of what might be coming, and making sure that we were not caught out. I said to them: 'Don't be surprised by anything that they throw at us and, when they throw something and they don't get anything out of it, then it's a win for us. So if they try and drive our lineout and get nothing out of it, it's a win for us. If they have a crack at our scrum, and they get nothing out of it, it's a win for us.' I only spoke for about two or three minutes, but that was enough this far ahead of kick-off.

We went out and were applauded onto the bus by all our families and friends, as well as some supporters. I was sitting in the front row, alongside Ger Carmody, looking out the window. I think I was one of the few who witnessed what happened next, although everyone saw the aftermath.

Billy Stickland, the Inpho photographer who is part of our support staff, had gone onto the road to take a picture of the players boarding the bus. Billy was standing there, his camera going '*click, click, click,*' when all of a sudden I saw this car coming around the corner. 'What's this ...?' but everything happened so quickly that there was nothing I could do to prevent what followed.

The car hit Billy from behind, and he and his backpack were thrown up in the air, before landing on the windscreen and smashing it. I think there might be a video of the incident. If the car had been any bigger, it could have seriously injured him, but because it was a small car it literally scooped Billy into the air. I'm sure the Lions bus probably distracted the car driver – it does tend to draw eyes, especially when surrounded by police cars with their lights flashing – but it wasn't the driver's fault, and the security guys and the police dealt with the matter. Billy's back was sore and stiff, but he looked OK, which was a huge relief. Billy went to the match, and did his job like the true pro that he is.

It only took twenty minutes to drive to the ground. We were given a police escort and all the traffic lights en route were turned green. That journey was amazing. Fans lined the road all the way from the hotel, chanting '*Li-ons! Li-ons!*' and then when we arrived at the ground it seemed like everyone was wearing red.

I went into our changing room for about ten minutes and then did my pre-match interviews with Ian Smith from SkySports NZ, Graham Simmons from SkySports UK, and Russell Hargreaves from talkSPORT. Graham asked me: 'Warren, rugby doesn't get much more giddy than this. How have you and your team tried to contain and channel all the adrenaline and excitement of the last eight to ten hours?'

'I think in the last week it's sort of picked up with all the fans arriving into New Zealand so it's pretty exciting,' I said. 'It's sort of what top-level sport is all about, isn't it? Players get pumped up, everyone gets pumped up. The fans get excited about it. So that's what you do all those hard hours of training for on the training paddock. It's for big occasions.'

Then he asked: 'You said earlier this week that you wanted your team to be bold. Specifically where and how do you think fortune might favour the brave tonight?'

'Well, I just think you have to take your opportunities, and if it means getting an offload away and somebody has a bit of X-factor or something a bit special, you've got to have the courage to be able to do that and we're encouraging players to try and do that. We saw some of that on Tuesday night. We've been creating opportunities, and often when you look at the All Blacks, it's something that they do especially well. It's an offload out the back. You saw the game against the Blues when Sonny Bill Williams gets an offload away and Ihaia West scores a fantastic try. We've got to try and be prepared and have the courage enough to do the same sort of thing.'

Out on the pitch, I just had a look around. The stadium was already filling up, but the wind was also picking up. It was quite blustery. The coin toss was about fifty minutes before kick-off, which we'd won. Some people like to play into the wind, which is fine. I think those sort of things are up to the captain, after he talks to the '10' and maybe other teammates. In the other games when we'd won the toss, we'd kicked off and got a good return from them. Peter O'Mahony discussed it with Owen Farrell and made the decision that we would play from right to left into the wind, so the All Blacks had the kick-off.

Before the warm-up, I had a quick chat with the All Blacks' Assistant Coach Ian Foster on halfway and then with Steve Hansen as well.

'How's it going?' Fozzy asked.

'It's been an interesting couple of weeks, with the media stuff,' I said.

As we had brought in extra players, the three '9s' warmed up together, and so did the three '10s'. As we had sixteen forwards, the pack did a few lineouts, ran a few calls and did two or three scrums of eight-on-eight.

The coaches ran the drills. We covered defensive lineouts, a little bit of mauling as well as pick-and-go, and a few scrums. We did a handling drill, a couple of 'stride outs' and then we came together to run some attack patterns and defence plays for the starting fifteen. We hit some bags at the end and went back into the changing room with about ten minutes to go before kick-off.

I thought we were in good shape. The room was quiet, but that's no bad thing. Sean O'Brien was good, telling the guys to be vocal, and to front up. I stressed the same things. 'Take your opportunities. Believe in yourselves. You're good enough to win this.'

The players were putting their jerseys on while the coaches and the rest of the squad went around shaking everyone's hand and wishing them all the best. There were no more speeches. It had all been said. Myself and the other coaches left. We liked to leave the players on their own, for the last two or three minutes, before they were called out.

We were in the coaches' box for the national anthems and the *haka*. They did the *Kapa o Pango* rather than the *Ka Mate haka*. Because we have faced so many *hakas*, I don't think they're an issue for the boys.

We dealt with the All Blacks' kick-off, and Ben Smith couldn't take Conor Murray's first box-kick which Anthony Watson chased well. When Aaron Smith came through too soon on Conor, we had an 'in' from a lineout in their half. We got our runners going and we could easily have scored a try in the first two minutes.

Foxy (Jonathan Davies) made a great break and Conor was in support.

When Elliot Daly dived in by the corner flag, I couldn't see clearly from the box because of people jumping up. At first, we thought he had scored, so we were pretty excited. 'What a great start.' But the replay showed that Israel Dagg's tackle had forced Elliot over the touchline.

Brodie Retallick had retreated on the blindside to defend, but not enough so that he was behind the offside line. As a result, Owen Farrell had to dive pass because Retallick was straight on him. Otherwise Owen would have been able to pick and go, Dagg would have had to hold and Elliot may have got in for the try.

Instead, it was their lineout and we were then penalised for offside. I was going mental in the coaches' box. The message to the players throughout the past three weeks has been: 'When you get a team in their 22, whatever you do don't give away soft penalties,' but our discipline has been a hugely disappointing element of the tour. The number of penalties we have conceded has been our most significant problem; not territory, possession, scrums, lineouts, the breakdown or anything else. Penalties have been the biggest momentum shifters in almost every game.

Soon after this, Beauden Barrett had a grubber-kick blocked by Conor in our half, turned, picked-up one-handed on the run, transferred the ball from his right to left hand and glided away in one movement. Even I said: 'F***, that's pretty cool.'

The All Blacks started attacking the narrow channels off Aaron Smith. In the twelfth minute, they were generating some momentum, when Kaino came hard off '9', as did Sonny Bill with a big carry. There were five carries in a row to put us on the back foot.

Toby Faletau was unlucky to be called offside when he came back into the defensive line. It didn't affect the pass to Ben Smith, and it wasn't as bad as the Retallick offside earlier. But that's a penalty and 3–0 to them.

We had a maul which they sacked, fair enough, but we were going forward and the ball went to ground. Sitting in the coaches' box I thought: 'How's that a scrum to them?'

Our lineout and Conor's box-kicking were putting us on the front foot again, but Tadhg Furlong went for an offload to Liam Williams. It was one of those when he should have held onto the ball. It wasn't the right time to offload, but it's kind of a Catch 22. When it's on, that's how you get in behind teams and stress them.

They started launching one-off runners again and George Kruis was penalised for not rolling away. Aaron Smith had the ball in his hands. It wasn't a quick tap, because it took about seven or eight seconds and he had a look around. Barrett shouted to him twice, he heard the second call, tapped, gave it to his out-half and we just didn't react quickly enough.

It was great skill by Smith, Barrett and Dagg for Codie Taylor to score, but Elliot Daly got caught there. He left himself in no-man's land. He either had to come up hard or stay out on his man. Then he would have forced Dagg to throw the pass over him, or maybe get an intercept and score at the other end. We think it is a forward pass from Dagg to Taylor. Looking at it again, we're convinced of it. When we spoke at half-time, Elliot acknowledged that he got caught.

Barrett kicked the conversion from the sideline to make it 10–0. A few minutes later, Elliot beat Dagg in the air to a cross-kick by Owen, and if he'd got his pass away to Foxy it would have been a try, but Ryan Crotty made a great tackle.

Our lineout was excellent. We got one penalty for sacking and then another one when Owen Franks came through on Conor. It's hard to get momentum in their 22. Any time you start to do so, they give away a penalty. Anyway, Owen kicked that, but when Aaron Cruden took the re-start, because Ben Smith had gone off and they'd moved Barrett to full-back, there was a bit of a miscommunication and we didn't take it, which was really disappointing.

Kieran Read made a good bust for them, and in the same move Crotty did his hamstring before Aaron Smith purposely passed the ball into Jamie George's back, which was clever, but Jamie just had to stay down on the ground. Barrett kicked that again and we were 13–3 down.

When Cruden then kicked in behind us, Anthony Watson covered it well, as he'd done with a cross-kick by Barrett earlier. He passed it back to Liam Williams, and what he did next was typical Liam. Read chased really hard, but Liam stepped him. Then he saw space and beat Cruden and Sonny Bill. He also did well to offload to Foxy. He gave it to Daly, who took on Anton Lienert-Brown and passed back inside to Foxy. Sean O'Brien was there for the offload to score.

Sean had worked so hard to be in that position. The in-and-out by Elliot was unbelievable, and Foxy had the awareness to do a 360-degree turn before offloading to Sean. It was a great try.

There was some shouting in the box. We were relieved, as well as pleased, because we had missed three chances before then.

Barrett had kicked 100 per cent until this point and we needed to kick the conversion, but Owen missed it, making it 13–8 instead of 13–10. I know we've got great goal-kickers, but we left two points behind there again, and that would have been so different going in at the break.

At half-time in the changing room, we gave them a little bit of time to themselves as usual and then split between forwards and backs. We were happy with the way we were scrummaging, and the lineout was going well. We were also putting their lineout under pressure. In attack, we needed to be a bit more aggressive at the breakdown.

We felt like we were really in the game, although we had to improve some of our contact work. We knew they were coming hard off '9', so Andy and myself said we needed to narrow up a bit, come up hard and win those collisions.

Obviously we had switched off for that quick tap. We were annoyed that we conceded the seven points from such a soft try. But there was no sense of panic at all.

I finished off by saying we needed to be accurate, disciplined, and to come hard off our line to stop their go-forward off Aaron Smith, and when we got chances we had to take them.

The second half had just started by the time we got up to our coaches' box again. It's not a great box to watch a game from. It's enclosed and soundproof, so you don't hear the crowd and experience the atmosphere of the game. It's like watching in your living room with the noise turned down. I prefer one of the windows being open so you can hear the crowd.

They started running hard off '9' again, but Tadhg made a good tackle and Toby dislodged the ball. George and Owen shifted the ball on to Liam, who counter-attacked again.

I think Foxy passed a little bit early to Conor after fending off Taylor, but then Anthony and Liam took it on. After two rucks, Owen passed left to right to Ben Te'o. They were stressed, and Ben just had to pass. He had Retallick and Kaino in front of him, but he had Sean and Toby outside with a two-on-one against Sonny Bill. If we'd just put the ball through the hands, it was another try, 13–13 with the conversion to come, and potentially that could have completely changed the last thirty minutes.

We had an advantage because they were offside from the ruck. Again, the All Blacks were happy to concede a penalty rather than five or seven points. Jaco Peyper warned us in the second half about giving away penalties, but every time we were on the attack in their 22, it was a penalty. Every single time.

We decided to go for the corner. We'd had some success from our lineouts. In this game, they had looked to bring the lineout down, but you've still got to back yourself.

Read then came in from the side. How that was not picked up was unbelievable, but Sean won the ball back with a brilliant turnover. We made some good yardage, but a foot prevented Conor from making a clean pick-up.

Peyper said 'ball backwards' but then changed his mind for a knock-on. I couldn't see any knock-on.

They won the ball anyway, and Dagg kicked long. Elliot gathered, and passed infield to Liam, who worked a switch with Anthony. He beat four tackles, one after the other. Great footwork. We had them stressed again, but there was no need to try the offload to Conor. We'd got back into their 22, but instead of keeping our momentum going, it was another turnover.

We decided to bring Maro Itoje on then, and we had a big discussion whether we took Alun Wyn Jones or George Kruis off. It could have been either, but George is a very good lineout caller and our lineout was going well. We needed to have Maro's energy, coming off the line quickly and bringing that physicality and urgency. We brought Jack McGrath and Sam Warburton on early as well, for Mako Vunipola and Peter O'Mahony. Pete had done well at lineout time, but we weren't dominant in the tackles. We were soaking them up.

We were in the game up until the fifty-fifth minute, but then we had one bad scrum and paid a heavy price for it. Our front-row got caught a little high and the loose-forwards came off. The All Blacks went for a second shove and had a penalty advantage.

Owen was defending on the blindside, but once the scrum screwed around, I thought he probably could have gone to the openside, particularly as the loose-forwards could then defend our left-hand side once the scrum turned.

Read offloaded off the ground, Aaron Smith stepped Ben, and then Foxy was caught a bit in no man's land and missed Dagg. Anthony Watson also came in and Dagg got the ball away to Rieko Ioane for a try. When it went to replays to check for a possible knock-on by Read, you can only admire his skill. It was an incredible offload as he dived onto the ball. It would have been a better end result had we not let them play off the scrum and limited it to a penalty.

We felt that we needed to get Johnny Sexton on, so we shifted Owen to '12' and took Ben T'eo off. Ben had defended very well but hadn't passed the ball in the game. We needed more in our attack then. But then there was a period of eleven minutes or so when we had no ball. Even when we had a chance to get it back, we just turned it over straight away.

Johnny was called offside and they had to take the three points, which put them more than two scores clear at 23–8.

Owen found a huge touch from a penalty and we brought on Ken Owens. They say you shouldn't bring on a hooker just before a throw-in, but they've got to come on at a break, and that's normally a scrum or a lineout, or an injury.

We lost the lineout when they got Whitelock into the air, but that wasn't Ken's fault. George made the call and the All Blacks made a really late shift. It happened just behind George and he didn't see it. If he had, he would have changed the call.

Even at 23–8 down I was thinking: 'If we get a try, we have a chance.' But then Johnny and Owen got their wires crossed. Johnny passed flat to Owen, but Owen didn't have his hands up for the ball, he was expecting a pass behind him to Elliot, and the turnover was conceded.

Liam couldn't hold Perenara's box-kick and Ioane latched onto it to score. That was another very soft try to concede. Sometimes with Liam you get the best in the world and other times not.

Of course, Barrett didn't miss once more. I was in the coaches' box thinking: 'Jesus, we shouldn't be 30–8 down.'

Now we had too much to do. The penalty count had been massively against us but then, typically, in the last seven or eight minutes we were awarded three or four penalties.

We finished the game with some good, direct carrying. Rhys Webb came on and gave us some impetus. He linked up well with Foxy off a scrum. Foxy made some great yards again, and then Rhys finished well. I think 30–15 was the least we deserved.

When the full-time whistle went, hardly a word was said in the box. I went down onto the pitch and shook hands with Fozzy and congratulated him, and Steve Hansen as well. I did the same when I saw their Scrum Coach, Mike Cron, in the tunnel.

I went into the changing room. There's no in-between after a game. It's either agony or ecstasy. You're in a lonely place, because you're hurting, and two or three minutes later you have to do the TV and radio interviews, and then face the press conference.

Before that, I said to the players: 'Look guys, we're obviously all disappointed. We've given away a couple of penalties, and if you look at the tries they've scored, two of them are not tries that they've created. There are things that are fixable from our point of view.' I also said we missed out on a few chances and we allowed them to dominate us in some of the collisions.

On SkySports UK, Graham Simmons asked me: 'What have you said to the guys in the changing room?'

'I think the message was there are things that we can fix, in terms of how we switched off for a quick tap and a try. The ball has gone through Liam's hands and Ioane scored. That was disappointing. In fairness though, there is no excuse in terms of the result. The All Blacks were very direct coming off '9'. They ran really hard and were better than us at the breakdown, and we missed a number of opportunities. But I think they're all things we can fix pretty quickly.'

As Steve Hansen was coming out from the press conference and we were going in, I shook his hand and said: 'Congratulations. Well done. You played well.'

He said: 'Thanks.' That was it. We were walking past each other, so it was just a quick exchange.

At the press conference, I again gave them credit. No excuses. The better team won on the night. I said we created opportunities but didn't finish some of them, that it was a great game of rugby and a great Test match.

After all my post-match media obligations, Dave Barton and I went back to the changing room. The other coaches were having a beer, so I sat down and had one with them. We weren't there for very long, as the buses were soon ready to go.

We continued our chat about the game back at the hotel. Andy was disappointed with our defensive performance. He felt we'd fallen off a few tackles and weren't dominant in the collisions. Graham Rowntree was hacked off about that one scrum, although apart from that we scrummaged pretty well. We spoke about things we did well, how we created some good chances.

In the lineouts we won twelve out of thirteen and they lost five of theirs – one was an overthrow and one not straight, so we did put their lineout under pressure. But even though we won twelve out of thirteen, it's the end result from the lineout that matters. We had one stolen, we were turned over twice from driven lineouts, we picked up off the back of another and turned that over, so the end result could have been better. There were about seven of the twelve where you could put a tick next to it, but there were four or five that although we won, still merited a cross.

The post-match meal for the players was in the team room at 11.45pm. I wasn't interested in eating. I called into the family room instead and met Trudi. It was a welcome escape after defeat.

Later, I went into one of the offices with Graham, Bobby and Ger for a couple of glasses of wine and reflected on the game some more. By the time I went to bed, it was around 2 o'clock.

You're always pretty wired after a game. Your head's going crazy thinking about what you could have done better.

This was definitely one of those nights.

## 17

# HURRICANES AND STORM CLOUDS

## Lions to New Zealand 2017

*Sunday, 25 June*

We had a busy morning, as we had an early afternoon flight to Wellington. After breakfast, the players had medicals, massage, pool recovery and ice baths between 9 and 11am, before a squad meeting at 12.10. As well as the reviews, we had to pick and announce the team to play the Hurricanes on Tuesday.

The analysts had worked pretty much through the night again, collating all the stats on the first Test. Going through the video confirmed much of what we had seen with our own eyes.

There were three or four avoidable penalties, and only two offensive penalties in the entire match. Both were for not releasing and both were against us, and yet there was one time when Sean was on the ball for much longer than either of those two. When those calls aren't going your way, you have to be almost 100 per cent accurate, especially in your discipline.

They stopped our driven lineout by sacking it. I thought they may have caught the ball and tried to out-drive us more. Apart from that one successful crack at our scrum, scrum-time was pretty even.

I also thought they might have kicked a bit more, but the main thing was they stopped our line speed by coming really hard off Aaron Smith at '9', through Sonny Bill Williams and other big runners. It wasn't a typical All Blacks performance in terms of throwing the ball around and being expansive. But it was effective and they were physical.

The analysts also provided us with stats on all the players: tackles, carries, passes made, rucks hit and tackles missed.

We had too many turnovers. When we have the ball, we've got to keep it better. They had some phases of play where they put us under pressure, and when we had a chance to get the ball back we turned it over straight away.

We have to be more physical in the contact area, especially with our tackling. We also didn't control key moments, like Liam Williams dropping that ball, and we were caught by one scrum and one quick tap.

All in all though, there wasn't a massive amount wrong and we were pretty clear about what needed to be fixed.

I got together with the coaches at 11.30 to pick the team for the Hurricanes game. That was pretty straightforward. It was the same pack and half-backs that played against the Chiefs, and we brought in Jonathan Joseph, George North and Tommy Seymour. We moved Jack Nowell to full-back and had Jared Payne and George Kruis on the bench along with the six players we had called up. Jack had played exceptionally well at wing, and we wanted to have a look at him at full-back, and Tommy also deserved to play.

Even though I didn't think Alun Wyn played as well as he could have in the first Test, George Kruis had that knock-on, had a ball stripped off him, gave away a couple of penalties and had fallen off a couple of tackles. I was however really impressed that he approached me and said that he knew his performance wasn't at the level it needed to be and that if required he would be better next week.

We didn't discuss the second Test team much at this meeting, but if there was to be a change in the second-row, we discussed whether Courtney Lawes or Iain Henderson would come into the equation.

We were looking at starting Sam Warburton in the second Test, because we thought he was good when he came on for that last thirty minutes.

We announced the Hurricanes' match-day twenty-three to the squad at 12.10, and were straight on the bus to the airport for our charter to Wellington at 1.30. On arrival we were taken by coach to the Rydges hotel.

Watching the video again, it was clear that the All Blacks had pinpointed Conor Murray's box-kicking as a strength. When I reviewed the incident where Jerome Kaino dives in on his leg, I thought: 'If he gets that wrong, he injures Conor.' It didn't look like he was trying to make a tackle, or like he was diving to try and block the ball. He hit Conor's standing leg after the ball had gone.

In other plays involving our scrum-half, Aaron Smith and Owen Franks were penalised for coming through before he cleared the ball, Brodie Retallick pushed him over twice after Conor got his kick away, and twice they came through and hit Conor after he passed.

So that afternoon I sent an email to Alain Rolland, with 'targeting our 9' as a theme. I said I was happy that Jaco Peyper protected Conor on two occasions; however I felt he was being targeted on our exit plays as well. We didn't send videos on everything but we noted that: 'Black 9 had come in and played 9'; 'Black 6 targeted 9 standing leg after kick has been made'; 'Black 3 playing 9'; and, in thirty-seven minutes and thirty-nine minutes, 'Black 4 had just pushed him over.'

We highlighted four incidents where the All Blacks had neck-rolled and this hadn't been picked up by the TMO. We asked for some clarity on the maul sacking and had a couple of questions on the lineout, such as coming in within the ten metres, and also, '2 going early outside the fifteen as a defender, before the ball is off the lineout.'

As a final point, we referred to entry into the maul by 'Black 8 just after half-time' when Kieran Read definitely came in from the side, and then Retallick on the other one that we lost. Most coaches will ask the ref to look at a number of situations and calls in a match to get some clarity and question some decisions.

Alain replied to say they'd already had a workshop that day concerning a number of issues, and they would send my email and the clips on to Jaco Peyper. Jaco would come back to me tomorrow as Alain himself would be travelling to Tokyo, but that he'd be in Wellington on Friday if I wanted to meet him.

At 7pm I went across the road with our media guys and Rory Best, who was captain again, for the press conference, where I raised the issue of the All Blacks targeting Conor.

I felt that I was well within my rights to defend one of our players by highlighting this. I wasn't bitching and moaning. I just asked that the officials look to protect Conor within the boundaries of the law. That's all I said, but I feel at the moment it doesn't matter what I say, it will be twisted into a negative anyway.

I had spoken to Conor about it. He knew that they would try to put him under pressure, but he felt that he had been roughed up a little bit.

Of course, once I raised the issue, this led to plenty of follow-up questions, both at the main press conference and then, in a separate session, with the travelling media.

I said: 'From my point of view, if someone pushes him afterwards, that's fine but diving at his leg? I know other teams have used that in the past and I think Joe [Schmidt] has come out and was pretty critical about that being a tactic other teams have used against Conor. It's just a safety issue for me. I'd hate to see someone dive at his leg and have him blow a knee and then wreck his rugby career.

'It's just a case of making sure he's being looked after and protected, and not harassed after he's box-kicked. We will probably just get some clarity from the referee later in the week.

'For me, it's just about protecting the players and making sure they are safe. That's my biggest concern. I will be asking politely that the officials look at that and make sure they protect him.'

## Monday, 26 June

A good night's sleep and a brand new day. It was time to park the first Test and focus on our last midweek match tomorrow against the Hurricanes. The kickers were down early as they were leaving the hotel at 8.50 to go to the Westpac Stadium. The rest of the squad had pool recovery and optional weights at 9.45. At 11 o'clock we had a meeting with Rory Best, Iain Henderson, Greig Laidlaw, Dan Biggar, CJ Stander, Justin Tipuric and Robbie Henshaw – the spine of the team.

Those guys had been excellent against the Chiefs, and this game was a chance to set us up in Wellington for the week. We discussed how the Hurricanes might approach the game tactically, and maybe do what the All Blacks did by coming hard off '9' and also attacking the short side. We also knew they would kick more.

At 11.15 we had a squad meeting. We reviewed Saturday's game and then previewed the Hurricanes match. The Analysts, Rhodri Bown, Mike Hughes and Vinnie Hammond, showed some footage on the video screen in the team room. They began with some scrums, and Graham Rowntree was obviously disappointed with the one that led to Rieko Ioane's first try, but the overall feeling was that we managed the scrum pretty well.

Defensively, Andy Farrell spoke about his disappointment with the collisions and just getting off the line when they came off '9'. We needed to be a bit more aggressive. We'd fallen off or soaked up a few tackles, and he stressed that was an area which needed to improve.

Rob Howley spoke mainly about finishing off the chances that we've created, showing examples of us getting in behind them. But we lacked a little accuracy with some of our calling. There were also a couple of unnecessary offloads, such as the ones by Tadhg Furlong and Anthony Watson which didn't go to hand. On those occasions, we needed to keep hold of the ball to maintain pressure.

I wrapped things up by saying tomorrow's game would be a big one for us, both in terms of the opportunities for players and to continue the momentum from the win over the Chiefs. Another win and a strong performance would be good for everyone's confidence.

I repeated that there were things that we think are fixable, and are not major issues. While we had to bring more physicality next Saturday, I questioned whether the All Blacks could bring the same emotion to the second Test. Four of the tight five had played against us for the Crusaders and would have been hurting from that game. They would have been grilled and pretty pumped up for the first Test, so they turned up absolutely 100 per cent mentally focused.

That was the key message. Can the All Blacks be as good next time? I didn't think they could. Will we be better? Yes, we will be.

We set off in two buses for the Jerry Collins Stadium, about twenty-five minutes away. The match-day twenty-three had their Captain's Run, and so the non-twenty-three departed twenty minutes after them. The ground is the home of the North club, or Northern United, and used to be known as Porirua Park. It was the club where Jerry Collins played and was officially renamed after him last year. Jerry had died tragically in a car accident in France in 2015. There were lights there if we needed them, and the pitch was in great condition. The Hurricanes play warm-up games there, and it's a really good facility.

The boys were nice and sharp for the Captain's Run, which involved a few exit plays, half a dozen attack plays off lineouts, some restarts and then finished with the forwards doing a few lineouts. The non-twenty-three guys were still pretty sore from Saturday, so it was mostly an organisational jog through. We went through some lineout patterns, including a chip-kick option using Sean O'Brien off a lineout, scrum set-up, and a kick and chase. Before the first Test we'd spoken about kicking the ball to Ioane's wing, because he's not great in the air, but we didn't put the ball on him once. So we had to target him this time.

We went back to the hotel for some lunch and gave the squad some downtime in the afternoon. Before dinner that evening, at 6.45pm, we met with Jamie George, George Kruis, Peter O'Mahony, Conor Murray, Owen Farrell, Sam Warburton and Johnny Sexton. This was a leaders' meeting to talk about the first Test.

I had spoken on the Monday before about all of us, senior players and coaches, making sure that we didn't overcoach and try not to overload. The players needed to monitor themselves over the week, so I asked them: 'Did we get that right?'

Jamie George said that two or three forwards had felt heavy legged and in the video they did look that way. Subsequently, when I met with the officials at 7pm in their hotel, Jaco Peyper revealed that first Test was probably the fastest game he had ever refereed, including the Tri Nations and the Six Nations.

The feedback from Jamie, in addition to our own review, confirmed we had done too much in the week. We did a double session on the Thursday, units in the morning and then in the afternoon, so this week we decided to have a session on the Tuesday and then just one on the Thursday.

At that leadership meeting, we also discussed the physical challenge of playing the All Blacks, taking opportunities, that one costly scrum and that there were a few things to work on in defence. We also spoke about the role which those guys had in generating excitement and energy for the whole group throughout the week.

Jaco Peyper had also emailed me back that day. He thanked me for the feedback and agreed that Conor had been targeted. He added that they had made it a focus for the assistant referees in the second half once Conor had made them aware of it, and would do so for the remaining games.

They didn't see any issues with the tackler releasing at the breakdown, but that they should have picked up a couple of the neck rolls in real time. On review, they also admitted that one maul sacking should have been a penalty, and after a discussion they agreed that the Kieran Read decision was a marginal call but that it probably was side entry.

All this was pretty unusual, because you don't ever get a response from the post-match referee's analysis along the lines of 'Yes. Yes. Agree.'

*Tuesday, 27 June*
*Hurricanes v Lions, Westpac Stadium, Wellington*

This was the morning that Luke Broadley and Dave Barton informed me that the *NZ Herald* had portrayed me as a clown. Again.

I didn't bother looking at it, but I was pretty disappointed. Everything I say is being twisted, particularly by the *NZ Herald*. I was so excited about the tour, but this kind of thing has really taken the gloss off it.

This is getting so personal. It's people writing about me who don't even know me personally; people I've never even spoken to, making assumptions about me as a person, as a coach, who's influencing me, and who's not influencing me in my decision-making.

Someone had told me that Steve Hansen had rung a radio station the previous day, which I found kind of strange. He said: 'It's a predictable comment from Gatland, isn't it? Like two weeks ago, it was we cheated in the scrums. Last week it was blocking and now he's saying this. But it's really, really disappointing to hear it, because what he's implying is that we're deliberately going out to injure someone and that's not the case. We've never been like that, and as a New Zealander I would expect he would know the New Zealand psyche. It's not about intentionally trying to hurt anybody, it's about playing hard and fair.'

I had just asked that the officials protect Conor Murray. I hadn't gone out of my way to accuse the All Blacks of cheating, or claim they had played dirtily, or criticised their tactics or anything like that.

I was very surprised about Steve ringing a radio station. It's not something I would do as a coach. Maybe he's reading everything and knows everything that is being said. I'm trying not to. But I was being briefed by our media guys. They were telling me what was going on, what the *NZ Herald* were doing, what some journalist or ex-player might be saying, or what Steve Hansen said.

At press conferences, I have been determined not to give anyone the satisfaction of thinking that the negative media coverage was affecting me.

I've had so many supportive texts from friends and people in general, and Trudi's getting plenty of them as well. She received one from a good friend of ours called Kevin. 'Hi Trudi, thanks so much for the kind offer of the ticket. I really felt for you guys over the last couple of weeks. I know this goes with the territory up to a point, but the media stuff is just trash and the best that can be said about the people that are pumping it out is that it shows how unprofessional and lacking in integrity they are. Enjoy Wellington, and best of luck for Warren and his team tomorrow.'

Another friend of ours, Rebecca, texted: 'Hi Trudi, I just wanted to let you know the incredible support out here in Joe Bloggs' land for the whole

Lions tour. It's been so amazing to have all the Lions supporters here last week, and then in Rotorua and Auckland. We have had wonderful chats with supporters in cafés and bars, they are a great lot. In addition they are also so complimentary of Warren and the players. Please don't take any notice of the media. As always they are running their own circus which in no way reflects what the public think. Congrats on Bryn's Blues contract. Exciting times for the family. Would love to catch up once you guys catch your breath.'

That morning, the players had breakfast and monitoring and then at 10am the non-twenty-three did weights, followed by units and rugby at the Jerry Collins Stadium. We took the forwards out a bit earlier. They wanted to do a few lineouts and scrums for fifteen minutes before the backs came onto the pitch.

After they warmed up, we came together and ran a contact drill. A big focus this week was the contact stuff and being much more aggressive with the All Blacks in clearing past the ball.

Then we ran an attack drill and focused on staying connected with the forwards; having the option out the back and a tip-on pass. We introduced another call where we could hit the backs flat, in front of the forwards.

We split again for about twelve minutes and the focus for the forwards was purely on scrums. We then did a defensive block in which we looked at collision dominance, and defending the All Blacks runners off '9'. After that we did some exits and some kick pressure, not driving the lineout and box-kicking, but just catching and giving a different delivery to Conor so we can put pressure on Ioane in the air.

This was followed by some kick-offs and attack kicks before we ran the attack patterns we'd walked through the day before.

We trained for forty-eight minutes. It was a good session. It was tough, there was an intensity there, and we were really pleased with it.

I saw John Plumtree that afternoon back at the hotel and had a great chat with him. He was Head Coach of the Sharks in South Africa and Forwards

Coach with Ireland before coming home to be the Forwards Coach with the Hurricanes. I asked him how his sons were getting on. One of them had done his anterior cruciate ligament, and had to have an operation, while the other boy was a second-row and hoping to make the New Zealand Schools side. Then he spoke to a few of our guys. I saw him talking to Conor.

The Hurricanes' CEO, Avan Lee, came up to me and said he couldn't believe some of the crap in the media, and wanted to tell me that ninety per cent of New Zealanders don't feel that what's been written is reflective of how they feel. That was nice of him to say that.

We had to make a late change after Eanna Falvey told me Jared had been suffering from a headache. You can't take any risks these days, and Eanna was worried whether it was related to the knock Jared got last week. So, we pulled him out of the game and we had to put Leigh Halfpenny on the bench.

Some of the match-day twenty-three had taken up the option of primers in the afternoon, before we met at 3.50 to take the bus to a little park up the street for our walk-through. There was no one there initially, but within fifteen minutes about thirty or so Lions supporters were watching us practise some lineouts. It was like a flock of seagulls at the beach once they see a bit of bread, appearing from out of nowhere and descending en masse.

The foyer in the Rydges hotel is quite small, and when we met up again at 6 o'clock someone said it was mad down there, absolutely jam-packed with Lions supporters.

I told the team that there were opportunities for the weekend. I thanked Rory. He'd done a brilliant job in leading this team, which they had begun to call 'The Team of Rory Best'. We had a bit of a giggle about that.

We again stressed how important the night was in the context of setting the tone for the week and Rory said: 'For some of us this may be our last game on tour, or our last game for the Lions.' When you put that in perspective, it should make for a highly motivated group of players.

As we came downstairs to board the bus for the match, we were almost mobbed in the hotel foyer as a cordon of family, friends and fans roared us on our way.

When we arrived at the ground, I went into the changing room and did my three television and radio pre-match interviews before we had the warm-up. Some of the players realised it could be their last game on tour and spoke about that, why it was an important game because it was the next one, and that it was important for the squad as a whole. They were in a good place.

Interestingly, the All Blacks camp had released a few players for this game: Julian Savea, Jordie Barrett and Ngani Laumape. The Hurricanes had nine of the starting team from the defeat to the Chiefs two and a half weeks ago which had ended their unbeaten home record this season. But this was good. We were playing the Super Rugby champions in front of another packed stadium, and it was a pretty strong Hurricanes side.

After leaving the changing room, we walked up the stands to the coaches' box. The amount of people, both Lions supporters and New Zealanders, shouting 'Gats, best of luck!' or 'Good luck Gats!' was remarkable.

But the goodwill didn't extend to the pitch. There was a fair bit of needle from the start. Our guys wanted to impose themselves and make a statement. Julian Savea was up for it too, and they stressed us at the start. But after a penalty by Dan Biggar, Tommy Seymour made a good read in defence, forced a loose pass which Greig Laidlaw read well, and Tommy supported him for the try. It was 10–0 to us and a great start. I was happy with that. But unfortunately Robbie Henshaw went off with what looked like a bad shoulder injury and so we brought Leigh Halfpenny on, moved Jack Nowell to the wing and shifted George North into '12' and left Jonathan Joseph at '13'.

Dan executed a nice chip-kick out of defence for JJ and he was tackled in the air. Dan made it 13–0 from the penalty, but then the Hurricanes came back and scored a try. Laumape made a big break up the middle, and they picked and drove until Callum Gibbins scored.

Laumape continued to cause us problems. But Dan kicked another penalty

**Maori All Blacks, Rotorua International Stadium, Rotorua, 17 June**

*Left:* Another warm welcome from the Maoris.

*Below:* Leigh Halfpenny slots one of his six successful penalties.

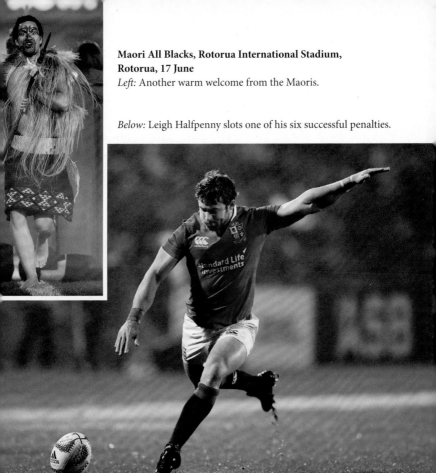

*Below:* The Maori All Blacks treated us to another *haka* at the post-match reception.

**Chiefs, Waikato Stadium, Hamilton, 20 June**
*Above:* A pre-match *haka* this time, courtesy of the Chiefs.

*Above:* Jared Payne goes over in our 34-6 victory.

*Right:* Dan Biggar enjoys the reception of the amazing Lions fans in the tunnel at the end of the game.

**FIRST TEST:
New Zealand,
Eden Park,
Auckland,
24 June**
*Right:* Codie
Taylor surges for
the line to score
the game's first
try.

*Left:* Sean
O'Brien goes
over to claw
back the deficit
to 13-8.

*Right:* Rieko
Ioane stretches
the All Blacks'
lead with the
first of his two
second-half
tries.

*Left:* Rhys Webb grabs a
consolation score in the
last minute.

**Hurricanes, Westpac Stadium, Wellington, 27 June**
*Above:* Tommy Seymour dives over for our first try, and the first of his two in the match.
*Below:* A rampant George North bursts through the Hurricanes' defence to score.
The game was drawn 31-31.

**SECOND TEST:**
**New Zealand, Westpac Stadium, Wellington, 1 July**
*Above:* Taulupe Faletau dives for the line and we're up and running in Wellington.
*Below:* Referee Jerome Garces shows Sonny Bill Williams a red card on 25 minutes.

*Above:* Conor Murray has the strength to go over for our second try.

*Below:* Owen Farrell slots the winning penalty to give us a morale-boosting 24-21 victory.

*Above:* Ken Owens and myself enjoy the beautiful backdrop during a training session in our time in Queenstown.

**THIRD TEST: New Zealand, Eden Park, Auckland, 8 July**
*Right:* Ngani Laumape crosses for the All Blacks' opening try.

*Above*: Elliot Daly makes his monster penalty.

*Left*: The emotion is there for all to see as Owen Farrell has just kicked the penalty 12 minutes from time which tied the game, and left the series drawn 1-1. A score-line of 15-15 barely tells the story.

*Above:* The two teams mingle to celebrate a monumental Test Match series.

*Left:* The two captains, Kieran Read and Sam Warburton, shake hands and share the spoils.

*Above:* I thought it would be fun to attend the post-match press conference with an accessory.

*Left:* With Steve Hansen, catching up after the game.

and then put up a good bomb, Leigh chased it really well and when the ball went loose Iain Henderson showed lovely hands and George North scored under the posts. At 23–7, we were pretty happy when we went down from the coaches' box into the changing room at half-time.

The main message during the break was to keep controlling the game, which only made what happened at the start of the second half so disappointing. We were walking up the stairs to the box when there was a huge roar and I turned around to see the Hurricanes had scored.

They shortened us up and Savea broke through the middle off an inside pass before Laumape scored. Dan couldn't stop him at that range. Barrett then kicked a penalty before Dan did as well to leave us 26–17 ahead.

Iain Henderson started carrying really well then, and he probably should have scored when he was held up on the line. CJ Stander carried strongly off the base of the scrum and after a few phases Dan, JJ, Jack and Leigh put Tommy over in the corner. That was a really nice try.

Unfortunately, Tommy slipped when trying to narrow the angle and touched down out wider than he intended, so Dan missed the conversion. It was his first miss of the night but it was another costly one, and we've had a few of those.

We were in complete control again, and it would have been game over after another big carry by CJ when JJ chipped through and George gathered to touch down. It was a lovely piece of play, but George had stepped into touch. If he had dived off his left, I think he would have scored. But, in taking another step, he put his foot on the touchline.

Then everything changed when Iain cleared out Jordie Barrett at a ruck, but in doing so lifted him and drove him into the ground. Initially Romain Poite had decided it was only a penalty but George Ayoub, the TMO, encouraged him to have another look at an angle that he had already shown Romain. A referee like Nigel Owens would have gone, 'No I've looked at that, I think it's a penalty but it's not deserving of a yellow card.' If the TMO had said straight away 'I think it's a yellow card' then, OK, I would have accepted that. I was disappointed in how the decision was reached. But in saying that, it wasn't very clever by Iain. It was unnecessary. He didn't need to lift him. It proved to be a massive turning point in the game.

It went from our penalty to theirs, and we were down to fourteen men again for ten minutes. We went from having sixty-eight per cent possession in the first sixty-five minutes, to twenty-five per cent in the last fifteen minutes, and then they scored two tries. We were 31–14 up, we've missed a conversion, squandered George's opportunity, had a reverse penalty and a yellow card, and all of a sudden it's 31–31.

During this period, they had a lineout five metres from their own line and Justin Tipuric was caught offside again. We'd spoken about this. That's the third time on this tour that we've encroached ten metres. It was another avoidable, soft penalty which has relieved the pressure on them.

Also, when we kicked, and kicked well, we put them under so much pressure. Yet we only kicked the ball eight times in the second half. We tried to get the message onto the pitch through Neil Jenkins.

'Jenks, tell them we need to try a little chip behind them.'

'I don't know how many times I've been getting the message on, they're just not doing it,' said a frustrated Jenks.

Some of our exit plays weren't good enough and we've made a rod for our own backs. At 31–31, I'm sitting in the box thinking: 'Jesus, we're going to lose this game that we've dominated and controlled because we've shot ourselves in the foot.'

But then, still down to fourteen men, we managed to survive twenty-one phases in defence before we got a turnover. The boys were brave there. Poite and Ayoub went back a few phases and penalised Laumape for a neck roll on Leigh. So we got the ball back in the last couple of minutes and, for me, it's an absolute certainty that they collapsed our lineout drive. We'd gone about ten metres. It should have been a penalty to us. OK, we would still have had to kick it from about forty metres.

I haven't seen anything as obvious as that for a long time – a player at the back of the maul collapsing it – and there was side entry too. The officials just didn't want to make such a big call at the end of the game.

That said, not for the first time, we have been the architects of our own downfall because of some of the calls and decisions we've made.

At the end, we went for a drop-goal which was too far out. We'd been closer before that and in a better position, but then ended up being further away. Dan had been screaming for the ball the first time but it wasn't passed to him, and then he actually ripped the ball back himself after we turned it over.

So we got out of there with a draw, although at the end it felt more like a defeat. Everyone was raving about what a great game of rugby it had been, but it didn't feel like that to us. We played some good rugby, scored a couple of good tries and sixty-two points were scored. Yes, fantastic. But as coaches we were disappointed, and the players were also disappointed.

As well as bringing on Leigh for Robbie in the first half and Finn Russell as a temporary replacement for Dan early in the second, we only made one tactical substitution when we replaced Courtney Lawes with George Kruis with twenty-five minutes to go. We left the other five late call-ups on the bench.

We talked about making more replacements. With seventy minutes gone, Dan Cole had run himself into the ground. But hindsight is a great thing. At 31–17, if we'd brought those guys on and had drawn or lost, the whole focus would have been on the quality of those players. We would have been absolutely slaughtered.

Then, with two or three minutes remaining, was it worth putting someone on at that stage? It would have been just a token gesture. Actually, during an injury break, before Dan Cole recovered, we were going to make that substitution. Tom Francis was down beside the pitch waiting to come on. I felt bad for him. I feel bad for all of them because they've come in, worked hard and haven't complained.

When all the squad were in the changing room after the game, I thanked the guys who'd come in. I said I knew they'd be disappointed that they didn't get a bit more of an opportunity, but they had been good for us. All the boys gave them a round of applause.

Then I spoke to the rights holders before going into the main press conference. Rory Best was getting some treatment so he wasn't able to join me. It was there where I admitted that the backlash to calling in the 'Geography Six', as they were now being referred to, was a factor in me not bringing them on. Many people were surprised by that admission and criticised me for it.

I was, inevitably, also asked about the *NZ Herald* clown stuff. 'I haven't seen that,' I said. 'Which newspaper was that? I don't know what that's in reference to. Was it in reference to Michael Cheika?'

I was told it was related to what Steve Hansen and I had been saying in the last few days. 'I haven't read anything from Hansen's quotes,' I said. 'The only thing I heard was that he had rung up a radio station. I thought that was quite unusual for an international coach. But I'm not worried about what Steve Hansen says or what any newspaper draws me up as. I just hope it was a happy clown!'

I had used that line before. I genuinely hadn't seen the story, but I didn't want to give them any satisfaction from it whatsoever. Journalists have egos as well. They don't like the idea that you don't read them, or that they have no impact on you.

We were on the bus by 11.30 and back in the hotel by 11.45. The hotel foyer was again packed. We couldn't go down there. We wouldn't have got anywhere near the bar for starters. So I had a couple of drinks in the room with Trudi and the kids, and then went down to the team room for a while and had a drink and a chat with the other coaches.

# 18

## Lions to New Zealand 2017

Damned if I did, and damned if I didn't. From the day I was announced as the Lions head coach, on 7 September 2016, I revealed that I had spoken to the Lions board about the possibility of bringing in additional players as cover, a week before the first Test, and have them sit on the replacements' bench against the Chiefs on the preceding Tuesday.

I highlighted that Wales were in New Zealand and Samoa, Scotland would be in Australia, England in Argentina and Ireland in Japan. I said: 'There is potentially an opportunity to maybe bring in four or five to sit on the bench. That is my thought process at the moment. You want to protect that Test twenty-three. It made a massive difference in 2013.'

Four years ago in Australia, we had brought players in to sit on the bench for the Brumbies game to protect as many of the Test twenty-three as we could. We didn't expose any of the first Test starting fifteen except for Alex Corbisiero, who was a sub in Canberra.

'That was important,' I said at the press conference. 'It's getting the balance right. You don't want the squad to be too big and unwieldy. How do you keep it small enough so everyone feels a part of it, feels like they have an opportunity, so you are not carrying two or three just for the sake of it?'

I had spoken with Joe Schmidt, Gregor Townsend, Eddie Jones and Robin McBryde, who would be the caretaker coach of the Welsh squad for their games against Tonga in Auckland and Samoa in Apia. The home nations were all on tour anyway and they were aware that if we had injuries they could have players called up. They also knew that we were going to be bringing players in to protect the match-day squad for that first Test. The original plan was that these call-ups would join the squad for a few days and then go home. But then we thought if they're going to be here anyway, we might as well keep them for the week of the second Test as well.

Ireland were playing one match in America and two in Japan, the second of which was the day of our first Test. Joe asked which players from his squad could potentially be called up. Garry Ringrose would definitely have been added if we lost any of our centres, and we also spoke about Simon Zebo if there were injuries to our outside backs.

Gregor was taking over at Scotland, who were playing Italy in Singapore, Australia in Sydney on the same day as our first Test, and Fiji in Suva a week later. Finn Russell was next in line at out-half, and Gregor kept me informed about some of the other players who were performing well on tour. I also spoke to Greig Laidlaw and he thought Allan Dell might be a good addition.

I had spoken with Eddie Jones a few months before, and then with Steve Borthwick, because he was in regular contact with Eddie. England were touring Argentina, where they played two games on 10 and 17 June, which was a week before our first Test.

We didn't finalise the six names until Wednesday, 14 June, the day after the Highlanders game. We outlined what we required. We needed cover at

'1', '2' and '3', in the second-row and at '9' and '10'. We decided to call in Kristian Dacey, Cory Hill, Tomas Francis and Gareth Davies from the Welsh squad the day after they played against Tonga in Auckland. We had to wait until they played for Wales before notifying them, so they could concentrate on that game. They joined us in Rotorua on the day we played the Maori All Blacks. We announced it publicly that morning.

We also called up Allan Dell and Finn Russell after Scotland had beaten Australia in Sydney the same day. Similarly, we had to wait until that night before notifying them and making it public, so they could focus on that match. They joined us the next day in Hamilton.

There were a few things to consider in all of this. I tried to look at it from everyone's point of view and we also looked back on past experience. In 2013 we brought players in who had to travel a long distance, and we also experienced what had happened to us in Whangarei on the first week of the tour, when a few of the players were still tired and jet lagged.

This time round, the Welsh players were already in New Zealand, and it was a relatively short hop for the Scottish boys from Sydney. It seemed the sensible thing to do.

We decided, given our experience, that there was a greater risk of players suffering from jet lag if we called them in from England's tour in Argentina or Ireland's in Japan. Ireland were playing their first of two Tests in Japan on that Saturday, England weren't even in Buenos Aires. They were another three hours away in Santa Fe for their second Test there.

I told the squad in Rotorua after lunch on the day of the Maori game that these guys were coming in, who the six guys were and that they were coming purely as cover so that we could give as many of the match-day twenty-three as possible an opportunity to prepare properly for the first two Tests. 'They'll be here for nine days and then they're flying out,' I said.

The players didn't say anything really. I didn't expect them to. I had to explain what we were doing, because I'd heard complaints from outside the camp that we were devaluing the Lions jersey. I spoke to Sam Warburton and he completely understood the rationale behind it.

I was asked why we didn't decide a little sooner and bring in, say, Joe Launchbury as well as Cian Healy and Dylan Hartley, a week earlier. To be honest, I wanted those players to come in as late as possible and we would have needed those coming in from Argentina and Japan to be there at least five days before they were involved in a match.

We also weren't really in a position to decide a week earlier. We wanted to wait until after the Highlanders game to see what the injury situation was like and whether we had a reasonably clean bill of health.

Maybe it was the wrong decision, but we made that call at the time and I thought it was the right one. I can understand people having different opinions.

On reflection, if I was to do this again I would do it differently. I would name the call-ups when the squad was announced, explaining when they would join the squad and how long they would be there for. Hindsight is a great thing. Two or three of the six we called in were the next in line anyway, and probably would have been out here sooner had there been injuries.

I like to think that I'm honest, and part of coaching is that you take on board the views of others, such as ex-Lions coaches and players, who thought we had been devaluing the jersey. That resonated with me. There was some validity to their views. I let that influence our decision not to bring those players on against the Hurricanes, but in hindsight I regret it.

I think it was the right decision not to bring them on in the first game, against the Chiefs, when we only used Allan Dell as a temporary replacement for James Haskell when Joe Marler was sin-binned. Similarly, we only brought on Finn Russell as a temporary replacement against the Hurricanes when Dan Biggar required an HIA, but I'm not sure that was the right decision.

Part of the reason we didn't make any subs against the Chiefs was because we were comfortably winning the game. I think that was also a good message we sent to the squad; it confirmed these players were here as cover. I thought that was important.

Against the Hurricanes, I don't think that would have mattered as much, and I can understand the disappointment of those six players. People were also really critical after the Hurricanes game that we didn't use more replacements.

But I also think we were in a lose-lose situation, because we were 31–17 up, Iain Henderson was sin-binned and then they came back to draw 31–31. Imagine if we put five or six of those guys on and it had been the same outcome? We would have been criticised for using them and the players themselves would have been accused of weakening the team. I'm not saying that would have happened, but if it had, some people would have taken that line.

Some of the squad thought that we should have brought in players from Argentina, and I respect that. But there is no doubt that the Test squad benefited from the presence of the call-ups in helping their preparation.

The game has changed, in that squads of twenty-three are now almost always used on match-days. In my playing days, it was the fifteen who started and replacements only came on if there was an injury. I don't feel particularly sorry for them, but I think we should have made some changes. I appreciate what they did, and their presence on the tour. I think it was critical to us winning the second Test. In our preparation for that game, we had a good week's training. None of our second Test starting fifteen were involved against the Hurricanes, and only three of the replacements – Jack Nowell, Courtney Lawes and CJ Stander – played on that Tuesday night.

We did something very similar in 2013 and there was much less of an outcry, but everything has changed since then. If you look back on the players we called up four years back, people would be much more critical of those call-ups now.

We brought Shane Williams out of retirement from Test rugby. He'd been playing club rugby in Japan. Christian Wade travelled from England's tour in Argentina to Australia, which is nearer than New Zealand, and his body clock was all over the place. He didn't have his greatest game against the Brumbies. But we made what we thought was the right decision then too.

I was talking to one journalist on this tour who came to training, and he said his boss was adamant that bringing in the players was a knee-jerk reaction to a couple of defeats. The journalist had explained to him: 'No, no, Warren mentioned this as far back as the press conference in Edinburgh last September, when it was first announced that he would be the head coach.' But his boss said: 'No, that's bull****.'

The journalist stuck to his guns, otherwise it would have been written up as a panic decision. That's what you're dealing with. Some people don't want the truth. They just want a negative headline.

Maybe bringing out six players this time is partly why there's been a bigger fuss; that and the advent of social media. But we haven't deviated from this or any of our messages all along. We haven't changed our tack. Everything we've done has been as we've said we were going to do it: preparing for the Test series, that we'll get better, and the need to protect as many players as we can before the first Test. In fact, it had been planned all along, and we thought it prudent to keep those players for the Hurricanes match.

I reflected on it all twenty-four hours after the Hurricanes game and thought: 'Actually, that wasn't the right decision. We should have made a few changes, and brought some fresh legs on.' It was the wrong call.

I suppose it's like everything in life, or everything in coaching. You make what you think is the right decision at the time and then you reflect back afterwards and think: 'What have I learnt from that situation? How would I do it differently in the future?'

That's life. That's coaching. I've made lots of mistakes, but I like to think

I've learnt from them. It's all very well people being critical when you're not the one making that call. And it wasn't just my decision, it was a collective decision along with the other coaches.

Against the Hurricanes, we were also asking some players to play eighty minutes for the second game in a row, something they wouldn't have done for a long time. So we could have made those changes.

Allan Dell went well for his brief time on the pitch against the Chiefs, especially for one scrum, and we could therefore have brought him on for Joe Marler. Tom Francis should have come on for Dan Cole, who had run himself into the ground. We also should have put Gareth Davies on.

I don't think there's anything wrong with people having opinions because it's all about opinions, isn't it? Selections are just a matter of opinion, as are tactics. Ironically, as I admitted before the tour, the model that Clive Woodward used in 2005 in New Zealand is probably the correct one. You virtually need two complete teams to be able to cope with such a tough fixture schedule. However, the same question applied then: were you devaluing the jersey by picking more players and having two different teams?

You could argue the case both ways. Maybe it is devaluing the jersey. But maybe it's also the best means of taking on a schedule like this one and giving us the best chance of success.

## 19

## LET'S GET PHYSICAL

### Lions to New Zealand 2017

*Wednesday, 28 June*

Our first day after a midweek game without any travelling; and our first week in the same city and same hotel. Everyone had a bit of a lie-in for the first time.

I spoke to Gabby this morning. She had come down the previous day and had been through a fairly torrid 24 hours. She and her boyfriend Sam had been the victim of identity fraud on social media, and Sam's picture had been put on a gay website. Apparently this is called 'catfish', where people use pictures from a person's profile on Facebook or Instagram to create a fake identity. I just laughed out loud, because I knew there was no way Sam would have known anything about that!

I was not due to meet up with the other coaches until 6pm. So I had some time to myself to think more about the team for the second Test. I was still disappointed that we'd let slip a winning position the night before. But, when I thought about it, apart from Beauden Barrett, TJ Perenara and Ardie Savea, who were all significant losses for them, the Hurricanes were pretty much at full-strength. It wasn't a bad performance overall, considering we were reasonably comfortable for much of the game before we allowed them back into it.

In our coaches' meeting, initially we talked about the Hurricanes' match, about our game management, our discipline and especially the yellow card. Iain Henderson was a bit unlucky but you can't really argue against that yellow.

Then we discussed the team and replacements for the second Test. We had quite a significant debate about the second-row, both the starting combination and the cover on the bench. We also talked about the back-row at length.

I felt that we needed to bring Maro in from the start. He has a physicality, an energy and a work-rate that we lacked a little in the first Test. So he was definitely going to return. Then we had to decide who was the best choice to partner him. Ultimately, we went with Alun Wyn because of his proven big-match experience.

We were happy with Courtney Lawes' performances on tour, and especially against the Chiefs and the Hurricanes. He'd played on the Tuesday, which would limit his training that week, so we chose him on the bench. This meant we lost a little at the lineout in deciding not to pick George Kruis.

We brought Sam Warburton back for Peter O'Mahony at blindside. Again, we needed Sam's physicality in the collisions and at the breakdown.

We also left a final decision until tomorrow as to whether we'd pick Pete or CJ Stander on the bench. I think we'll probably name CJ, as he brings a strong engine off the bench. So conceivably Pete could go from starting as captain one week to sitting out the next, which I realise is tough on him. But this is about picking what we believe is the best team and best combinations to beat the All Blacks and level the series.

We decided to start Johnny Sexton at '10' and move Owen Farrell to '12', and put Ben Te'o on the bench. Ben played well in the first Test. He carried and defended well, but he didn't pass the ball. He had eight strong carries and no passes. A prime example was after the break by Jonathan Davies. Ben had to pass the ball, but he tried to cut inside when he just had to attack the outside and then give it. We had Sean O'Brien and Toby Faletau on the outside — it should have been pass-pass-try.

We felt that Johnny and Owen together would surprise the All Blacks a little. We thought they might go after us again in that area, but we had to win to keep the tour alive. We would have to score tries, and Johnny and Owen gave us two playmakers with good kicking games. They're also both very experienced players.

It's interesting because in the last few years not many teams have had ball-playing '12s', but Owen gave us that option. He is one of those few players at the moment who can play '10' or '12' at Test level. Dan Carter could do that for the All Blacks and the Crusaders. I felt it was the right decision, and Rob Howley and Andy Farrell thought so as well.

The weather conditions were not meant to be great, but with New Zealand the long-term forecast may say one thing but come Saturday it could be completely different. We will have Ben on the bench so we could make that change if we need to.

We brought in Jack Nowell for Leigh Halfpenny on the bench. Again that was a tough call. But I had been impressed by Jack. He hadn't had a lot of opportunities in the first few games. It didn't go his way, but he's got energy, a great work ethic and he played well against the Chiefs and the Hurricanes.

Unfortunately for them, George North and Robbie Henshaw have been ruled out of the tour. George has a grade one tear to his hamstring, while Robbie has suffered a torn pectoral muscle. We all felt really bad for both of them. Although George has been around a while, they are both young enough to make another tour.

Later that evening we had a management dinner back at the hotel. I have still been getting lots of supportive messages and texts from people, including one from Malky Mackay, the former Scottish footballer whom I got to know when he was manager of Cardiff City.

I received another one from a good Kiwi friend who described the campaign against me as 'really disappointing and somewhat disgusting' and added: 'As I said earlier, just stick to your guns and back yourself to do what you do and I really hope you win the next two games. You were so close and could have won all your games, including last week's Test. So get on with it and shove it up them.'

### Thursday, 29 June

I was up early and went downstairs to meet with the other coaches. It was only a quick conversation. I asked the others: 'What are you thinking?' They thought CJ was the best option for the bench. We recognised it was really tough on Pete, and that we risked losing something in the lineout without either him or George in the match-day twenty-three. On balance though, we still felt that we might need CJ's energy and ball-carrying more.

We had a meeting at 10.15 to inform everyone of the team and replacements. I sought out Pete before we announced it. He was sitting at a table on his own.

'Can we have a chat?'

We went outside the room and I just said: 'Pete, you're not going to be there this week. We're going to stick CJ on the bench. I know you'll be disappointed, but you have done a great job for us.'

He took it well. 'Fair enough,' he said. 'Thanks for letting me know.'

He was the only player I took aside before the meeting. Faz showed some defence clips and spoke really well about our attitude coming into the second Test and how important our physicality would be. It wasn't as if we had to change our tactics too much. We just had to work on stopping their momentum, and being a little bit more physical at the breakdown.

Then I read out the team and outlined what we would be doing in training at the Jerry Collins Stadium. It was a beautiful day and we had a light session. The forwards went a little bit earlier than the backs, and just did a few walk-throughs and lineouts to warm up. We came together as a squad for some contact and offloading, before we split the forwards and backs for about ten minutes.

Faz did the defensive block, and then we did some exits, kick-offs and attack as well. The session was thirty-eight minutes, before the forwards had another seven minutes for a few live scrums. It wasn't a long session. Last week, we had overdone it when we had the two training sessions on the Thursday. On review, the forwards looked slightly heavy-legged, even though some of them said they felt good.

I don't think that was just from the training week. We've had three weeks together with no days off, no rest, just training – which eventually took its toll both mentally and physically. It had been an accumulation of factors. We weren't going to risk that happening again.

We went back to the hotel for lunch, which I skipped. Then myself and Sam, along with Dave Barton and Luke Broadley, went to Waterloo Quay for the press conference. I thought about what was going to be said over the next couple of days. What would the *NZ Herald* do to try to unsettle me?

The room was absolutely packed. There must have been over a hundred journalists in the room, and about fifteen television crews. If you say the wrong word or the wrong sentence, that will be the negative headline.

It was interesting to hear Steve Hansen, earlier that day, blaming the press for trying to create something between us. He's obviously made a few comments which they've jumped on and he's accused them of stirring things up. He made the point that 'you guys ask the questions and we give the answers.' That's fair enough, as the question is rarely reported, only the answer, and it's written up as if you said something without any prompting.

Steve had been asked about the clown stuff in the *NZ Herald* and said: 'I think it is really disappointing. It's one thing to have a bit of banter, and then you guys beef it up to make it bigger than it really is. Like, I have heard you say that I don't like him, and we won't have a beer. I have got a lot of respect for him. I think he is a good coach. I have got a lot of respect for the Lions, they are a good team.

'But to come out and do that, I think you are ridiculing somebody that doesn't deserve it. At the end of the day, we are all coaches trying to do what we think is right. Sometimes people don't always agree with what we do, but that's OK, you are allowed to have your opinion. But to ridicule someone is not right. It's a bit disappointing, really.

'I read somewhere that I lashed out at Warren Gatland. I haven't lashed out at Warren Gatland at all. I have got a lot of respect for him. I am looking forward to having a beer with him and a chuckle about life.

'We've got a lot of common interests. He likes racing horses, so do I, he coaches Wales — I've been through that experience myself. It's the media that ramp it up, because it sells you guys newspapers. Who am I to say, "stop it"? But I do look at it and think that's not actually how it went.'

When I was told that he had tried to stop the war of words between us, and how I felt about this given Steve 'had started it', all I said was: 'I think

I have been pretty mild and tried to be complimentary of the All Blacks. Obviously they are the best team in the world. It's been a great experience for us as a team. The hospitality in New Zealand has been unbelievable. The treatment we have had from the fans wherever we have been has been absolutely brilliant. I don't know if there is any hostility from this side. Hopefully, we can have a good game and maybe enjoy a beer together afterwards.'

As I was leaving, I spoke with Sean Fitzpatrick and Josh Kronfeld, who were at the back of the room. Sean had written a piece condemning the *NZ Herald* for portraying me as a clown and I said to him: 'Look, I heard about the piece you had written and how disappointed you had been with the *NZ Herald*. Thanks for that.'

He said it was the first press conference he had ever been to, which was interesting. I also spoke to Josh and Ric Salizzo, who's the executive producer of *The Crowd Goes Wild*, a sports programme on Prime TV, and who I know from my All Blacks days. Josh has been travelling around and doing pieces on the tour for the programme.

That evening, Gabby's boyfriend Sam arrived in a taxi from the airport. He was working in Wellington the next day. When the taxi pulled up outside the hotel, Gabby, Trudi and I were outside waiting for him and started singing the Village People's *YMCA*, and doing all the dancing and actions as well. I wasn't too sure if he got the joke, but when he told his mother Caroline about it she couldn't stop laughing.

## Friday, 30 June

I was down for breakfast at 8.30 and the first person I met was Eanna Falvey to go through the squad and the training stats, as we do most mornings. That was when we ruled Jared Payne out for the rest of the tour.

Jared had pulled out of the Tuesday night game with headaches, and he was feeling dizzy. He'd had a CT and MRI scan, which initially they were a bit worried about because they thought he might have a brain bleed, but the neurologist confirmed that wasn't the case. As a precaution though, we thought it was best for Jared not to train for the remainder of the tour.

After breakfast I had a coffee with Ger Carmody and Dave Barton. Ger said he'd had an email from Joe Schmidt about tickets, and Joe also said a lot of Kiwis were embarrassed about the negative media coverage that I was getting from the NZ Herald.

We saw that the All Blacks had announced their second Test squad. With Ben Smith and Ryan Crotty ruled out, they moved Israel Dagg back to full-back and brought in Anton Lienert-Brown. I was a little surprised they picked Waisake Naholo on the right wing, with Ngani Laumape on the bench.

Rob Howley showed some clips on the All Blacks, including some plays of Rieko Ioane and Naholo, and the need to put pressure on them in the air. We spoke about us taking our opportunities, varying our lineout delivery and, again, our defence around '9', which we had to improve if they were going to come hard off Smith again. We also needed to be sharper stepping forward. We got a little bit caught on our heels last Saturday. It's only a fraction, but it makes all the difference.

Graham Rowntree showed three or four clips of some really good clean-outs against the Hurricanes. We had been working hard on being very aggressive, going past the ball, cleaning the player out and creating quick ball. One good example was of Dan Cole doing precisely that.

Before the meeting I had a little chat with Sam Warburton. 'How are you?' He said: 'I'm feeling really good.' He was up for it.

At training, I spoke to Maro. George Kruis would usually call the lineouts for Saracens and England, and had been doing so for us. This was the first time Maro would be doing it on the tour. 'Look, we've got a huge amount of confidence in your ability to call lineouts.' I told him just to back himself; not to worry about it. He is smart, he has done it before, and he'll get better at it.

The skill in calling lineouts is understanding where the space is, where the opposition are defending and making a quick decision. It's also about maintaining a good tempo. Steve Borthwick has done an excellent job with our lineout. I have been really impressed with his technical knowledge and how he has conducted his forward reviews and previews of ourselves and the opposition. He has also been quite innovative; for example getting the forwards to practise our mauling up and down a bank in order to work on our height and tightness.

But the lineout is only one small aspect of the game. For example, against the Hurricanes we only had five in total.

Some of the VIPs and board members were there. I spoke to tour manager John Spencer on the bus on the way back. He was saying we looked really sharp. Courtney Lawes didn't train because his ankle was a little sore. That's not ideal, and some people will wonder why we still picked him ahead of Iain Henderson. The main reason was probably Courtney's defence. He's also a bit more aggressive in the breakdown area, although Iain was doing really well with his carrying. Courtney is possibly a better lineout forward too.

Ken Owens also rolled his ankle a little, so he pulled out of training. There hadn't been a lot of difference between him and Rory Best. Rory probably had to have a big game on Tuesday, with his carrying and physicality, as well as his throwing. He didn't play badly, but it wasn't a performance that was enough to put him in the Test side.

After the Captain's Run, the kickers went with Neil Jenkins to the Westpac Stadium – Johnny, Owen, Dan and Leigh. It was another beautiful day in Wellington which was a little unusual. It hadn't even been that windy up until then, although we knew tomorrow's forecast wasn't too flash.

We had the afternoon off, and I caught up with the family back in the team hotel. We had an early evening meal, because I had a meeting with the match officials at 7pm – Jerome Garces, the referee for the second Test, his assistants, Jaco Peyper and Romain Poite, and George Ayoub, the TMO – followed by a Lions gala dinner, which over 700 people attended as part of the package for supporters who were travelling with the official Lions travel agency.

After a busy night, I went back to the hotel and was on my way to bed at 11.30 when someone shouted: 'Hey Gatty!' It was Bruce Deans, an ex-All Blacks scrum-half whom I had played with. So I stopped and had a chat with him. He was with an Irish friend of his from his days playing and coaching in Old Belvedere.

'What have you been up to? I haven't seen you for years,' I said. He said he had 4,500 acres down in Canterbury and was busy farming. 'I've driven up here to see you. I came to the hotel earlier but someone told me you were out.'

So I had a beer with him. We used to room together quite a bit on tours. He has a really dry sense of humour and I've always liked him. We chatted for about half an hour, but then the hotel started to get mobbed with supporters. 'Can I get a picture with you?' 'Gats, a quick snap, please!' 'Just one quickie with me and my missus. . .'

Time to go to bed.

# 20

## Lions in New Zealand 2017

*Saturday, 1 July*
*Second Test: New Zealand v Lions, Westpac Stadium, Wellington*

I had breakfast in the room with Trudi this morning. Among the loads of texts and emails I had received overnight was one from Prince William, Duke of Cambridge to the Lions squad, sent to me via his equerry James Benbow who attends and assists members of the royal family.

'Dear Warren' was handwritten above the typed message. 'Ahead of the second Test against the All Blacks this weekend I wanted to write, to let you know how much support you and the squad have behind you back home across all four nations. The tour is proving hugely popular, and the scale of the challenge, and the ambition with which you are all approaching it, have really captured the public's imagination. It has been heartening to see how each performance has built on the last, and there is a huge amount of pride across the nations at each and every point the Lions managed to claw from these New Zealand teams. We all appreciate what an important match this will be on the tour. The weight of support behind you is phenomenal. Enjoy the challenge. Please pass on my very best wishes to the whole squad and support staff for Saturday and the rest of their time in New Zealand. [Signed] William.'

That was a nice gesture. I printed off the message and put it up in the team room. Then Trudi and I went through all the texts and emails from people during the night wishing me well before I went downstairs.

The first person I spoke to was Rob Howley. I had initially planned on meeting Alain Rolland at 7.30 the night before. I had emailed him but he hadn't picked it up. When I finished my meeting with the officials last night, I rang Alain, and he had actually been at our hotel.

Alain told me that Rob had spent twenty-five minutes with him and said: 'I've just spoken to Rob and he has told me that he will pass on all that stuff to you.'

So this morning I asked Rob: 'Well, how did that meeting go with Alain?' Rob had said to him that we just didn't feel we were getting any 50/50 calls, but Alain doesn't really give away a lot. Understandably, he backs his officials and very rarely admits there was a mistake or that things were done wrongly. For an away team not to be getting any of the 50/50 calls is not unique in sport. I suppose it's how away teams in football always feel when they play Manchester United at Old Trafford.

Then I spoke to Johnny Sexton, and just asked him to be careful with these officials. They are aware of his tendency to gesticulate. He can be inclined to wave his arms about and complain to them. He knows this himself, and is constantly trying to temper this side of his game, but when he's in the moment he just can't seem to help himself.

I also had a chat with Tadhg Furlong because he had been penalised twice in the scrum for not taking the weight, which was absolutely ridiculous. There's no way we're going into scrums not trying to take the weight. If the New Zealand teams have pushed early, rather than them being penalised for pushing over the mark, it's us who have been penalised. So I said to Tadhg: 'You've just got to load up. We can't get caught.'

Then we had a management meeting at noon, with the coaches, Bobby, Rhodri, Ger and Eanna, to go through the following week's programme. We are going to Queenstown tomorrow and staying until Wednesday, giving all the boys three days off. We did this in 2009 and 2013 at the start of the final week. We have done a similar thing with Wales on a number of occasions. We decided that after units tomorrow morning and then flying at lunchtime, we would have the rest of the day off, as well as Monday and Tuesday, and then train and travel to Auckland on Wednesday. We'd have one session on Thursday and the Captain's Run on Friday.

Later in the afternoon we all met up in our team room, which is on the second floor, before going to the hotel car park, where the team walked through a couple of plays and some patterns. This was easier than taking the bus to an indoor area, although there wasn't much room in the car park. That took about fifteen minutes before the boys headed downstairs for their pre-match meal.

After the meal I went back to the room at 4pm. That's when the nerves usually hit me, about two or three hours before the game. I tried to have a nap for half an hour or so, something I only do occasionally. I put my alarm on, just in case. Missing the team meeting is always the biggest fear and, of course, the thought of that usually prevents me from falling asleep anyway. Bryn was with me and we ended up watching horse racing on the TV to relax a bit.

The non-twenty-three departed for the ground at 6pm and I went downstairs for the team meeting with the match-day twenty-three, which was at 6.05. I was early and poured myself a coffee. The coaches, as usual, came down about ten minutes before the meeting and sat down for a chat.

We had a room next door set aside for the meeting, with the chairs arranged in a semi-circle. Normally a couple of players are there early. We don't mind the boys arriving early, so long as they're all there on time. I think Kyle Sinckler was the last one to arrive, about a minute before the meeting started.

I didn't speak for long. We all knew the importance of this game, and about staying switched on for every moment. 'When you're playing against the All Blacks every carry, every clean-out, every tackle, every collision has got to be 100 per cent.' The players just have to be 'in the moment' the whole time.

From a tactical perspective, I said: 'Just because we didn't get any success out of our drives last week, don't be afraid early on to go there because they may not be expecting that.' We had to be stronger and stay on our feet, and not allow them to sack us like they did in the first week. 'Don't be afraid to have a crack at their scrum as well, particularly on our ball, because you have to put them out of their rhythm a little bit.'

The other thing which annoyed me was the soft penalties we have been giving away. They are so costly, particularly at this level. Rugby goes through cycles during which some factors are more influential than others, and I think penalties are the most important aspect of the game currently. If a team gives away eleven penalties, like we did last week, the All Blacks will almost certainly never lose. So we had to improve on that area. I told them to play with discipline and accuracy, to keep the ball and to take our chances. The defence was about winning the collisions, and we needed to pressure their wingers by winning the collisions in the air too.

Then it was on to the bus, through a sea of red, with fans chanting the by now familiar 'Li-ons! Li-ons!' It was awesome. It made the hairs on the back of my neck stand up. It also reminded me that they have paid a hell of a lot of money to come here and support the team in the way that they do. It's a memorable day in their lives as well.

● ● ●

The drive to the Westpac Stadium was only five minutes and I was pretty calm when we arrived. After going into the changing room, I did my interviews with the different rights holders and the press. Graham Simmons said to me that it was very unlike a Warren Gatland side to have a 10-12 combination with a ball-playing '12'. I was thinking that at Wasps, Stuart Abbott wasn't a bad ball-playing '12', was he? Scott Williams is a ball-playing '12' with Wales as well.

You pick from what you've got. At Wales, we know Jamie Roberts isn't the best ball-playing '12' but there have been few better at getting a team across the gainline. Why would you not pick him, and instead pick someone else? Just to look pretty and then lose?

Ian Smith, from SkySports NZ, asked me about the week and how things had gone. I said: 'Oh, we've had a good week's training.' I also didn't mind saying before the game that we needed to stop their momentum off '9', and that our kicking game needed to be accurate in putting pressure on their back three. We needed to finish off some of the chances that we were creating, and I was looking forward to a good game.

I saw Steve Hansen coming out of their changing room around 7pm. I just shook his hand and did the same with Grant Fox, the former All Black who is now a selector.

The warm-up was the same as the week previously. The forwards went out a little bit earlier, as they usually do a few lineouts, and Graham Rowntree also did a couple of three-on-three or four-on-four scrums.

Funnily, Steve Hansen took no part in their warm-up at all. He just stood on their 10-metre line and watched us, with his back to their warm-up. It's not the first time I've seen him do it. He did it last year here with Wales. I might have a look at a couple of things the opposition are doing occasionally, but not all of it. Grant was with him this time but often he's on his own.

Sometimes you get a bit of a feel from the warm-up as to how things will go, but it was quiet, and it was wet, and in one handling drill we put a couple of passes down. The pitch was good but the rain was pouring down and it was blustery. After a lovely week, Windy Wellington had arrived.

After the warm-up, we went back into the changing room and the boys started putting their jerseys on. It was still pretty quiet. Only a few words were spoken. Sean O'Brien was good again. He has taken a really important leadership role in the squad, especially at training and in the matches. He said: 'Let's take it to these f***ers. Don't give them any time. Don't give them any space.' Sam Warburton was good too. He talked about no one letting themselves down, being aggressive, and getting on the front foot from the off.

Myself and the other coaches went around the room shaking everyone's hand and left about three minutes before the boys were called out. This time, because we were a little bit late coming out, we stood there and waited for them. Along with the rest of the squad, we clapped them through the tunnel and wished them all the best.

At the Westpac Stadium you have to climb the stands to the coaches' box through a lot of supporters. It was a mixture of Kiwis and Lions fans, and there's always a bit of banter with some of them. I remember at half-time against the Maori, as I was walking down the steps from the box, one woman said to me: 'How much did you pay the ref?'

'Two grand!' I said.

Andy Farrell chipped in. 'No, it was two and a half, wasn't it?'

Despite the rain, we played some good rugby at the start. When Owen Franks took it up from Aaron Smith's first pass, Alun Wyn came off the line hard and put in a great hit. It's the second minute. We were putting in big tackles. There was intent there. That's what we wanted. Our set-pieces were good, and Sean and Tadhg made some good carries before Maro dropped the ball.

But we had talked about being aggressive, and they were some really strong carries. Mako Vunipola made another big charge and Johnny tipped on a pass from Owen to release Liam Williams, but it was called back for a forward pass. It didn't look forward to me. Liam was slightly in front of Johnny but he caught the pass behind him. If that's forward, then have a look at Codie Taylor's try in the first Test – where Dagg passes and where Taylor catches it. The 50/50 calls again!

Sean went for a poach but was judged to be off his feet. He was a bit unlucky there. He put his hand on the ground past the ball, so hadn't gone onto the ground. The referee Jerome Garces was quite pedantic about that. When Barrett missed a kick from in front of the posts, I was thinking: 'Hmm, maybe it's going to be one of those nights.'

But then Mako got pinged for collapsing a scrum, when Tadhg got caught a little bit high as well. This time Barrett didn't miss.

I've been pretty happy overall with the scrums, but that's what can happen at this level. Tadhg is still learning his trade as a tight-head prop. He is going to be world class in a couple of seasons, and with him and Jack McGrath Ireland are going to have a very good front-row for a long time. There isn't a front-row forward who at the top level hasn't had his head shoved up his backside at some stage of his career. That's how you learn.

A couple of minutes later they were penalised for blocking. Considering the wind and the rain, Owen kicked a great penalty from 45 metres. It was bucketing down now.

When Sonny Bill Williams put in a big hit on Anthony Watson, you could immediately see the reaction of our players. Conor and Toby raised their arms, and Johnny came running in with arms flailing. So much for our chat!

I saw the hit at the time, and when they were showing the replay I was thinking: 'This is going to be a red card here.' That was the general consensus in the coaches' box. Sonny Bill led with the shoulder and caught Anthony in the head. I don't think the referee had any choice.

After the first view of the video, Garces said to his assistant referees: 'There is a clear shoulder charge to the head. Do you agree? In the face. I think it's deliberate. I think it is a red.'

As they studied the replays, the TMO, George Ayoub, said: 'Jerome, would you like to have another look?'

I'm sitting there thinking: 'Is the TMO trying to dissuade him from giving a red card here and give him a yellow instead?' It seemed like the reverse of Tuesday night's yellow card for Iain Henderson, when the referee initially thought it was only a penalty. Then, after Poite yellow-carded Iain, the TMO said: 'Good decision. Well done.'

After Garces sent off Sonny Bill, there was no 'Good decision, well done' this time.

They brought on Laumape and took off Kaino. I was really surprised they opted to go down to seven forwards, particularly given the weather conditions. They were defending with another forward out in the backline on a lot of occasions anyway. You can always take forwards out of scrums or lineouts and put them in the back line.

Anthony went off for an HIA as a precaution, and we put Jack Nowell on, but Anthony passed his HIA and returned. We tried to get the message through to the players, from Neil Jenkins, that we had to play territory. We've been guilty on this tour of trying to play too much around halfway, and we needed to keep turning them.

There was a really good example from a scrum. Conor gave the ball to Liam, and he needed to put it on his boot but instead he did a switch with Anthony. Sam Cane got on the ball and we were penalised for not releasing. We just had to keep the pressure on them and be better than that.

When Conor was pinged for not rolling away, Barrett made it 6–3. When Sam Whitelock was penalised as well, Owen made it 6–6. At least Garces was being consistent.

But when Mako went for a poach, his knee hit the ground for a split second before he bounced back up, and Garces pinged him. I thought: 'Gosh, c'mon ref.' I think he had enough time to say: 'Let it go, let it go.' It was slow ball anyway. In those conditions that penalty was pretty severe. Barrett made no mistake and it was 9–6 to the All Blacks.

At the next scrum, Graham Rowntree gave the signal from the touchline to have a crack at them. They only packed down with their seven forwards, and we won a penalty. We went up the line, and after Jonathan Davies made a good break we won another penalty. Conor played the advantage by cross-kicking to Toby, where Ioane was defending on his own. Ioane couldn't hold it and Anthony just needed to be a bit quicker there. If he had chased it, he would have dived on the ball and scored. Toby didn't really go for it either. It was a curious one.

We started walking down to the changing room as Owen lined up the kick. We went in at 9–9, and against fourteen men.

At half-time, the emphasis was on making sure that our scrum and lineout were good. If they didn't have eight in the scrum, then there was an opportunity for Conor to recognise that and we could either attack there or go for a second shove, and see if we could squeeze a penalty out of them.

Faz just spoke about maintaining the emotion and desire to win, and Rob spoke about playing the game in the right territory. He said: 'We win this game by being smart and being accurate.'

I told the players: 'They're going to try to slow the game down. They're going to try and squeeze us for momentum.' We had allowed them to dictate the pace of the game. They were going down for injuries and everything. The other thing I said was: 'We are under no pressure, so don't give away any silly penalties.'

We ended up spending the third quarter in our own half. We were terrible in that period. Barrett missed another kickable one but then Conor was done for a high tackle on Lienert-Brown. I think that was a penalty. Barrett put them back in front.

They were having all the possession and they were playing all the territory. And we kept giving away penalties. Barrett had another miss, but we immediately gave him another shot when Mako was pinged for a late hit on the fly-half. I didn't think there was a lot in that. Mako didn't change his line. It was just a collision, but he was penalised for being late. Sitting in the box, I was so frustrated. A few minutes earlier, when Codie Taylor caught Owen late, it was every bit as bad.

A few minutes later, the TMO said: 'I want to have another look at a clean-out by number one red.'

Mako had dived onto Barrett. I didn't think red. He didn't make contact with the head. But Mako was binned and Barrett kicked the penalty. Now it's 18–9 to them and it's fourteen-a-side. How did it get to this?

We brought on Courtney Lawes for Alun Wyn, but I was furious because we were completely the authors of our own downfall. All those penalties were avoidable, whether it was Conor or Maro or Mako. We had talked about being disciplined and being accurate.

Our territory suffered in that second half. It was horrible. We tried to get the message down to the players: 'Guys, we've got to play for some territory. We've got to get down there and get the ball.'

But then, ironically, with fourteen against fourteen, we started to play again. Johnny hung the restart high and long, and finally, we had a set-piece in their half – our first of the second half – and we attacked off a lineout. Johnny looped around Owen, and Elliot showed what great hands he has. I actually didn't realise it until I watched it again afterwards. The ball slightly deflected off an All Black hand and Elliot caught it low and transferred it for Liam to put Anthony away down the right.

Then Maro made a good carry and Sean made a really good clean-out. Johnny pulled the ball back for Owen, Liam gave Toby a one-on-one and he went through Dagg. It was a great finish.

It was the first time in the second half that we got down in their territory, kept the ball and actually stretched them. I've been critical of Liam in the past for not passing the ball, or not passing it early enough. But he gave Anthony space for the run and also Toby the chance to finish.

As Owen lined up the conversion, I was thinking: 'Jeez, kick this and it's a two-point game.' But it skewed well wide. Still, it was 18–14 and I'm thinking: 'We're back in this now.'

We brought on Kyle for Tadhg, and Elliot saw a good kick unluckily keep rolling until it went dead. Then Kyle was penalised for not getting back onside. That wasn't clever. Barrett made it 21–14, and we needed to score twice to win.

Johnny's restart again hung long enough and high enough for the chasers, and Smith kicked out to give us another attacking lineout. Maro called it on himself at the tail, and a couple of phases later Johnny gave a little flat pass for Jamie George to break the line.

We had gone out the back a lot in attack and Laumape was expecting that again, but Johnny hit that flat run by Jamie. Johnny did that in the first Test, when Owen wasn't expecting it, and the ball hit him in the side. That was when TJ Perenara box-kicked and Ioane scored.

This time we were behind the defence, and from the ruck Conor did really well to dummy and go for the line, and he had the quickness of mind and the legs to get there. It's another very good finish. Owen kicked a tough conversion to make it 21–21.

We had a discussion about bringing Ken Owens on, but Jamie had been playing well. We also talked about bringing on CJ Stander. But for who? Do we bring off Toby? We felt the loose-forwards were working well. Warby had fallen off a tackle or two, but I thought he was very, very good. Sean was great and Toby has been awesome all tour. When I explained this to CJ in the changing room afterwards he said: 'No problem at all. I understand.' I really have a lot of time for CJ.

Courtney and Kyle added to our energy in defence, which was brilliant then. Maro, Sean, Warby, all of them stepped off the line and put in hits. We drove them backwards and Laumape dropped the ball.

Now it was our turn. Off our scrum, Owen and Courtney showed good footwork, and then Charles Faumuina tackled Kyle in the air and was penalised. Conor's pass had made Kyle jump. It's a slightly tough call on Faumuina, but he does go really low on Kyle. Owen kicked it to make it 24–21 to us with three minutes to go.

Nobody said a word in the coaches' box.

They got the ball back from the kick-off, but Jack McGrath made a great hit on Read. We came off our line really hard and aggressively. Then Barrett countered and Cruden's cross-kick went over the touchline. They've always backed themselves to do those things, but this time it was a little overcooked.

It's our lineout. I'm not sure throwing it to Warby at the front was the best call in the world. Retallick went up against him, and the ball came back awkwardly to Conor. He found touch inside their 22. It was the line-kick of the tour. It was perfect. I thought that trying to play the ball out from there for two minutes was going to be hard for our boys.

When Barrett countered again off the quick throw, the chase was just all red and Sean gathered his chip. Then all we had to do was go through two or three phases. Courtney did well on one of the carries. They couldn't get anywhere near it. The 80 minutes were up, and the ball was there. Conor kicked it dead.

When the whistle went, I just screamed, 'Yesss!' Rob screamed as well, threw his arm around me, and punched the air. We all shook hands. We were pretty happy in the box.

Coming down the stairs I met Trudi's uncle and aunt. Then I saw Trudi, Bryn and Gabby, and gave them a hug and a kiss.

The security guys went down in front of us to make a path. If we'd been on our own, it would have taken forever. The banks of red were mostly to our right and the Lions supporters were going absolutely mental.

The reaction inside the stadium was remarkable, and again it was Kiwis as well as Lions fans with the congratulations.

'Well done!'

'All the best!'

'Great win!'

'All on for next week now!'

We made it to the changing room. All the other support staff were coming in, shaking hands and exchanging hugs. Then the boys came in. I had asked some of the other coaches if they wanted to say anything, but they said 'nah'. So I said a few words.

'Congratulations. Well done. This hasn't been the Lions twenty-three. It's always been the forty-one, and everyone has been a part of this.'

I added: 'We've not finished. We have a couple of days off. Enjoy yourselves tonight. Look after each other. And then we start thinking about next week.'

Everyone burst into song with *The Fields of Athenry*. The singing as a group has been pretty cool, and we have definitely improved too. We had a few beers in the changing room, then I had to do my usual media duties. I said to Graham Simmons: 'What tricky questions have you got for me tonight?'

'What do you mean?'

'Asking me about the twelve one was a bit tricky,' I said.

Graham always tries to be a little different. When the SkySports cameras rolled, he started the interview with: 'Not bad for a clown.'

'I'm a pretty happy clown this week. Yea look, it's great to have tied the series up and we go to Auckland next week with everything to play for. Even with the red card, and we got a yellow card, I thought we were the better team and deserved to win. I think we played some good rugby. We gave away some soft penalties which was disappointing. We need to fix that for next week, but I thought the better team won tonight.' I feel like a broken record talking about unnecessary penalties we have given away. But I said I was proud of the performance and proud of the players, which I was.

To be fair to Ian Smith from SkySports NZ, he has been really good. We had ended the All Blacks' forty-seven match-winning streak at home, a record that had endured since they lost to South Africa in Hamilton in 2009. Yet he was very positive about the Lions and our performance.

We had taken the series to the last game in Eden Park and I think most observers thought that this was great for rugby, for the series, and for the future of the Lions. I think many people wanted that, even Kiwis, in a strange way.

From there we went into the press conference. The night before, I had chatted with our media guys, Dave Barton and Luke Broadley, about the best way to respond to the *NZ Herald* and their clown stuff. We agreed that we should do it in a light-hearted way rather than go on an all-out attack, and we came up with the idea of me wearing a clown's red nose to a press conference.

Luke went out on the morning of the first Test and found one. He told me: 'That took me half the bloody day.' He had bought me a clown's nose and a clown's bow-tie, but I didn't think it was quite the right time to wear it now. No, not just yet. We hedged our bets that we'd have the opportunity after the third Test.

The room was rammed. Going into the press conference I was thinking to myself: 'Right, just don't say too much. You don't want to give the All Blacks any extra motivation.'

There was a tape of them in a huddle on the pitch after the game which we subsequently looked at. Jerome Kaino was saying to them: 'We use this for next week. We use this for motivation next week.' I think it might be one of the views that wasn't shown on TV, even though one of the match-day cameras picked it up. Rhodri Bown had spotted it and deciphered what Kaino was saying. He told me about it back at the hotel that night. We decided we'd show that to the boys later in the week, just to illustrate what kind of response we could expect from the All Blacks.

So, going into the press conference, I said to myself: 'Another week to go. Be humble. Don't give them anything.' At the same time, I thought it was a good opportunity to have a little dig back at the *NZ Herald*.

I said: 'The last couple of weeks in terms of the criticism and personal attacks have been a little bit tough to take, not so much for myself, more for family members. Ironically, the Kiwi public are probably the fairest people you will ever come across.

'There is a huge proportion of Lions fans and Kiwis who want us to do well and are saying the criticism has been unfair. Ironically, it's actually been a huge positive. So whoever's been doing it, keep doing it because it's actually worked for us.'

I enjoyed that, although I'm not sure some of these guys are bright enough to get the subtlety. Even when I said: 'We are going off to Queenstown for a few days for a bit of skiing and stuff,' I then had to say: 'That's a joke.'

Both sets of players had been into each other's changing rooms to swap jerseys by the time I got back there, and it was actually pretty quiet. We were on the bus at 11.30pm.

The Rydges hotel was packed. I thought: 'I can't stay downstairs or I'll get absolutely mobbed.' So I went up to my room where there was a magnum of champagne that Simon, the hotel manager, had left for me. Gabby said: 'That's mine.' We took that down with the glasses to the family room, to join Trudi and Bryn, their friends and other family members.

After finishing the champagne, we had a few beers and a few glasses of wine. What happened next is really not like me.

'Why don't we go out?' said Trudi.

'OK,' I said.

I went up to the room to get changed, put some jeans and a shirt on. Two of the security guys, Sean and Ray, took us about 300 metres down the road to an Irish bar called D4 on Featherston. It's owned by Barry and Dermot Murphy, two brothers from Ringsend in Dublin. Barry and Dermot are good friends with Kevin 'Smiley' Barrett and his family, and the oldest of the Barrett boys, Kane, came over and congratulated me. He had captained the New Zealand Schools team and played for Taranaki and the Blues, but had to retire due to concussion problems when he was only twenty-four. He's a huge lad.

Smiley was a teak-tough number 8 who had a great career with Taranaki. I played against him plenty of times and I've known the Barretts for a long time. They have a dairy farm in Pungarehu, a little town on the coast of southern Taranaki, and I really like them because they're just good down-to-earth people. We had seen them at church a few years ago in Waihi and I remember talking to Beauden Barrett.

'Well done, you had a good year,' I told him.

'Yea, it was good. How is Bryn getting on?'

When I told Bryn that 'Beauden Barrett was asking for you' he couldn't believe it. But that would be typical Beauden.

It was good to get out of the hotel. In fairness to the Lions and All Blacks supporters in the D4, they realised I was with my family, so not too many people came over and asked for photographs. Barry told me: 'We've had our best day ever in the history of the bar.' He probably made a few grand more after that, so he was pretty happy. It reminded me again of the effect of the tour on the New Zealand economy, and how it has heightened interest in rugby over here.

We left the D4 at about 3am and walked back to the hotel. There were one or two puzzled onlookers, who probably thought: 'That can't be Warren Gatland, can it? He must just look like him.'

We had a couple of glasses of wine back on the second floor with Graham Rowntree and Rob Howley in the team room. Obviously, the win smoothes over everything. Bryn and Gabby had gone to bed, and myself and Trudi took the lift to the room at about 4am.

The exciting thing was that now we had a decider next week. John Feehan, the Lions boss, had come up to me in the changing rooms afterwards and just said: 'Today makes up for all the disappointments of 2005.'

Some day. Some game. Some night.

# 21

## Lions in New Zealand 2017

*Sunday, 2 July*

When will they ever learn? How many times has that happened? They decide to really climb into me, and then? Don't write me off too quickly boys. It could backfire on you.

But the day began with bad news. Sean O'Brien had been cited following an alleged swinging arm against All Blacks winger Waisake Naholo during the second half of yesterday's game. I had a look at the match video and I showed it to Bryn. He said: 'That's not a red card.'

The hearing was scheduled to take place in Wellington that evening, so while the rest of the squad set off for Queenstown for a couple of days off, I stayed an extra night in the Rydges hotel along with Sean, Ger Carmody, John Spencer and Dave Barton. I thought I should be at the hearing. It was sending the right message. But it made for a long day.

The hearing over Sonny Bill's sending off started at about 5pm, and that went on a bit longer than expected. Sean's case was due to commence at 8pm. We met up an hour before in our hotel, where we were all briefed by Max Duthie, the Lions legal representative. He had been doing some work exchange in Sydney, from where we had flown him across for the disciplinary hearing.

When we got a message saying things were running behind schedule, we had some fish and chips, and then hopped into two taxis to attend the hearing at the offices of New Zealand Rugby. While we were waiting I saw a board where the staff write and post positive messages about their co-workers. I decided to get a piece of paper and wrote 'Buck is awesome' and signed it 'Gatty'. I was referring to Brent Anderson who works for New Zealand Rugby and is in charge of the community game. Buck and I played a large number of games together for Waikato. I still don't know if he has seen it!

There was an independent judicial committee made up of Adam Casselden SC, who was the chairman, and David Croft and John Langford, two former Australian internationals. It started off a little ropey. The ref had said he hadn't seen the incident, but we had evidence to say he had commented on it at the time. He actually said: 'There's nothing in that. I thought he was going for the ball.' So that upset the chairman of the panel a little.

The hearing lasted over three hours. Sean spoke well. He explained that he was going for the ball and there was no closed fist. It wasn't a stiff arm. He might have made contact with Naholo's head, but Elliot Daly also made contact with his head.

We left the room while they deliberated and waited half an hour for the verdict. That was a long half hour. I think having two ex-players on the hearing panel probably made a difference. When you look at it in real time you think: 'There's nothing in that.' The end-on views were only in slow motion, and they made it look worse. We were called back in and told that the citing complaint had been dismissed.

It was a relief to have that over and done with. We got another two taxis back to the Rydges, with myself, Sean and Max Duthie in one of them. I joked with Sean: 'We weren't even going to select you this week,' to which Max said to me: 'If you weren't, I don't think you would be here, would you?'

I chuckled. 'Oh yea, that's a good point.'

Back at the hotel, John Spencer and I had a beer at the bar. Two women staying at the hotel came over to me. They were Northampton supporters who had been on the last tour and one of them told me she had spoken to me in Melbourne after the second Test. I said: 'Yes. Oh, sorry, I don't remember that.' She also told me they had been chatting with Alain Rolland, and one of the things she said was: 'We asked him if he thinks the Lions have a chance, and he said, "Not a hope in hell".'

## Monday, 3 July

We had booked a couple of taxis to take myself, John, Ger, Sean and Dave to the airport for our flight from Wellington to Auckland, and then our connecting flight to Queenstown, as we had missed out on the direct charter the day before.

At Auckland, our landing gate was also our departure gate, so at least we could hang around there without having far to walk. Even then I caught up with some people I knew and some I didn't for a few more photographs. All were Kiwis who were also on their way to Queenstown. Among them were Chris Clapcott and his family, who are farmers in the King Country on North Island. Their son, Doug, had been at Hamilton Boys with Bryn, and their daughter Lucy had rowed with Gabby. We chatted for a while about how all the kids were doing and the tour.

After being up so early, I had a good sleep on the second leg of the journey. We landed at midday and were picked up by the Liaison Officer, Brad. He organised the various activities while the squad were based there.

We checked into the Hilton on the shores of Lake Wakatipu, an absolutely beautiful spot, and I had a quiet afternoon in my room. I looked back over the video of the second Test again, and then went through all the data which the analysts had broken down. Once again, I found myself hugely disappointed at the number of penalties we'd given away. The penalty count was 11–7 against us in the first Test and I'd said we wouldn't win the next Test with a repeat of that. Yet last Saturday we conceded thirteen penalties to eight, and ten of them were in kicking range.

That said, I still felt we weren't getting the close calls. The best example of that was the one against Mako for colliding with Beauden Barrett when he tried to charge down the kick. Codie Taylor had done exactly the same thing with Owen Farrell. Putting the two clips side by side, they're virtually identical. In fact, Mako put his hands up. Taylor didn't even do that, he just dropped his shoulder. One was given as a penalty, and one wasn't, yet if anything they should have both been penalties or not at all. When I go to see the officials on Friday evening, that will be one of the examples I will highlight.

In the first two Tests we have outscored the All Blacks by four tries to three, and created other chances as well. All those Kiwi journalists who were describing the Lions as boring and one-dimensional are pretty quiet now. We're not being given much credit but, of course, a certain newspaper would be pretty embarrassed to admit all of this.

The All Blacks haven't played an awful lot rugby so far. But no one is saying that, because they can't criticise the All Blacks. They say the Lions need to play more rugby this week. They'll have to, they say, because Warrenball – whatever that is – is not working for them. Everyone seems a little confused.

Going back over the match, I noted that Romain Poite had come in on the mic from the touchline to the referee, Jerome Garces, eight times – and five times, it was against us. I know that's not a lot on its own. But Jaco Peyper, the other assistant ref, came in twelve times from the sideline, and eleven times it was against red. I need this week to persuade the refs that we are capable of winning the third Test in Auckland where the All Blacks' record has been so good.

We held onto the ball better on Saturday night. We didn't throw those stupid passes away like we did in the first Test. A good example was from a nice little offload to Liam Williams when he looked to offload again, but there was nothing on and instead he kept hold of it.

Monday was a proper day off for the players. Even the team room was closed. Everybody was out doing different activities, from jetboat rides and bungee-jumping to helicopter trips. We had laid on buses to drop them into town every hour on the hour, and to pick them up as well.

I'd been told the boys had a good time the night before in Winnie's, which has a rooftop bar with an area sectioned off for the players. To their credit, they didn't go absolutely mad.

It was the sixth week of a demanding, intense tour at the end of a long season. We have had no time off. But we've just beaten the All Blacks in New Zealand. Finally, we have a couple of days off in Queenstown, so why not go and have a drink and celebrate? I had no problem with them having a few beers six nights before the third Test. They'd earned it. A few of the players who weren't involved in the second Test and don't have a midweek match this week stayed out a little longer, but they didn't go overboard. They kept their counsel. No dwarf-throwing. James Haskell had joked that the only dwarf in the squad was Dave Barton, so Dave may have dodged a bullet, or a throwing anyway, by also being one of the Wellington six who had stayed behind on Sunday for the hearing. I know Sean O'Brien was pulling his hair out because he was stuck with us in Wellington while the players were partying in Queenstown.

## Tuesday, 4 July

Breakfast or a lie-in was optional. The players could get up whenever they felt like it. We just wanted their bodies to recover, and to refresh themselves mentally.

I pride myself on understanding the dynamics of a team, and getting them right for big matches. Of course, no one is always right, and when I looked back on the first Test some of the forwards, in particular, were heavy-legged. As I've said, it wasn't just that we may have overtrained slightly with the double session on the Thursday. Everything had caught up with us; arriving in New Zealand, playing twice a week, days off were still travel days, and even if the training was light there were still meetings, walk-throughs, and gym sessions. I felt it just caught up with us a little.

For the second Test, we still had the intensity required but it was much lighter week; less volume of work and shorter training sessions. As a result, we had plenty in our legs last Saturday, and that should be the case next Saturday after another light week.

I know the All Blacks were in the gym yesterday, because I saw them on the television news. They'll be on the pitch training today, will probably take tomorrow off and then train again on Thursday before their Captain's Run on Friday. It's not that much more than us, but I'm quite comfortable with this anyway. We did the exact same in Noosa in 2013, and in the week of the third Test in South Africa, taking off Sunday, Monday and Tuesday before going back to training on the Wednesday. This was no different. It's the end of a long season for us, whereas it's two-thirds of the way through their season. Not a huge amount is going to change between the second and third Tests. There were things that we worked on in the second Test that we didn't get a chance to use. You never get to use all your moves and all your plays, but they're in the bank for us. We'll make a few subtle lineout alterations, and adjust one or two other things.

Last Thursday, I had spoken with CJ in the team room. He told me his grandmother's funeral was on Saturday, so I spoke to him again today.

'Did you write something for the funeral?' I asked him. He said he had.

'How did it go?'

'Oh, they gave her a good sending off and they finished up at the farm at about midnight, so they had a good day. It was a good celebration of her life.'

We caught the bus into town at midday. It was a shopping day for the girls. Gabby bought some jeans and other clothes, while Trudi bought some clothes for herself and stuff for the beach house. Walking around the shops, it was the first time I wasn't stopped by fans for photos.

It was almost a rugby-free day, but not quite. Back at the hotel, I met up with the other coaches at 7pm to pick the team for the third Test. The meeting lasted for a brief ten minutes. We all agreed it should be the same team. We had a discussion about the second-row, and considered starting Courtney Lawes. He made a good impact off the bench in Wellington, but we decided that he would keep that role. Ultimately, we didn't think it was fair to make any changes, even though we had made it tough on ourselves, particularly in that third quarter.

There had been some speculation that we might bring Jack McGrath in for Mako Vunipola, because Mako had conceded four penalties. But when you examined them, he was a little unlucky. One was very harsh, for his knee briefly going to the ground at a ruck. The scrum penalty against him was as much of a problem on the tight-head side. As for the late hit, he just tried to make a charge-down. The other one on Barrett wasn't clever, but that's been going on every single game. I thought there were a few penalties by others that were dumber than those four.

Jack had been great coming off the bench, but we thought Mako had carried very strongly, and he's an intelligent rugby player. He's been vocal, he's been communicating really well with the other players and I didn't think he'd make the same mistake again. Considering what he gave us in those first two Tests, I thought he deserved another opportunity.

I'm a great believer in that. Sometimes you make changes because you have to freshen things up. Other times you hold back on making a change, because you want the player to think: 'I'm the lucky one. I get a chance to redeem myself.' It really is a balancing act.

We spoke more about our game management and applying more pressure with our kicking game to turn them more, and also our discipline. In both Tests, we had one scrum where we'd been caught, but we still felt we scrummaged a lot better in the second Test. There were a couple of times where we had the All Blacks stood up at the scrum and had them on the ropes.

Our lineouts have been pretty good. The last lineout couldn't have worked out any better, but we questioned whether it was the right call to the front when Retallick was there. We could have done a decoy but in any case Conor Murray kicked it seventy metres down the sideline. But what was amazing was the kick-chase. You just see this blur of red, of seven guys in a line. It was fantastic. We decided we'd highlight that clip to the players.

Earlier that day, we had been given the GPS figures which showed that we finished the game much stronger in the second Test than we had done in the first. Our sports scientist, Brian Cunniffe, gave the data to the fitness trainers, and we decided we'd show them to the players the next day as well.

That evening, we had made a reservation at the Wakatipu Grill Restaurant in the Hilton, which has a terrace overlooking Lake Wakatipu. Trudi, Gabby and I had a lovely meal there with Rob Howley and his daughters Megan and Rebecca. Rob and I have known each other a long time now and get on well together. One of the things I've learned about the management on this tour is that while you need some freshness, having continuity among people who know and trust each other from working together is hugely important. You need that to have any chance of success.

## Wednesday, 5 July

We were scheduled to have weights and units this morning at the Queenstown event centre, but we changed our plans and only did one training session in the morning.

After breakfast and a walk-through and meeting with the forwards, we met with the entire squad and announced the unchanged team for the final Test. I'd said to the guys before: 'All I want is to show the penalties.' So we played all thirteen of them from the second Test, one by one. 'Unlucky. Unlucky. Avoidable. Avoidable...' and so on.

'Guys, we can't give away this many penalties and expect to beat the All Blacks. I know a couple of them are tough, but we're not getting anything from the officials. So we've got to be squeaky clean. They're not giving us any calls, so you just have to make sure.'

I usually like to finish on a positive and so then I said: 'Alright, this is what we're about.' I showed them that kick-chase in the last minute and then how we controlled the endgame, culminating in Conor kicking the ball out.

Then Bobby spoke to the players and put the graphics up to compare the GPS figures from the Hurricanes game to the first and then second Test. The figures show a falling off of metres per minute. You expect the guys to get tired and for those average metres to drop off in the last quarter. Even when you use all of the bench, the same thing happens, but in the second Test the cumulative numbers had gone up in the last quarter. We had never seen that before.

We also showed clips and GPS figures demonstrating how the intensity of our training sessions have been higher than the games. We haven't been training for too long, but the intensity has been there.

We wanted to give the players that belief and confidence, in where we're at, and what we've done. The message was: 'We're in great shape and we've done a lot of work.'

Rory Best spoke to the team. He recalled that the Irish team knew what was coming when they played the All Blacks two weeks after beating them in Chicago. But Ireland made a couple of mistakes early on in Dublin, and that really let the All Blacks off the hook. He also said they probably didn't react quickly enough to the physicality that the All Blacks brought that day. They'd have loved another opportunity. He said not to have the same regrets. We needed to make sure that we didn't get caught out by that physicality; to be ready for that and meet it head on.

Rory's been an awesome tourist, despite the personal disappointment of not making the Test twenty-three. It's been hard on him. He could have played in one of those games against the Crusaders or the Maori, and then might have been the guy playing in the first Test. He hasn't performed badly at all. It's just that sometimes you're fortunate to be in the right place at the right time. He started the first game, Ken Owens started the second, and then Jamie George played against the Crusaders. So Jamie's already into that Saturday cycle and we won that game. Rory has just been unlucky. It's very similar to Dan Biggar who has been excellent. I have been really impressed with him, how he has trained, played and been very positive in the squad.

At about 9.50 the forwards got on the bus and went to training first. It wasn't our greatest session, but after our experience in 2013 we expected that. It was better than the Wednesday in Noosa four years earlier. That wasn't great at all.

As we'd had a couple of days off, we walked through a few options. Then we did some contact. After that we ran an offload drill. We split the session for twelve minutes before we came together and ran a defensive block. We did some kick-offs and exits, and then we finished with some attack drills. The forwards had another seven minutes for some scrums. So they trained for about an hour and seven minutes, and the backs for forty-five minutes.

The feedback I received from the players after training was that they really enjoyed their two days off. They all felt they needed it. This wasn't just because they had no training for three days. It was the freedom of movement, to be able to get out of the hotel and do a few activities, or whatever else they wanted.

They're not robots. They're people, and we wanted them recharged mentally for the third Test. It's a model we've used with Wales in the World Cup and on the last two Lions tours.

The session was a little bit longer than planned because we did some organisational work, but we only did the one session. From there we went straight back to the hotel to shower and pack. We were supposed to be out of our rooms at noon but we didn't get back until about 12.30pm. Ger said to me: 'We could have asked for a late checkout until 2 o'clock.' They wanted to charge us for another full day's rooms. I said: 'Ger, it won't hurt us to get out in a bit of a hurry.' We got the bags onto the bus by 1 o'clock to catch the plane for Auckland.

We didn't go through the airport terminal. The bus drove us onto the tarmac and we were straight onto the plane. The flight was an hour and fifty minutes, and we slept through most of it. Well, I did anyway. From a coaching perspective, it has been unbelievably tiring. You want to spend a bit of time with your family and to socialise a little. But you are always up early, and your mind is going all day. There are some days when you're absolutely shattered. So you get on a plane and think: 'I've got to get an hour's sleep here.'

We were back in Auckland's Pullman hotel by 7pm. I had a meal in the hotel restaurant with Trudi and the kids, and just a couple of beers afterwards before calling it a night.

## Thursday, 6 July

It was an 8am start, and the first person I spoke to was Eanna Falvey, who updated me on Rhys Webb and Liam Williams. Both had groin problems, but he was confident that Liam was going to be alright whereas Rhys was a little bit more of a concern. Neither of them took much part at all in that Thursday training session. They pulled out of it effectively.

The All Blacks team had been announced at 5am. We had heard the day before that Jordie Barrett would be playing at full-back and, with Sonny Bill suspended, that Ngani Laumape and Anton Lienert-Brown were going to be the two centres, and that Israel Dagg was moving back to the wing. Waisake Naholo had failed his HIA in the second Test and hadn't completed the return-to-play protocols.

Julian Savea was in, replacing Rieko Ioane. Apparently Ioane was a bit crook. My initial reaction was surprise. I thought Jordie Barrett might have been picked for his goal-kicking. I also thought, for the first time, that there was a bit of inexperience in that back line with him and Laumape starting their first Tests. Maybe that was why Savea had been brought back in. Laumape is a strong ball-carrier, a smaller version of Sonny Bill, but obviously not with the same offloading skills. Maybe they were going to play Warrenball. Whatever that is.

I've heard that some ex-players have forecast we're going to get beaten by twenty points, that we've poked the bear. I can't see them beating us by twenty points. I don't know where that's coming from. Where are they going to run over the top of us?

The first bus went at 9.30 for weights, and the second went at 10.30 to the QBE Stadium for training. We had a meeting there at 11.25, when Rob went through the attack strategy, and talked about what we would be doing at training.

Once again I spoke about the four pillars that we've been working hard on during this tour: being the best at everything that requires no talent; not being out-talked by the opposition; being more physical than the opposition and making sure that we stay alive and don't get caught out by the unexpected.

The other thing, of course, is discipline. So as not to be repeating myself, I tried to rephrase it. Rather than writing on the board, 'Let's not give away stupid penalties', I wrote it in a different way. I tried to change the language a little, making it a positive rather than a negative message. You have to be conscious of not giving the exact same message over and over, or you lose the focus.

So I wrote: 'We will give away less penalties than the all blacks.' Writing All Blacks with a small 'a' and a small 'b' was just me trying to play a little game psychologically. My mantra was: whatever it takes.

The meeting was in a large room upstairs. At the end of it, we cleared the chairs away and walked through some attack patterns. Then we went down onto the pitch. We had a warm-up for six minutes. We did a bit of contact and then we split the forwards and backs, only for twelve minutes. We ran a defensive block for six minutes, and some exits and kick-offs for another six. Then we did some attack plays and went through three in-game scenarios.

We replicated what happened in the second Test by having a lineout in our own 22 with two minutes to go. We also went through a drop-goal scenario. We set up two options, with Johnny and Owen, although Johnny didn't hit his very well. But at least we'd gone through the scenario. The third scenario was a kick-off, on the basis that we were leading in the last minute of the game, where they'd go short and how we would deal with it.

Then we went through some attack stuff which completed a forty-minute session, before the forwards did another seven minutes of scrums, both with the machine and live as well. It was a good session. In total the backs trained for forty minutes and the forwards for forty-seven minutes, and that included a six-minute warm-up. I'm not sure you can be any shorter for a Test match session.

We returned to the Pullman hotel for lunch, after which I had to do my Thursday press duties along with Sam Warburton at 2pm. The first questions were from SkySports' Gail Davis, and she began with a couple of negative ones. I was a bit taken aback.

'How tempted were you to make changes?'

'Not very.'

'Given how much you have talked about discipline this week, did Mako Vunipola's four penalties and yellow card make you think about a change in that position?'

'No. I didn't think there was anything wrong with the first one where he has gone to charge down a kick and he has followed through. . . The one where the referee has penalised him for going on his knee is absolutely marginal where he has competed on the ball. He hasn't connected with Barrett's head [for the yellow card] and then there's a scrum penalty.'

'So you haven't called him to one side to have a word with him about it this week?'

'We've had a word with the team about making sure we give away less penalties than the opposition. I just thought there were a couple of times where Mako was a bit unlucky. There were dumber penalties given away in the game by other players. Those are the ones that are avoidable.'

'How surprised have you been by some people questioning the intensity of your preparation this week?'

'I always get questioned about everything. It's not unusual for people to have a pop at me and question things. We had a pretty testy session today, with some verbals. Everyone is pretty aware of how important the game is. It's about having emotional control. You want to take it to the edge, but you don't want to go over the top as well.'

I thought that put a dampener on the whole mood of the press conference right from the start. Gail had only been out here for a couple of days so she hadn't captured the tone of the tour and the week, and how excited New Zealand was about a series decider. I had gone in there thinking how much we were looking forward to the weekend and how well we had trained.

## Friday, 7 July

I woke up at 3am and couldn't get back to sleep for a couple of hours. I was going over what I was going to say to the match officials later that day.

We left at 10 o'clock for the QBE Stadium, to have our squad meeting out there before the Captain's Run. As we had done attack drills yesterday, Faz showed some defensive clips from the second Test which demonstrated how effective our line speed was and also our physicality in the collisions. He also showed some clips where we needed to be a little bit more 'front line' in shutting the space down, taking the legs from them and reacting a little quicker in getting off the line.

Faz told the guys that we hadn't reached our potential as a team yet. We feel that we've improved as the tour has progressed, but that there is another level in us, and we should embrace the excitement about tomorrow night.

We knew that was the case. We knew that as coaches and as a team.

The Captain's Run was really sharp. It was completely over to the players again. At the end of the team meeting I asked Sam and Johnny Sexton: 'What do you want to do?' They wanted Faz to run a defence drill, which worked on our line speed and then it was over to Johnny. He ran a few plays, put the subs in for two or three of them, and then finished with the starting team again. The forwards did a few lineout spotters, and we were done and dusted in fifteen minutes.

It's a strange feeling, but watching the players today I don't see fear or even trepidation in their eyes. I see nervous energy, excitement and self-belief. They also know it's going to be incredibly physical but that if they play to their potential they're good enough to win.

I think that has been a huge turnaround psychologically, for all of these players who have played against the All Blacks in the past. A few unusual things have happened this week that, as a Kiwi, gives me confidence as well, and I also said this to the players at the meeting.

I know the All Blacks said Ioane was a bit crook this week, but having thought about it, they may have brought Savea back in anyway given his greater experience of playing against our players. Traditionally the All Blacks have never worried about the opposition when it comes to selection. It's always been about themselves. 'We pick the team. We'll play how we want, and we'll worry about ourselves and not the opposition.'

But this time there seems to be a little bit of a focus on us. In the first two games they haven't played the expansive rugby they normally play – whether we've allowed them to do that or not. I saw yesterday that Steve Hansen had said: 'We're only playing a rugby game. We could win it, we could lose it, we could draw it. But we'll be a better team for it. We're a young side who are in the infancy of where we're going.' That had me thinking: 'That's unusual.' It's not the picture they normally paint going into a big game at home, and especially at Eden Park.

I said to the players: 'Every nation has its strengths and weaknesses and, as a Kiwi, I can see signs of some frailties at the moment. They are saying and doing things that they don't normally do.' I was also thinking, if there's only a score in it with twenty to go, they might be a bit more nervous.

We've trained really well this week. There's just a good edge there. They're bubbling underneath the surface. But we had a few laughs at training today as well, which was good.

I went for lunch to Mission Bay with Trudi and Bryn to a nice café. In Bryn's car we passed several Lions supporters walking along the waterfront. 'Come on the Lions,' I shouted out of the window. They all waved back but didn't realise who it was. Small things amuse me. During our meal a few people came over and said: 'Well done for last week' and 'Good luck for tomorrow'. It's a little hard to get away from rugby in New Zealand at the moment.

I had a quiet afternoon upstairs in my room and then went to see the match officials in their hotel at 6.30pm. After highlighting the near identical incidents involving Mako Vunipola and Codie Taylor, all I asked was that they have an open mind. 'We believe we're good enough to win. I need you to think that the Lions can win.'

At dinner that evening, I met a guy called Martin Graham, a Welshman who works for the casino and lives in Sydney, and he had a glass of Pinot Noir with us. Clive Woodward was at the next table, so I went over, shook his hand and said: 'I hear you've been very positive about the tour.' He said: 'Well, you've done a great job, and well done.' Funnily enough, he had lost his voice and couldn't say much!

I was feeling very positive. It was only the second time on tour when we could prepare for a match without having to coach another group of players for an upcoming game. I had nothing else to worry about apart from the match, and I knew I could actually have a sleep-in.

# 22

## Lions to New Zealand 2017

*Saturday, 8 July*
*Third Test: New Zealand v Lions, Eden Park, Auckland*

The first person I met this morning was Neil Jenkins. It would probably be our last meeting on tour as he was leaving early tomorrow. I asked him about the kickers, and he said he was pleased with the way they had gone yesterday.

I spoke to Eanna Falvey again and Prav Mathema, one of our physios, about Rhys Webb and Liam Williams, and they were both confident that the two of them would be OK.

After a quiet morning with some of the family, we met up with the match-day twenty-three in mid-afternoon for our walk-through at the gym. The players went through a few team plays, before the forwards did some of their lineout calls and the backs jogged through some plays.

We came back to the hotel for a pre-match meal. By now, I was actually pretty nervous. I didn't feel hungry at all, so I didn't have anything to eat. All the boys were having some food, so I decided to go up to my room again and get myself organised.

At 4.30pm we had what had become our pre-match pie ritual. This had started in Christchurch, when Bobby went out and bought some pies. We ate the pies, the Lions played really well and won, so Bobby said: 'Shoot, now we have to do pies before every game!'

When Bobby came up to the room he announced proudly: 'I've got the pies! And I'm also going to go and strap my leg. I don't need to, but I had a strapping on in Wellington so I'm going to go and strap it again.' Welcome to our superstitious Bobby. He's the Strength and Conditioning Coach and all he eats is fish 'n' chips, and pies.

I came down ten minutes before we were due to met up at 5.50pm in the team room, which is below the ground floor, and popped my head into the family room to say hi to Trudi and the kids before they were brought outside to cheer us onto the bus.

As well as the match-day squad, the coaches, some of the staff and John Spencer were all at the meeting, but only I spoke. I was a little more animated than I normally would be.

'Just a few points. Firstly, as a group of players I think you guys have been absolutely fantastic on this tour. And as a group of coaches I think you guys have done a brilliant job as well. It's been absolutely superb.

'I think Steve [Borthwick] has spoken to the forwards on a number of occasions about winning the series – about us having to be the best forward pack in the world. Faz spoke yesterday about there being another level in us. I haven't thought today about anything other than being positive. There's not one negative thought that's come into my mind about the result. We're good enough to win and we're good enough to win well.

'There is another level in us. We saw that in the GPS numbers going up. We've never seen that before as coaches. It's taken a while and we've built, and we've built, and we've built. We've got a great opportunity to win a Test series in New Zealand. Seven of you were involved in the third Test in Australia four years ago. Guys here have won Premiership finals, Heineken Cups, European Cups. You're here because you've been involved in big matches.

'We've got a great opportunity tonight to do something really special. Going through it, I don't think anyone is going to be here in twelve years' time. Maybe Maro has a little chance, as a thirty-four-year-old. You get these opportunities in life and you want to make the most of them. And for us as coaches and you as players, it may be the last time you even put that jersey on. Don't let the moment slip.

'If this is the last time you ever wear that jersey – because we never know what's going to happen in the game – make it count. Do something special. Something you're going to remember for the rest of your life. Something you can look back on and go: "I was part of 2017. We won a Test series in New Zealand. We beat the back-to-back world champions. We were the best team in the world in 2017."'

I finished by repeating the words again. 'Let's do something special.'

● ● ●

The journey to the ground was quick; police escort, green lights all the way, which makes a difference. Again the roads were paved in red, as the army of Lions fans were winding their way to Eden Park, and were noisy about it too. When they saw the blue lights of the police bikes coming, and then the Lions bus, up went the usual chorus. *'Li-ons! Li-ons! Li-ons!'* They were everywhere, and even the Kiwi fans were clapping and waving.

Arriving at Eden Park an hour and a half before kick-off, I noticed thousands of Lions supporters were already milling around outside the gates. Banks of fans in red roared us off the bus. I was in the changing room for about ten minutes, and I spoke to Johnny Sexton and to Owen Farrell, telling them: 'These are the kind of games when big players step up and make a difference, and you guys are that.'

Then I went to do my last pre-match interviews with the usual rights holders, and Graham Simmons, Ian Smith and Russell Hargreaves from TV and radio. They were pretty innocuous really. I spoke about how well we'd trained, and hopefully it would be a great Test match and we expected it to be pretty close.

Before the warm-up, I saw Steve Hansen out on the field, shook his hand, and just said: 'How's your week been?'

'Really good.'

Steve asked me the same question and I said: 'Yea, we've had a good week as well. It was nice to get a bit of a break.'

Then he watched some of our warm-up again, and we had a little bit of a look at theirs as well. We'd been doing pretty much the same warm-up all tour and the guys were very familiar with it at this stage. It was quiet again. You could see how focused they were. They seemed ready.

We went back into the changing room. I didn't say a lot then. There didn't seem much need. More than once though, I said: 'Don't let this moment pass you by. Take the opportunity that's presented to you.'

Sam Warburton and Sean O'Brien talked about believing in themselves. That was the main message, and there was a lot of belief in that changing room.

I had chatted with Sam the day before and we'd spoken about the *haka*. We hadn't decided on any specific way of facing it. A couple of times, as coaches, we'd discussed whether the players should form a semi-circle with the captain in the middle, but decided against this. I said to Sam: 'Look, let's be in control of it. When they finish the *haka*, stay standing still for about five seconds. Compose yourselves.'

Sam spoke to the players during the walk-through that afternoon and said that this is what he wanted them to do as well. 'When they finish the *haka*, I'm just going to count to five and walk away then.' It was our way of saying to the All Blacks: 'Look, we're here to accept your challenge and we're ready to go as well.' It wasn't being disrespectful, but we were drawing emotional energy from them throwing down the challenge to us.

Here at Eden Park, we watched the *haka* from the coaches' box, and sure enough the boys stood there for five seconds after the All Blacks broke up. I bet not too many people even noticed.

We won the toss and decided to kick-off. We've won a lot of tosses on this tour actually, including all three Tests. In the first Test we decided we were going to play into the wind, but this time we opted to kick-off and put them under pressure.

Johnny's kick-off was good, but after Savea ran it back, Liam Williams caught Aaron Smith's box-kick and jumped over the touchline. I went absolutely nuts in the box, because early on in the tour we'd shown the players the law change on video. The ruling is that the ball has to pass the touchline before a player can put his foot into touch and catch it. Before the rule changed, they could plant one foot on or over the touchline before catching it to ensure it was your throw-in or the ball had gone out on the full. But the ball hadn't crossed the line when Liam caught it in the air and then jumped out, so it was their throw-in.

'Does he not know the rules? We've covered this.' I was furious. Instead of it being our throw-in on halfway, they had the throw-in and we were on the back foot. The advantage of winning the toss had gone in the first minute.

When players don't know the laws, that really, really frustrates me, because as a professional that's part of your job.

Sean and Sam combined well at the breakdown, and Sam seemed to win a clean turnover, but Romain Poite ruled he'd played the ball off his feet and penalised him. Sam clearly thought that was a tough call, and I know this is hardly a surprise, but so did I. Sam was on his feet. That was a fantastic steal. I looked at it again and said: 'Oh my God, that is an absolutely shocking decision.'

Beauden Barrett took the kick but pulled it, and like a week ago you're thinking: 'Right, is it going to be one of those nights where things go our way?'

Elliot Daly did well to cover a little grubber but we were still under the pump. We were relieved to see Savea drop a pass from Jordie Barrett after Beauden's break and offload.

The All Blacks were playing with more width. They threw everything at us in that first ten minutes. But they were making mistakes as well. I didn't realise how greasy the conditions were until I spoke to Johnny after the game. He said the ball was just like a bar of soap.

It looked like Maro Itoje had eased the pressure when shooting up out of defence to actually rip the ball, except that Owen kicked the ball out on the full. He didn't have a brilliant first twenty minutes.

Toby Faletau put their lineout under pressure, and as a result Maro won another turnover. Conor Murray put up a box-kick, and Elliot made an outstanding take, like something out of Aussie Rules or Croke Park. We then played some great rugby, really stretching them for about fifteen phases. We looked like we were going to score, but then Owen threw a skip pass for Anthony Watson on the wing and Beauden Barrett intercepted it.

When I looked at it again maybe Liam should have come short, instead of drifting out. If he had, I think he would have been straight through a hole; or, if he had come short, that holds the defender and Owen could throw that pass. But because he's drifted out, that's brought them out too. Owen should possibly have just given the pass though. Just put it through the hands. He could even have grubbered it into the in-goal area. But I suppose it's easier from the coaches' box and looking at the video after the incident.

It could have been a fourteen-point swing in favour of the All Blacks but for some great defending. In fairness to Liam, he turned and tackled Barrett, Jonathan Davies chased down Laumape, and Anthony intercepted the offload to Savea. And he stayed on his feet really well.

It was still a big turning point though.

From their lineout they stressed us again and Beauden cross-kicked to his brother. Jordie got above Elliot and tapped it down for Laumape to score. We should have stopped that, but when I spoke to Jonathan afterwards he said he was gone. He knew if he worked harder he would have tackled Laumape, but he was absolutely shattered from that period of play, which had lasted for about three-and-a-half minutes. He said: 'My mind was telling me "go, go," but there was nothing there.

'I'm sorry about that.'

I said: 'Look, sometimes that's sport, isn't it?'

Elliot knew he probably could have done better too. He didn't really get up in the air. Beauden even kicked the touchline conversion, to make it 7–0 to them.

But Toby won a deflection off Smith's box-kick and then there was a great example of us not forcing the pass as we had done in the first two Tests. Conor feinted to offload, but held on and then gave it to Tadhg Furlong. Jonathan Davies put in a good kick to force an attacking lineout. That's what we needed there. When Foxy then took it up, Poite penalised Barrett for not rolling away, and Owen kicked the penalty to make the score 7–3.

Jordie won Beauden's restart, but Liam and Owen did well to stop Savea when he gathered Beauden's cross-kick. Then Cane knocked on. They won a turnover from our scrum, but Smith fired the pass at Beauden Barrett and he couldn't hold it. They normally take those chances, but the ball was very slippery.

We were also hurting ourselves with turnovers. When Liam caught a Smith box-kick, Dagg's hit forced a knock-on. I just cursed again.

We needed someone or something to lift the pressure, and Johnny made a good read to force a knock-on from Jordie Barrett. Johnny had a big game defensively. Then Foxy made a good read on Jordie, we counter-rucked and Sam made a good steal. That won us a penalty.

There was a long break in play. Then we were all ready, but they stayed in a huddle. When Poite blew his whistle, Owen tapped it and gave a terrible pass to Anthony. He caught it but slipped in doing so with Liam on his outside. We had a chance of scoring there. That could have been pretty special.

But we got another penalty against Lienert-Brown for offside and Owen made it 7–6. We were happy with that.

The intensity was huge. Despite the weather, there was no let-up except for injuries. Sean had copped a blow to his left shoulder and Johnny to his left ankle, which needed strapping. But they carried on until half-time.

With thirty-five minutes gone you're thinking: 'Let's get to half-time at 7–6 and we're in this game.' They made a mistake at a lineout but got lucky. Their lineout was under pressure, and we probably should have won it. No one went up in the air, but we didn't react quickly enough. Retallick caught it and by running ten metres it got them on the front foot.

Then Laumape offloaded in a double tackle from Owen and Jonathan. It was just a phenomenal piece of skill and Lienert-Brown put Jordie Barrett over. Maybe Jonathan should have gone a bit higher and stopped it. He just reacted a bit late. Barrett missed the conversion to leave it 12–6. It was disappointing to concede before half-time, but it was still only a one-score game.

When the boys came in we gave them a couple of minutes to rehydrate and re-group. We split into units – Graham and Steve with the forwards, and Andy and Rob with the backs. Then we came together. Andy spoke about getting off our line and winning the collisions, that when we win the collisions we are in control. That was his focus. It was just a mental thing about getting off the line, and Rob emphasised the need to be accurate.

While Johnny was being heavily strapped again, Sean was sitting on the table. Eanna was examining him, testing his arm strength, and it was a little bit better but it still wasn't right. We had a chat with him and he said to me: 'I haven't been able to do anything on that left shoulder for the last six minutes. It's no good.' So we said: 'CJ, you're on.' We put him at blindside and Sam at openside.

Sean has had an unbelievable tour but CJ was a bit unlucky last week. We knew he was going to come on and bring energy and carry. We had been thinking it was the type of game that we'd need all our subs, to keep our momentum going and bring fresh resources.

There wasn't a lot to be said. It was a case of being accurate and keeping hold of the ball. We spoke about turning them around and playing some territory. I felt that we just hadn't kicked enough. I think that we've played too much rugby around halfway again. I said to the guys: 'Look, this is simple. We're in this game. We haven't played that well, with mistakes and turnovers. We've got to keep hold of the ball and we'll win this.'

We were back in our box for the kick-off by Barrett, which didn't go ten, and Read was penalised for pulling Liam to the ground off the ball. That was a good spot by Poite.

There was a bit of discussion in the box about what to do next. We decided to send the message down to Jenks: 'Give Elliot a kick at goal.' Steve and Faz were sitting in front of me and Rob, and Steve said: 'I think it's the wrong decision. I think we should kick to the corner.'

But then he added: 'Hopefully I'm wrong.' Thankfully he was.

Elliot landed a brilliant kick. That is a huge lift for any team, when you see a goal-kicker do that from his own half. We'd just conceded before half-time, but it was only five points because they missed the conversion, and now we had three of them back. It's a big difference psychologically.

Our discipline was much better. The penny had finally dropped. But I felt again that there were a couple of decisions against us which were pretty harsh, because Johnny was then penalised for offside, when the call came from the assistant Jaco Peyper. Johnny was sixth man out and we can't see where he's offside. It's the most marginal of decisions.

The penalty was straight and forty-five metres out, but the All Blacks decided to go up the line. I was surprised by that, but it was a big kick by Beauden Barrett, to within five metres of our line. Although we held their maul up, they created an overlap for Savea. But Jordie Barrett's pass was well forward. Liam did well to push up and force the pass. That was good pressure. We were just a little bit slow coming off our line. I thought if Anthony came up a little bit earlier he had a chance of an intercept.

Then we had a scrum on our own ten-metre line. It was a great chance to turn them, to get a kick away and put the ball behind them, try and squeeze them down in their 22. But Toby went on his own from a scrum and was turned over.

Johnny had to go off for an HIA and we brought Ben Te'o on. When we had another scrum from almost the same position, Owen gave Ben a run rather than kick it and I was surprised when Alun Wyn lost the ball in contact.

It's not like him. When I saw that, I thought: 'What's going on there?' Then, when the TMO had a look at it from an end-on view, it showed Kaino had led with his arm into Alun Wyn's head. I thought: 'That's going to be a yellow card here.' Poite thought so too and Kaino was off for ten minutes.

As Alun Wyn required an HIA as well, we brought on Courtney Lawes. Meanwhile, Johnny passed his HIA.

But we kept on hurting ourselves. Jamie's next throw to the tail was crooked. Then Jerome Garces called a forward pass by Anthony when he released Liam up the touchline. We were on our feet in the box. I looked at it again. There's no way that was forward. A flat ball at worst.

Still, we had a third lineout in those ten minutes against fourteen men after another good defensive read by Foxy on Jordie Barrett. But then Foxy couldn't hold a flat pass by Johnny.

At this stage, it felt like the momentum was starting to swing towards us, and they were slowing the game down as much as possible. We didn't get the chance to play a lot in that ten minutes because of that.

Elliot couldn't keep a long clearance from Dagg infield and instead gave them a lineout on our ten-metre line. 'What are we doing to ourselves?'

But mistakes happen, and CJ, Jamie and Mako executed a choke tackle to win a turnover. That was a big moment, because it led to Retallick catching Courtney high. Owen landed a great kick. It was 12–12.

We had chances to put them under more pressure at this point, but Courtney knocked on. Then Conor put us under pressure when he slightly hooked a box-kick too far infield. Jordie Barrett made a great catch and Beauden put in a long raking touch-finder.

Conor then made up for his error and found touch on halfway with a huge box-kick and Toby's tackle forced a knock-on from Beauden Barrett.

Graham Rowntree had problem-solved our scrum at half-time. He showed Tadhg some clips of two scrums. We knew there wasn't a lot of difference between the front-rows, and even after bringing on Jack McGrath and Kyle Sinckler, the scrum was still going to be OK.

Our scrum was much better in the second half, but then they were awarded a penalty on our put-in. I've looked at that again and again since, and both packs went down. He penalised Kyle for collapsing under our posts. 'Come on, give us a break here.' I thought that scrum was going nowhere.

They were not going forward against us. Normally, Poite is one of those referees who, if the ball is at the number 8's feet, he says play on. Although the ball was still sitting in the front-row, why not re-set?

The score was now 15–12 to them.

We brought on Rhys Webb for Conor because Rhys had given us impact in the first Test. Then when Jamie had his second crooked throw, we put Ken Owens on.

Beauden kicked to the corner again, but Anthony covered back and beat Savea to help get us out of there. Liam did well to deal with a kick from Jordie Barrett but then fumbled one by Aaron Smith. We brought on Jack Nowell for Anthony, and Ben Te'o for Johnny, while Sam returned after passing his HIA.

Rhys and Owen held up Dagg in a choke tackle. Lions scrum. When the first one went down, Poite re-set it this time. The next one was better. Kyle stayed straight and strong, and it was our penalty. Owen found a good touch on halfway.

Wyatt Crockett tackled Maro but didn't roll away. Rhys fell over him trying to clear the ball away. He did well to force that penalty, although Poite took a while to give it. We had to go for the kick. The clock was past seventy-seven minutes. It was forty-eight metres out. Owen hadn't had his greatest game, but that's the thing about quality players, they put the bad moments behind them, and step up when it matters. And that's what Owen did. What a kick! It was all-square at 15–15.

It was their kick-off. We'd practised this scenario the day before; receiving a short kick-off from them with the last play of the game, and to be prepared for that. We had different players nominated to receive the ball on either side, and Liam was one of those. But he couldn't gather it under pressure from Read, and then Ken played the ball. Poite awarded them a penalty. Our first thoughts were: 'That's it. Game over.'

But Sam asked the referee to check the challenge in the air. I thought Read was in Poite's ear too much all night, whereas Sam played him nicely. Maybe that contributed to Poite going to the TMO.

When I looked at it in real time, I didn't think Read had a chance of getting to the ball. When it went to the TMO, I looked at it again. I'm thinking: 'We've gone up early. Is there contact in the air? I'm not sure that Read can actually get to the ball from where he is. His arm is stretched, but it doesn't look as if he can reach it and hook it back. So he's made contact in the air and the ball has gone off Liam.'

I thought Poite could potentially penalise Read for making contact in the air. The next day I was shown a freeze frame of Barrett's re-start, and Read was in front of the ball. They didn't go back to check for him being in front of the kick-off, which is quite significant because then he wouldn't have got anywhere near the ball.

Poite called the two captains together. 'We have a deal about the offside by sixteen.'

Sam: 'Red or black?'

Poite: 'Red. He didn't play, deliberately, the ball, OK. It was an accidental offside.'

Read: 'No. No. No.'

Poite: 'It was an accidental offside. We go for a scrum for black.'

When Read again queried the ruling, Poite said: 'The ball touched him. It wasn't him playing the ball.'

The end result was an All Blacks scrum.

I think if we'd lost the game and the series on that call, it would have been very tough. You can go back to the kick-off and see that Read is in front of the ball and offside. It's also not certain if the ball did go forward from Liam before Ken instinctively played it and then pulled his hands away. It could even have been a penalty against Read for the challenge in the air. It's a tough one for the officials. They could have made any one of five decisions.

I felt for Ken, because he must have been thinking: 'Oh my God, I'm going to have to emigrate somewhere.' He thought it was going to be the worst day of his career. In those situations it's every player's instinct to play the ball.

I didn't think we'd been getting the 50/50 calls but when Poite decided it was an All Blacks scrum I thought: 'We're getting a call here! And now we have just over a minute to hold them out.'

The ball actually squirted out of their scrum and Rhys picked it up and started running with the ball. Someone shouted 'KICK IT!' I wish Rhys had booted it. If he had just kicked it down the left, they had no one back there. But he passed inside and although the ball seemed to deflect backwards off CJ, Garces called a knock-on from the touchline. Another close call and another scrum to them.

Then they came at us in waves. There have been so many occasions where the All Blacks have scored in those situations, in the last minute and up against it. They do it so, so many times. And then they very nearly did it again, but Liam made a good tackle on Jordie Barrett in the corner. CJ, Owen, Ben and Elliot all scrambled back and Elliot forced TJ Perenara into touch.

Full-time: New Zealand 15 Lions 15. A draw, and a drawn series.

No agony and no ecstasy.

There wasn't much of a reaction in the box. I shook hands with all the coaches and the analysts, and said: 'Well done. Some achievement.' And it was an amazing achievement, to come here having been completely written off, everyone expecting a 3–0 whitewash for them, and then to draw the series.

Everyone spoke about the schedule, saying it was suicidal to take it on, playing the best team in the world in their own backyard, and then we've lost the first Test. So when you think about it, it's some accomplishment for this group of players, support staff, coaches and everyone else who was involved.

Our emotions were a little scrambled. In the last minute we went from losing this game for not taking a kick-off to them getting the scrum, to then fleetingly having a chance to win it, and then finally holding out. So you're thinking: 'I'll take that.'

I went downstairs and then on to the field and shook all the players' hands. I went over and shook Kieran Read's hand and just said: 'Congratulations on your 100th cap, that's some achievement.' Then I waited for the presentations.

Wayne Smith came over and said: 'Congratulations. You did a fantastic job in the last six weeks with what you have done with this team.' I thought it was really nice of him to say that. He also said: 'It was a day for defence coaches today, wasn't it?'

The first presentation was to Read for winning his 100th cap. Some Kiwis who I spoke to later were a little embarrassed that it was nearly all Lions supporters who were still in the stadium for Read's cap presentation.

Then Read and Sam were interviewed and handed the trophy together. They invited all the players up to mingle and pose for photographs.

I thought it was fitting for our players to then go and thank the fans. Their support has been remarkable. They've just been absolutely phenomenal. Incredible.

Back in the changing room, I said: 'Look guys, well done. Congratulations. That's an unbelievable achievement. What we've done as a group, it hasn't been about the fifteen or twenty-three, it's been about everyone.' I thanked all the players and all the staff.

Then we had a big sing-song. We sang our four anthems, with all the squad, management and staff as a group in a big circle. There was room for all of us, just about. It was a nice time. We really belted them out.

Peter White, who did a fantastic job as our liaison officer, managed to locate Trudi and the kids and brought them down through a little back alley with some stairs. So when I left the changing room they were standing right outside, and I gave them a big hug. Normally Trudi and the kids know my mood will largely be dictated by the result. But this time they were clearly unsure how I'd taken a draw.

Trudi said: 'How's it going? Are you OK?'

'Yes, it's all good.' That seemed to put their minds at ease.

I had to do all my media interviews, and then the main press conference. Graham Simmons asked me would I take the draw or would I have liked to roll the dice?

'You always want to roll the dice, don't you? It's all about winning. It's a great achievement coming here and drawing the series. We knew how tough it was from the start, but we got better as the tour went on. I don't think we played that brilliantly tonight. The message at half-time was: "We're still in this game." We'd made a lot of mistakes and didn't have a lot of territory and possession, but the boys showed some real courage. I think speaking to the players afterwards, they said how slippery the ball was and that's probably why there were mistakes from both teams.'

I said I thought it was a fair result and that 'we would have been pretty gutted to lose the game' to that late penalty.

'Finally,' he said, 'you've been head coach twice. If they asked you to do it again, would you do it?'

'I'm a great believer in, what will be will be, so I won't be looking too far ahead. I'm looking forward, hopefully, to the next couple of years with Wales and seeing what other opportunities are out there after that. We'll see what happens.'

On my way to the press conference I said to Luke Broadley: 'Have you got that clown nose?' He'd also brought the big clown bow-tie. I didn't think that was appropriate, but I thought the red nose was fine.

Some people said: 'You're not going to do that?'

'Yes, I am.'

So I put it on, walked into the room and sat down, before taking it off after a few seconds. It got a laugh, but I don't think too many photographers got the picture.

You have to be able to laugh at yourself. In my time in coaching this job has changed hugely, with the impact of social media in particular. Everything has become so much more magnified and opinion-driven, and there are a lot of people out there who can be quite vociferous and vicious. You really need a thick skin to be involved in professional sport nowadays. Twenty-odd years ago it was just an occasional journalist writing an opinion piece, and no one really had any right to respond to that unless you went down to your local pub and spoke to a few of your mates about it. It's just changed dramatically.

Back in the changing room I put on my burgundy smoking jacket and changed ties, while we had a couple of beers. The coaches and the players were in a reflective mood, and the scale of what we had achieved was only slowly dawning on them. I went around to some of the guys and said: 'Some of you have been on two Lions tours and you're undefeated in both Test series. Not many players can claim to have done that.'

That's one hell of a feat for those players. Even someone like Tadhg, who has played the All Blacks five times, has won two and drawn one. What's more, if some of them get another chance on the next Lions tour, and if they win the series in South Africa, they will go down as legends, because that would be 2–1 in Australia, the draw in New Zealand and a win in South Africa.

We boarded the bus to Skycity for the after-match ceremony. They said they were having problems with the lifts in the Skycity Grand hotel, and the post-match reception was on the fifth floor, so we had to walk up five flights. We reached the fourth floor and Andy Farrell said, 'We're on 4a'. Then we go up another flight and it's 4b. Then he said: 'OK, we're at 4c now,' and I'm thinking: 'You've got to be joking.' Finally we reached the fifth floor.

Players, coaches and officials from both squads were standing around in a big room. There was finger food and I had a couple of beers. I spoke to Wayne Smith and his wife Trish. We had a good chat. We reminisced about the days when he was with Northampton and I was with Wasps. We spoke about when he was finishing up, and he said that after the Rugby Championship he was going to take a year out and go travelling.

I chatted with Steve Hansen and asked him what he was doing. He said he was going to take a week's holiday before coming in for the Championship.

Then it was time for some speeches. Maurice Trapp, President of New Zealand Rugby, spoke on behalf of the All Blacks, while Lions Tour Manager John Spencer spoke on our behalf. John talked well about the hospitality, how tough it's been but how we enjoyed the tour. He congratulated all the staff. Scotty Stevenson was the master of ceremonies and they had a couple of pictures in the background on the projector screen, including the DHL ones of the two squads together for the trophy presentation. It captures a nice moment in rugby history. Draws aren't the worst thing in the world. They create scenes like that.

The two captains spoke and then the All Blacks made their three cap presentations to the players who'd made their debuts against Samoa a week before the start of the Lions series: Vaea Fifita, Jordie Barrett and Ngani Laumape.

I chatted with Smiley Barrett. I didn't see Vaea Fifita, but I saw Jordie and congratulated him. Then I went up to Ngani who was sitting there with our two Tongan boys, Mako and Toby, and congratulated him. He was very respectful and said: 'Thanks very much, it's an honour to meet you.' That was nice. I always try and do that when guys win their first cap, just to acknowledge that big day in their lives. I think it's important to say 'congratulations' and 'good luck for the future'.

From Skycity we were driven to the Soul Bar & Bistro overlooking Viaduct Harbour. We were taken in through the back kitchen up a staircase and through the top bar. That was full of some fairly weary-looking fans, but we were brought into this lovely room which was just for the Lions players, management and families. There must have been around 100 of us in there.

By 4am we were ready to catch our bus back to the hotel. Even at that time of the early morning, there were hordes of Lions fans gathered in front of the bus, chanting and banging on the windows. So poor Rob and Sean, our security guys, had to go in front of the bus and try to push people back. They were just getting battered and the bus was progressing an inch, another inch, then another inch. Other fans climbed onto the top of a taxi to get closer to the bus. They weren't being aggressive, just buoyant after a few drinks.

The crowd just kept swelling. The next day Rob said that he'd been a bit concerned it was going to get out of hand, but it turned out OK when the police arrived and calmed everything down.

So that was a happy ending to a really momentous day for us.

## 23

# THAT WAS THE TOUR
# THAT WAS

## Lions to New Zealand 2017

*Sunday, 9 July*

We got about five hours' sleep, and had time for a shower and a light breakfast. We had a meeting with Peter White, our Head Liaison Officer, and Johnny McLaughlin and Glen Marsh, who were our Liaison Officers in Auckland. We wanted to thank them for looking after us so well.

Liaison officers are the main contact on the ground. They hold close relationships with the training venues, bus drivers and hotel staff. Basically, they know people who can get stuff done. They help make everything run smoothly.

We like to acknowledge them when we are leaving a location for the last time. As Peter had spent the entire six weeks with us, John Spencer presented him with a signed and framed Lions jersey in recognition of all the work he had done.

All the squad were there, and some were the worse for wear, having lasted until about 5am. The players were planning to have a court session at 3 o'clock that afternoon.

At 12.30pm we did our final press conference and then a group of us went out to Peter White's house in Browns Bay. His wife Jane put on some food and we had a few beers and glasses of wine. There were about twenty of us there.

I was speaking to Dan Sheridan, the photographer. This was Dan's third tour and he gets on very well with the players. He and Shane Whelan, the Head of Digital, were great for having a laugh and bringing some balance to the tour. Dan asked me: 'Out of the three tours you've been on, which one did you enjoy the most?'

'Oh, probably Australia,' I said.

New Zealand is a great country, but some of the external stuff made it a bit tougher. I enjoyed Australia. He loved South Africa. He said that was the best tour he had been on.

Bobby entertained us all with a few card tricks. Rala was there with his wife Dixie. I was sitting on Pete's couch when Rala came over, sat next to me, shook my hand and said: 'Thanks very much, I've loved it. Thanks for ringing me and bringing me on the tour.' While we were sitting on the couch we heard it crack. I got up straight away and left Rala there as it collapsed, so he copped the blame.

Then Dan took some photos of us all outside, before Trudi and I went back to the hotel. About twenty of us were reconvening at Soul down by the Viaduct. We left the hotel at 7.30pm on the bus. We had a nice meal there. I had the salt and pepper squid, and the tarakihi, a New Zealand fish that's a bit like snapper. At one point I went to the toilet and was asked for a photograph. Once I stop for one, this leads to a trickle which soon becomes a flood. After about twenty minutes, Trudi had to come and rescue me!

We were back in the hotel at about 11.30pm, by which stage it was pretty quiet. Some of the players were going out again. I went outside for a quick chat with Elliot Daly and Jonathan Davies. Then I had a drink with John Spencer and finished by having a couple with Ger Carmody.

We reminisced about the tour, and all the planning that had gone into it. Ger's first reconnaissance mission to New Zealand was back in June 2015, and to transport forty-one players, around forty support staff, twenty tonnes of luggage and taking in roughly 50,000 km of air and road transport, required detailed planning. It's twice the size of any normal summer tour in effect.

We were lucky that it went off without a hitch. Gemma Crowley, our Team Services Manager, did a lot of the organisation and Ger has put in hours and hours of his time. He did a great job. He loved doing it too, and will be compiling his report then taking a week's break, before returning to the IRFU in September but in a different capacity. Gemma was absolutely brilliant on tour: she was always there lending a hand and doing much more than her job description required.

We talked about the future, both ours and the Lions, and how this tour went. The key component to any Lions tour is harmony within the team, picking the right players, and by that I also mean the right characters.

We had three or four players who have become detached from the tour in the last week or so. You could see it in their body language.

It's something that everyone has picked up on, whether it's been some of the medics, the strength and conditioners, the coaches, players or other staff members. It happened in 2009, and again in 2013. You know it's likely, so you just try to keep everyone together for as long as you possibly can. We had a chat about those individuals. They weren't a particularly negative influence but it showed me what their real character was like. The vast majority have been brilliant, even those not involved in the match-day twenty-three for the third Test.

It was quite late when we called it a night, probably about 1am. But it was a fitting way to sign off the weekend. Back in September 2016, two days after I was appointed, Ger and I went to New Zealand for our first two-week tour of all the hotels, gyms, pitches, pools and stadiums.

It seems like a long, long time ago, and now it's all over.

## Monday, 10 July

Today is our last day but an important one for the Lions squad of 2017. It's the medical day for the players. All of them have to be examined for insurance purposes before they return to their clubs.

We had arranged to meet Michael Holland and his wife Susan, who had hosted some of the Lions management on a pre-tour planning trip in their chateaux near Perpignan, as well as his brother Dave and his wife Jan. He had flags and shirts printed for the tour, and before every match he laid on pre-match food in a pub at his own expense for maybe fifty people.

He had come to the Rydges hotel and given me a big hug after we won the second Test in Wellington. He'd also met Trudi in the Westpac Stadium not long after the match had ended.

'When did I see you?' he said to Trudi.

'Maybe twenty minutes after the final whistle.'

'Oh yes, before I lost it.'

'What?'

'I broke down,' he said.

So did Dave, his brother. When Dave saw him crying, he was in tears too. Susan and Jan were going: 'What the heck?' But it demonstrates what a supporter he is.

The tour has had that effect on people. Even when Lions Chairman Tom Grace first came up to me in the hotel this morning to say 'well done', he broke down and then just walked off. He came back over to me later and said: 'Sorry I lost it earlier on.' But there was no need to apologise.

Rob and Ceri Howley joined us before they went out for breakfast. Jan is quite new to this whole thing; she probably hadn't been on a rugby tour before. She asked: 'Can I have a photo of the group of us?'

Dave volunteered to take it, but we could see Sam Warburton standing at the bar talking to someone. So Trudi said: 'Ask Sam to take the photo.'

Everyone laughed, but she went over to him. 'Sam, would you mind taking a photo for us?'

Because he's so polite, Sam said: 'No problem.'

Then he looked up and saw me laughing. 'Oh, OK.' People do that to him, as a mickey-take. They would say: 'Oh can you take a photo for us?' and not: 'Would you be in it?'

Sam took the picture, and then, obviously, he got into the photo as well. He's such a good sport.

Last night when we got back to the hotel and went down to the team room, Sam was sitting there making sure everybody was OK. He had been out and about, but had come back, caught a few hours' sleep and got up again at about 11.30pm. He was pretty much stone cold sober, just chatting to people in the hotel, probably just watching guys coming in and out, and making sure there were no dramas.

Otherwise, today was a quiet day. Bryn came in and then we picked up Gabby from Sam's and went into Takapuna for some lunch. Then we came back to the hotel.

It was also a day of more goodbyes, as some of the coaches and staff were leaving before the squad flew home the next day, either for home or going from here to their various holiday destinations. I am staying on in New Zealand before we fly to Fiji on Thursday for a week's holiday.

Graham Rowntree was leaving at lunchtime because he and his family are moving house from Leicester to London on Tuesday. Wig came over to me in the foyer bar and gave me a hug before heading off to the airport. He said: 'Thanks very much for everything. That was a really wonderful experience. It's been emotional.'

'Yea, it was very good. You coached really well.' Wig's a good coach. Coaches improve over time. You gain experience and, definitely, four years on from our last tour together, he's moved on to another level. He's also had that experience of coaching with England and now with Harlequins. I had a good chat with Andy Farrell as well. He did a fantastic job.

Saying all the goodbyes, I found it almost sad as well as a relief that it's finally over. I am whacked. I've a cough and I'm probably coming down with something. It was hard work. But I knew that would be the case right from the start.

I look back on it all now and think: 'I've coached two Lions tours and we haven't lost a series. We've won one and drawn one. That's a pretty good achievement, playing away from home.' It feels pretty special.

Of the two, this is probably the bigger achievement. The All Blacks had won forty-seven in a row on home soil since they lost to South Africa in Hamilton in 2009. They had won thirty-eight Tests in a row at Eden Park going back to a draw with South Africa in 1994. What's more, that's the first time under Steve Hansen that the All Blacks have lost a game and haven't won the next one.

The second Test win in Wellington was obviously the highlight. I was pretty stoked after the Crusaders game as well. We had to win that one, and we played well that day.

Of course, all the coverage of the final Test focused on Romain Poite changing his decision from an All Blacks penalty to a scrum. No one noticed that Kieran Read was in front of the ball from the kick-off. It's a pity that this has slightly overshadowed what was a great game and a great series.

As I've said, to have lost it to a penalty in that manner would have been sickening, and I think we deserved a draw.

When the dust settles, I think more and more people will appreciate what an accomplishment it was to draw this series, and how successful this Lions tour has been. There have been great rugby matches all the way through, finished off by three epic Tests. It's been a huge boost for the New Zealand economy and the Lions brand.

So many of these Lions fans who have been over here for the last six weeks must have been saving and planning this trip for years. It could be with their father, son, mother, daughter, brother, sister or other relatives or good friends. These are huge days in their lives. And yet there are people in the game of rugby who, for their own selfish reasons or agendas, want to get rid of the Lions. I find that amazing.

On Sunday a supporter shook my hand and said: 'Gats, thanks for last night. I had the best night of my life!' When I think about it, how cool is that?

Then you think about these narrow-minded people back in the UK who want the Lions' itinerary reduced or even scrapped altogether. You'd like to say: 'Come on the tour. Come and experience it. And if you did, you'd find it magical.' Why would anybody want to get rid of that?

I don't know whether I'll ever be involved again, but I am passionate about the Lions. That's why, in the final press conference, Sam Warburton said it was 'the pinnacle'. I think we should actually be doing everything we can to give the Lions more time and better preparation, in order to protect the tours.

We've had one faction which has tried to undermine this tour from the start, unsuccessfully, even though it is a major national newspaper with an agenda. If I were them, I would be a little bit embarrassed.

Once every four years is the right time to tour, as is once every twelve years in one of the three southern hemisphere countries. It's the biggest event in rugby outside the World Cup. How much money has this tour generated for New Zealand rugby, for the four home unions and for the New Zealand economy? The head of tourism in Auckland was at the second Test and he couldn't stop smiling. All the bars in all the cities where the Lions have played have been packed and buzzing.

The Lions board hadn't communicated with me what they had agreed to say as a policy in public about the future of the Lions. John Feehan told me: 'I'm just letting you know that Ian Ritchie [outgoing CEO of the RFU] is not happy about some of the comments you made about the Lions and the future of the Lions.' So I said: 'OK, fair enough. If Ian Ritchie has a problem, tell him to come and talk to me.' I didn't have an issue with that. But it's a hard one. You're out here and you're asking yourself: 'Who's fighting for the future of the Lions?' There seems to be different agendas out there. Apart from John Spencer, who's been a really strong advocate for the Lions, there haven't been too many vocal others.

Last Friday, I sat beside John on the bus back from training. He had a board meeting the next day to discuss what needed to be done to protect the future of Lions tours, to make sure they continue long into the future. There are individuals out there, whether it's chief executives or club owners, thinking about their own interests. That is perfectly understandable. But not enough people are fighting for the Lions.

You think about what this tour has meant for the players and the fans. If we were to lose the Lions, it would be a sad indictment of the game. Like I said, the timing is perfect. Every twelve years in one of the three host countries generally limits players to one opportunity against the Lions. So when the tour comes along everyone – players, coaches and fans – is excited about it and looks forward to it.

I said to him: 'John, you guys have to be careful that whoever the next coach is in 2021, he doesn't try to re-invent the wheel.' That runs the risk of too many mistakes being made without time to rectify them, because these tours just go by very quickly. Whoever comes in will have a huge amount of control over the direction of the tour. I told him that the Lions board needs to be aware of that. There will be a lot of water under the bridge in four years' time and whoever comes in could easily forget all the lessons we've learned.

John is due to address two Lions board meetings over the weekend and when I said goodbye to him for the final time today, he looked as whacked as I did.

● ● ●

At about 8pm, we finished packing all our bags and took them downstairs in the lift. Trudi and the kids wheeled the bags to the car outside, while I checked out before the drive home to Hamilton. I saw Rala and Dixie, and said goodbye to them too.

Walking through the lobby of the Pullman hotel for the very last time, I was approached by a Kiwi lady who showed me an old-fashioned scrapbook, with pictures and cuttings stuck onto the pages, as well as hand-written messages. The lady explained: 'My boss's two daughters did this for him.'

The inscription on the front was: *'To Dad. Love Elsie and Matilda, Lions tour 2017.'*

She added: 'Elsie picked a draw for the series because she didn't want anyone to lose or win. Would you be able to sign it for me please?'

'Of course,' I said. 'Is this really for your boss?'

'Yes, his two daughters did the whole thing right from the word go. So they're hoping that maybe we could get a few of the Lions to sign it.'

As I was flicking through it, the lady said 'well done', and that it had been a brilliant tour.

'Yea, we did well,' I said, 'despite some people trying to derail it.'

Then she pointed to a page. 'Do you see what the girls wrote about you there?'

I looked to where she'd pointed.

*'We don't think he's grumpy.'*

---

After the third Test, Sam passed around voting slips for the players' Player of the Tour award, or the Lions' Lion of the Tour. Charlie McEwen counted them on the spot and Nuala Walsh, Global Head of Marketing with Standard Life Investments, presented the award.

We were speaking as coaches and I was asked: 'Who do you think will win it?'

I thought about it for a few seconds: 'That's a good question. Maybe Sean O'Brien'.

As I mentioned earlier in the book, coaches are often more critical of their own players than they are of other players; so I was delighted when Jonathan Davies won the vote. It clearly showed what a good tour he has had. I think he has had a great tour, actually. He's carried well and hasn't made many mistakes.

He had the experience from 2013, although I think it took him a while to rediscover his form after returning from France. I don't think going to

Clermont was the best thing for him. His game really dropped off, but in the last four to five months he has started to play some good rugby.

At Scarlets and Wales we got him running hard again, attacking inside shoulders. He has a good left boot on him and put through a couple of nice little kicks, particularly against the Maori. He has defended really well and performed in that key role as a conduit between the back three and the guys on the inside.

He's quieter in the Lions' environment than elsewhere, but he is really well liked by all the players and the staff. They have a huge amount of respect for him. Eanna Falvey said to me: 'Foxy will ask you if you can use the scissors to take his tape off and twenty minutes later he'll come back and hand you the scissors in your hand.' Other players would just leave them lying around the changing room. I really like the small things like that.

I think Sam Warburton will still improve as a captain. He's better when he has other leaders around him to help support him. I know how nervous he was in 2013 but he was much more comfortable in the role this time. What I love about him as a captain is it's not about him, it's about the team first and that was one of the reasons I chose him again. I was 100 per cent sure that he would be comfortable if we felt that someone else deserved to be picked.

Including him in the first Test on the bench was important. It was Graham Rowntree who said to me: 'I think you've got to have your captain in the twenty-three. Keep him on tour. Keep him involved.' I think it was the right decision; then, when we brought him back for the second and third Tests, I think he played exceptionally well and brought some physicality.

It was tough on Peter O'Mahony. He had done a good job as captain in the first Test. He's a fantastic lineout forward. But sometimes you pick horses for courses: that's how we felt with Sam.

I feel sorry for Sam sometimes in Wales because the Welsh media like to create this battle between him and Justin Tipuric, and continually report that he's under pressure for his place. They used to create this sort of rivalry and debate about the '10s'. In New Zealand they don't do that. They celebrate how lucky they are when they have the likes of Richie McCaw and Sam Cane competing for the same jersey.

I know that Sam has struggled with that at times and his decision not to captain Wales in the Six Nations was a good chance for him to get away from it. When I first picked him as a captain, from day one I thought: 'Yea, it's going to take him a bit of time but as the years go by he will get better and better.' We saw that with Richie McCaw, how much he improved as an All Blacks captain. Now we're seeing it with Sam, especially in the way he speaks to referees and the relationship he has with the officials.

In my view, he's as close to a southern hemisphere '7' as we've got in the northern hemisphere, in the sense that he is extremely strong over the ball. He's physical at that breakdown area and slows down opposition ball or wins turnovers as well as any '7' around.

## 2017 British & Irish Lions Tour Summary

*3 June, New Zealand Provincial Barbarians 7, British & Irish Lions 13, Toll Stadium, Whangarei*

**NZ Provincial Barbarians:** Luteru Laulala; Sam Vaka, Kaveinga Finau (Jonah Lowe 19), Dwayne Sweeney, Sevu Reece; Bryn Gatland (Joe Webber 58), Jack Stratton (Richard Judd 53); Aidan Ross (Tolu Fahamokioa 49), Sam Anderson-Heather (capt) (Andrew Makalio 40), Oliver Jager (Marcel Renata 61), Josh Goodhue, Keepa Mewett (Peter Rowe 61), James Tucker (Mewett 64-68), Lachlan Boshier (Matt Matich 46), Mitchell Dunshea.

**Scorers:** Try: Sam Anderson-Heather. Con: Gatland.

**British & Irish Lions:** Stuart Hogg; Anthony Watson, Jonathan Joseph, Ben Te'o, Tommy Seymour; Johnny Sexton (Owen Farrell 48), Greig Laidlaw (Rhys Webb 58); Joe Marler (Mako Vunipola 49), Rory Best (Jamie George 49), Kyle Sinckler (Tadhg Furlong 49), Alun Wyn Jones, Iain Henderson

(George Kruis 49), Ross Moriarty, Sam Warburton (capt) (Justin Tipuric 66), Taulupe Faletau.

**Unused replacement:** Elliot Daly.

**Scorers:** Try: Watson. Con: Farrell. Pens: Sexton, Laidlaw.

*7 June, Blues 22, British & Irish Lions 16, Eden Park, Auckland*

**Blues:** Michael Collins; Matt Duffie (TJ Faiane 38-40), George Moala (Faiane 66), Sonny Bill Williams, Rieko Ioane; Stephen Perofeta (Ihaia West 51), Augustine Pulu (Sam Nock 70); Ofa Tu'ungafasi (Alex Hodgman 57), James Parsons (capt) (Epalahame Faiva 70), Charlie Faumuina (Sione Mafileo 57), Gerard Cowley-Tuioti (Jimmy Tupou 57), Scott Scrafton, Akira Ioane, Blake Gibson (Kara Pryor 66), Steven Luatua.

**Scorers:** Tries: R Ioane, Williams, West. Cons: Perofeta, West. Pen: West.

**British & Irish Lions:** Leigh Halfpenny; Jack Nowell, Jared Payne (Liam Williams 48), Robbie Henshaw, Elliot Daly; Dan Biggar (Johnny Sexton 36), Rhys Webb (Greig Laidlaw 75); Jack McGrath (Joe Marler 54), Ken Owens (capt) (Rory Best 68), Dan Cole (Kyle Sinckler 55), Maro Itoje, Courtney Lawes (Iain Henderson 75), James Haskell (Peter O'Mahony 54), Justin Tipuric, CJ Stander.

**Scorers:** Try: Stander Con: Halfpenny. Pens: Halfpenny 3.

**Yellow card:** Williams.

*10 June, Crusaders 3, British & Irish Lions 12, AMI Stadium, Christchurch*

**Crusaders:** Israel Dagg; Seta Tamanivalu, Jack Goodhue, David Havili, George Bridge (Tim Bateman 66); Richie Mo'unga (Mitch Hunt 74), Bryn Hall (Mitchell Drummond 61); Joe Moody (Wyatt Crockett 50), Codie Taylor (Ben Funnell 50), Owen Franks (Michael Alaalatoa 50), Luke Romano (Quinten Strange 55), Sam Whitelock (capt), Heiden Bedwell-Curtis (Jed Brown 61), Matt Todd, Jordan Taufua.

**Scorer:** Pen: Mo'unga.

**British & Irish Lions:** Stuart Hogg (Anthony Watson 19); George North, Jonathan Davies (Johnny Sexton 27), Ben Te'o, Liam Williams; Owen Farrell, Conor Murray; Mako Vunipola (Jack McGrath 61), Jamie George (Ken Owens 65), Tadhg Furlong (Dan Cole 65), Alun Wyn Jones (capt), George Kruis (Maro Itoje 61), Peter O'Mahony, Sean O'Brien (CJ Stander 55), Taulupe Faletau.

**Unused replacement:** Rhys Webb.

**Scorer:** Pens: Farrell 4.

*13 June, Highlanders 23, British & Irish Lions 22, Forsyth Barr Stadium, Dunedin*

**Highlanders:** Richard Buckman; Waisake Naholo, Malakai Fekitoa (Marty Banks 12-17), Teihorangi Walden, Tevita Li (Patrick Osborne 68); Lima Sopoaga (Banks 55), Kayne Hammington (Josh Renton 75); Daniel Lienert-Brown (Aki Seiuli 60), Liam Coltman (Greg Pleasants-Tate 68), Siate Tokolahi (Siosiua Halanukonuka 68), Alex Ainley (Josh Dickson 55), Jackson Hemopo, Gareth Evans, Dillon Hunt (James Lentjes 60), Luke Whitelock (capt).

**Scorers:** Tries: Naholo, Coltman. Cons: Sopoaga, Banks. Pens: Sopoaga 2, Banks.

**British & Irish Lions:** Jared Payne (Elliot Daly 63); Jack Nowell, Jonathan Joseph, Robbie Henshaw, Tommy Seymour; Dan Biggar (Owen Farrell 68), Rhys Webb (Greig Laidlaw 48); Joe Marler (Jack McGrath 55), Rory Best (Ken Owens 25-29, 49), Kyle Sinckler (Dan Cole 49), Courtney Lawes (Alun Wyn Jones 27), Iain Henderson, James Haskell, Sam Warburton (capt) (Justin Tipuric 67), CJ Stander.

**Scorers:** Tries: Joseph, Seymour, Warburton. Cons: Biggar 2. Pen: Biggar.

*17 June, Maori All Blacks 10, British & Irish Lions 32, Rotorua International Stadium*

**Maori All Blacks:** James Lowe; Nehe Milner-Skudder, Matt Proctor (Rob Thompson 53), Charlie Ngatai, Rieko Ioane; Damian McKenzie (Ihaia West 62), Tawera Kerr-Barlow (Bryn Hall 74); Kane Hames (Chris Eves 61), Ash Dixon (capt) (Hikawera Elliot 70), Ben May (Marcel Renata 70), Joe Wheeler (Leighton Price 70), Tom Franklin, Akira Ioane, Elliot Dixon (Kara Pryor 74), Liam Messam.

**Scorers:** Try: Messam. Con: McKenzie. Pen: McKenzie.

**Yellow card:** Kerr-Barlow.

**British & Irish Lions:** Leigh Halfpenny; Anthony Watson, Jonathan Davies, Ben Te'o, George North (Elliot Daly 62); Johnny Sexton (Dan Biggar 66), Conor Murray (Greig Laidlaw 66); Mako Vunipola (Jack McGrath 59), Jamie George (Ken Owens 64), Tadhg Furlong (Kyle Sinckler 64), Maro Itoje, George Kruis (Iain Henderson 59), Peter O'Mahony (capt) (Sam Warburton 62), Sean O'Brien, Taulupe Faletau.

**Scorers:** Tries: Penalty try (7 points), Itoje. Con: Halfpenny. Pens: Halfpenny 6.

*20 June, Chiefs 6, British & Irish Lions 34, Waikato Stadium, Hamilton*

**Chiefs:** Shaun Stevenson; Toni Pulu (Chase Tiatia 12), Tim Nanai-Williams, Johnny Fa'auli, Solomon Alaimalo (Luteru Laulala 66); Stephen Donald (capt), Finlay Christie; Siegfried Fisiihoi (Aidan Ross 65), Liam Polwart (Hikawera Elliot 60), Nepo Laulala (Atu Moli 65), Dominic Bird, Michael Allardice (Mitch Karpik 65), Mitch Brown, Lachlan Boshier, Tom Sanders (Liam Messam 55).

**Scorer:** Pens: Donald 2.

**Yellow card:** Brown.

**British & Irish Lions:** Liam Williams; Jack Nowell, Jared Payne (Elliot Daly 77), Robbie Henshaw, Elliot Daly (Tommy Seymour 60); Dan Biggar, Greig

Laidlaw; Joe Marler, Rory Best (capt), Dan Cole, Iain Henderson, Courtney Lawes (Alun Wyn Jones 50-58), James Haskell (Allan Dell 14-24), Justin Tipuric, CJ Stander.

**Unused replacements:** Kristian Dacey, Tomas Francis, Cory Hill, Gareth Davies, Finn Russell.

**Scorers:** Tries: Nowell 2, penalty (7pts), Payne. Cons: Biggar 3. Pens: Biggar 2.

**Yellow card:** Marler.

*24 June, New Zealand 30, British & Irish Lions 15, First Test, Eden Park, Auckland*

**New Zealand:** Ben Smith (Aaron Cruden 26); Israel Dagg, Ryan Crotty (Anton Lienert-Brown 32), Sonny Bill Williams, Rieko Ioane; Beauden Barrett, Aaron Smith (TJ Perenara 56); Joe Moody (Wyatt Crockett 53), Codie Taylor (Nathan Harris 66), Owen Franks (Charlie Faumuina 53), Brodie Retallick, Sam Whitelock, Jerome Kaino (Ardie Savea 45), Sam Cane, Kieran Read (capt) (Scott Barrett 77).

**Scorers:** Tries: Taylor, Ioane 2. Cons: Barrett 3. Pens: Barrett 3.

**British & Irish Lions:** Liam Williams (Leigh Halfpenny 72); Anthony Watson, Jonathan Davies, Ben Te'o (Johnny Sexton 57), Elliot Daly; Owen Farrell, Conor Murray (Rhys Webb 67); Mako Vunipola (Jack McGrath 51), Jamie George (Ken Owens 67), Tadhg Furlong (Kyle Sinckler 60), Alun Wyn Jones (Maro Itoje 47), George Kruis, Peter O'Mahony (capt) (Sam Warburton 53), Sean O'Brien, Taulupe Faletau.

**Scorers:** Tries: O'Brien, Webb. Con: Farrell. Pen: Farrell.

*27 June, Hurricanes 31, British & Irish Lions 31, Westpac Stadium, Wellington*

**Hurricanes:** Jordie Barrett; Nehe Milner-Skudder, Vince Aso, Ngani Laumape, Julian Savea (Cory Jane 68); Otere Black (Wes Goosen 61), Te Toiroa Tahuriorangi (Kemara Hauiti-Parapara 68); Ben May (Chris Eves 55), Ricky

Riccitelli (Leni Apisai 61), Jeff Toomaga-Allen, Mark Abbott, Sam Lousi, Vaea Fifita, Callum Gibbins, Brad Shields (capt) (Reed Prinsep 55).

**Unused replacements:** Michael Kainga, James Blackwell.

**Scorers:** Tries: Gibbins, Laumape, Fifita, Goosen. Pen: Barrett. Cons: Barrett 4.

**British & Irish Lions:** Jack Nowell; Tommy Seymour, Jonathan Joseph, Robbie Henshaw (Leigh Halfpenny 18), George North; Dan Biggar (Finn Russell 42-48), Greig Laidlaw; Joe Marler, Rory Best (capt), Dan Cole, Iain Henderson, Courtney Lawes (George Kruis 53), James Haskell, Justin Tipuric, CJ Stander.

**Unused replacements:** Kristian Dacey, Allan Dell, Tomas Francis, Cory Hill, Gareth Davies.

**Scorers:** Tries: Seymour 2, North. Cons: Biggar 2. Pens: Biggar 4.

*1 July, New Zealand 21, British & Irish Lions 24, Second Test, Westpac Stadium, Wellington*

**New Zealand:** Israel Dagg; Waisake Naholo (Aaron Cruden 59), Anton Lienert-Brown, Sonny Bill Williams, Rieko Ioane; Beauden Barrett, Aaron Smith (TJ Perenara 66); Joe Moody (Wyatt Crockett 52), Codie Taylor (Nathan Harris 79), Owen Franks (Charlie Faumuina 52), Brodie Retallick, Sam Whitelock (Scott Barrett 73), Jerome Kaino (Ngani Laumape 26), Sam Cane (Ardie Savea 64), Kieran Read (capt).

**Scorers:** Pens: Barrett 7.

**Red card:** Sonny Bill Williams (25min)

**British & Irish Lions:** Liam Williams; Anthony Watson (Jack Nowell 25-31), Jonathan Davies, Owen Farrell, Elliot Daly; Johnny Sexton, Conor Murray; Mako Vunipola (Sean O'Brien 66), Jamie George, Tadhg Furlong (Kyle Sinckler 62), Maro Itoje, Alun Wyn Jones (Courtney Lawes 59), Sam Warburton (capt), Sean O'Brien (Jack McGrath 64), Taulupe Faletau.

**Unused replacements:** Ken Owens, CJ Stander, Rhys Webb, Ben Te'o.

**Scorers:** Tries: Faletau, Murray. Con: Farrell. Pens: Farrell 4.
**Yellow card:** Mako Vunipola.

*8 July, New Zealand 15, British & Irish Lions 15, Third Test, Eden Park, Auckland*

**New Zealand:** Jordie Barrett; Israel Dagg, Anton Lienert-Brown, Ngani Lau-mape (Malakai Fekitoa 66), Julian Savea (Aaron Cruden 72); Beauden Barrett, Aaron Smith (TJ Perenara 73); Joe Moody (Wyatt Crockett 57), Codie Taylor (Nathan Harris 72), Owen Franks (Charlie Faumuina 57), Brodie Retallick, Sam Whitelock (Scott Barrett 77), Jerome Kaino, Sam Cane (Ardie Savea 60), Kieran Read (capt).

**Scorers:** Tries: Laumape, J Barrett. Con: B Barrett. Pen: B Barrett.
**Yellow card:** Jerome Kaino.

**British & Irish Lions:** Liam Williams; Anthony Watson (Jack Nowell 72), Jon-athan Davies, Owen Farrell, Elliot Daly; Johnny Sexton (Ben Te'o 48-52, 72), Conor Murray (Rhys Webb 69); Mako Vunipola (Jack McGrath 60), Jamie George (Ken Owens 69), Tadhg Furlong (Kyle Sinckler 60), Maro Itoje, Alun Wyn Jones (Courtney Lawes 49), Sam Warburton (capt) (Jones 66-72), Sean O'Brien (CJ Stander 40), Taulupe Faletau.

**Scorers:** Pens: Farrell 4, Daly.

# ACKNOWLEDGEMENTS

## Warren Gatland

There are so many people to thank, and I must apologise if I forget anyone.

Firstly to John Feehan and the board for giving me the opportunity to lead the Lions on what was an incredibly challenging but rewarding tour.

To John Spencer: your experience and wisdom was invaluable. You must have attended a lifetime of functions in one tour and represented us superbly with dignity and grace.

Charlie McEwen was the conduit between the board and the squad and was always there to support us in what was needed.

I must make special mention of Ger Carmody, whose meticulous planning and preparation made everything run so smoothly. I certainly respect your support and loyalty.

Thanks to Peter White, our New Zealand liaison man, who worked tirelessly with Ger to ensure we had everything in place and anything that was required.

Also, the medical team, lead by Eanna Falvey, was sensational. To undertake a tour of the magnitude we did and to have so few injuries is quite remarkable. The Strength and Conditioning / Sports Science team of Bobby, Phil Morrow, John Ashby and Brian Cunniffe found the right balance in helping to prepare the players, and to help them recover, and also worked very closely with the coaches in planning and preparing our sessions.

To Anna Voyce, our head of commercial: your job was one of the hardest on tour. The Lions are funded almost entirely from our commercial partners and you had that horrible job of ensuring that the coaches, staff and players fulfilled our obligations. I know how challenging this was at times.

Our 'comms' team of Dave Barton, Luke Broadley and Christine Connolly continually kept us informed of what was going on in the media and worked hard to ensure that the values and integrity of the Lions were very much protected.

To Gemma Crowley, our Team Services Manager: all I can say is that your work was above and beyond what was required. You were such a star.

I must make special mention of Shane Whelan and his digital team. Your unique humour was a welcome relief to the pressures we all felt at different times on the tour. I hope Dan Sheridan has stopped stalking you. Bobby is so delighted you have named your son after him.

Thanks to Ben Uttley and his team from Stamp who produced the tour video. Your previous experience made it so easy in the way you were able to fit so seamlessly into the squad without being intrusive.

Billy Stickland and Dan Sheridan were once again the tour photographers and you were both very much part of the whole team.

I have so much respect for the coaches: Steve Borthwick, Graham Rowntree, Andy Farrell, Rob Howley and Neil Jenkins. Only you guys know how tough this tour was in preparing two teams a week with the quality of opposition we faced. The long hours you put in were a testament to your dedication and hard work.

I couldn't fail to mention the supporters of both teams. The atmosphere at some of the matches was truly incredible and there is no doubt that your contribution to the tour cannot be underestimated.

Thanks to Gerry Thornley for all his hard work and long hours with this book. It was definitely challenging for both of us to get this completed in time.

Thanks to Justin Paige and Jonathan Harris, and to Jonathan Taylor and all those at Headline Book Publishing.

Thanks to 'The Laughing Men', some great mates from school, for your support and for always keeping me grounded.

And finally, to the players. I really hope that most of you will look back on this in a few years and appreciate that you played the back-to-back world champions in their own back yard and while we didn't win, we drew the series. Some result.

## Gerry Thornley

First and foremost, I'd like to thank Warren for his time, patience and commitment, and also Trudi, in many respects the rock upon which this was built, and Gabby and Bryn.

I'd like to thank Jonathan Harris, who helped it all run so smoothly, as well as Jonathan Taylor, Tom Whiting, Katie Field and all at Headline Book Publishing.

I'd particularly like to thank Ger Carmody, who was a readily available source of information, clarity and help throughout it all, and also Luke Broadley and Dave Barton in the Lions' media team for their assistance, as well as Paul 'Bobby' Stridgeon.

To Agnes, Olga, Radek, Caroline, Rebecca and Diego in The Orange Goat in Ballsbridge, for their fine coffee, food and Wi-Fi. Likewise, to Kieran, Gerry, Paul, Ian, Jamie and Jemima in Mulligans of Sandymount for the same. They were my libraries.

To my sports editor at the *Irish Times*, Malachy Logan, for granting me the time to write this book, and to Noel O'Reilly for his proof reading.

To the great AK, for being the great AK.

To Fergal, for his technical wizardry. Every luddite needs one. To Una, Dylan and Shana.

Huge thanks, again, to 'the team', Yseult, Evan and Marian, and, most of all, to Petria. Still our guiding light.